# The Alcoholic / Addict Within

**Also available from this author:**

# A Trip Through the 12 Steps
# with a Doctor and Therapist

A comprehensive guide to the 12 Steps, from a doctor and therapist in recovery.

Finally... science meets spirituality!

Whether you're new to the 12 Steps, going through them again, sponsoring someone through the Steps, or just want to deepen your knowledge about them, this is the book for you. "A Trip Through the 12 Steps with a Doctor and Therapist" is a comprehensive how-to guide to the 12 Steps, combining the most up-to-date science with the 12 Step literature. This is the most in-depth and insightful guide to the life-changing 12 Steps available, and an important tool for optimizing the therapeutic value of the 12 Steps. "A Trip Through the 12 Steps with a Doctor and Therapist" is the perfect companion to the Big Book and other 12 Step literature.

**Available now in eBook and paperback at amazon.com**

# The Alcoholic / Addict Within

Our Brain,

Genetics,

Psychology,

and

the Twelve Steps as Psychotherapy

## Andrew P. MD

Contact the author at alcoholism.addiction@gmail.com

or

visit the author's website at

www.alcoholism-addiction-psychology.com

# Contents

This book is for three different groups of people: 1) the addict or alcoholic who wants to know more about how and why we become addicted, and how to use this knowledge to strengthen recovery, 2) the family and loved ones of alcoholics or addicts who wish to understand their addicted loved one and help them get better, and 3) for those who work with alcoholics or addicts and wish to sharpen their knowledge of root causes and therapies of alcoholism and addiction. This group includes medical professionals, addictions workers, teachers, social workers, and those who sponsor fellow addicts or alcoholics.

Our brain weighs 3.3 lbs and makes up a measly 2% of our body mass, yet alcohol or other drugs can befriend it and manipulate it into consuming our lives. We explore how the brain becomes addicted to alcohol, drugs, and addictive behaviors, how addiction comes to override and dominate brain processes, and what happens to the brain in recovery. We examine how we can use this information to strengthen our recovery.

Between 40 and 60 per cent of our vulnerability to addiction to alcohol or drugs is decided by the DNA in our genes. How does that happen? Does having bad genes mean we have no hope? Do we pass these genes on to our children? Does it mean they will be alcoholics or addicts too? Should we feel guilty about this? How do we know if we have the "alcoholic gene"? In this chapter we answer these and other questions, and discuss how to protect ourselves and our children from our "bad" genetics.

Our memory is not like a video recording, it can be corrupted by many influences. Alcohol and drugs are able to worm their way into every crack in our memory system and manipulate it to keep us shackled under their spell. We discuss how they do this and how to turn the process around to break free. Taking back control of our memory processes is a commanding tool for recovery.

Alcoholism and addiction turn our mind into a liar and bully. Addiction to alcohol or drugs takes over all higher brain functions and pushes them outside their normal limits of function. These hijacked brain functions are used against us to keep us drinking or using, and to derail our efforts at sobriety. These processes include how we view ourselves and others, our belief-system, learning, recall, planning, reasoning, decision-making, and dreaming. This chapter describes how they are taken over and used against us. These brain processes are automatic, and we aren't even aware of them, so learning about them will help us to take back control. We show how the Twelve Step program addresses these problems specifically, and we discuss how to use our new-found knowledge of psychology to enhance our recovery.

It's brain function and psychology gone bad. Alcohol or drugs are in control and turning our own mind against us, thereby keeping us under their spell. We lay out the science behind the "insanity" of alcoholism and addiction, and what can we do to wrestle free from its power.

Our disease's natural history is broken down into four phases. We discuss the mental processes involved in getting us to the readiness, willingness, acceptance, and open-mindedness that is a prerequisite to finding and maintaining sobriety. We find out how to help someone along in that process.

You have to spend thousands of dollars to attend psychological therapy (psychotherapy) to get better, right? Wrong. The Twelve Step program is a form of psychotherapy, and we explore what makes it so much better at treating alcoholism and addiction than traditional clinical psychotherapy. For free! Even those who are not Twelve Steppers will gain from this knowledge.

Did you know that addictions involve the same brain chemicals and involve many of the same genes that cause mental health disorders such as depression, anxiety, schizophrenia, and PTSD? Is this why 54% of alcoholics and addicts also have a mental health disorder? Is this why people with mental health disorders are so vulnerable to alcohol and drugs? How do we know if we have a mental health disorder? What are the symptoms? Which should be treated first, the addiction or the mental health disorder? We answer all these questions and more. The more we know about mental illness the better we can protect ourselves and others.

Enter if you dare. Where I was, what happened, and where I am now. My convoluted story of military service, sport fighting, becoming a doctor… and my fall. I fell prey to the bottle and my own prescription pad. How I beat it and came to write this book.

Disclaimer: The information in this book is not intended to be medical advice. Anyone who thinks they may have substance use or any other mental health disorder should consult a licenced health practitioner.

# Introduction

"The rewards of sobriety are bountiful and as progressive as the disease they counteract. Certainly among these rewards for me are release from the prison of uniqueness, and the realization that participation in the A.A. way of life is a blessing and a privilege beyond estimate – a blessing to live a life free from the pain and degradation of drinking and filled with the joy of useful, sober living, and a privilege to grow in sobriety one day at a time and bring the message of hope as it was brought to me" (Big Book, page 451).

Isn't that a great passage? Those are the words of a "hopeless" alcoholic whose life had hit rock bottom and even then kept falling, but who found sobriety and life through the program of recovery offered in the Twelve Steps. His story can be found on pages 446 to 451 of the book *Alcoholics Anonymous*, the so-called Big Book, the manual of the Twelve Step program of recovery.

Hope! How could that passage fail to stir hope in the alcoholic or addict in the throes of slavery to that drink or drug, who lives the deadly paradox: "I can't continue living with my drink/drug, but I can't live without it"?

And it isn't false hope!

Those words from the Big Book could be spoken by any of the millions of people who have found freedom from their addictions through the program of recovery of the Twelve Steps. I am grateful to be one of those people.

"Can't live with our drink or drug, can't live without it"; our very existence had become a paradox, a contradiction, a miserable lose-lose quagmire. Alcoholism and addiction are a disease of paradoxes, and it is our brain processes corrupted by our substance that create them. In this book we will find out how and why our brain biology, our DNA, and our natural mental processes are responsible for our alcoholism or addiction and why they make sobriety so unattainable. We will also uncover exactly why we nose dive again with that first drink or drug even many years into recovery. The information is shocking, because we see that our own biology and brain functions cripple us – alcohol or drugs seduce them into allies as they devour our lives. Scary as this information may seem, we will feel relief at understanding why our lives went the way they did… and unburdened by discovering firsthand that alcoholism and addiction are a disease of biology and not an issue of morality.

Why are we alcoholics or addicts? Most people can drink or even use a drug only on occasion and not even think about it in between, but with us one drink or hit and we're done in. My sister will nurse a glass of wine all evening and then cork the bottle for another day. It may sit there untouched for weeks. If I tried that I would burn with obsession until I grabbed that bottle of wine and finished it off. What's the difference between those people and us? After you read this book you will be able to answer that question with authority.

It is true that knowledge alone will not make us sober. Knowing how alcohol and drugs collide with our brain and mind will not suddenly reverse our powerlessness over them. However, once we accept and admit our powerlessness and decide to get off the runaway train of endless bottoms this "insider" knowledge (literally) is a commanding weapon for fighting back. Why?

For one, it is eye-opening and fascinating stuff, because we learn about ourselves. And by learning the inner workings of our mind many new doors open wide for a deeper level of self-discovery than we have previously known. Most people go through their entire life without any real knowledge about how their mind works and why it makes them behave as they do. They are missing an opportunity to recognize and address behaviors that cause them many problems, including alcoholism or addiction. Awareness of our mental processes – our psychology – allows us to arrest harmful dysfunctional thought processes as they are at work. As alcoholics or addicts this can only strengthen our sobriety and our ability to help others who suffer, as we pass on this new-found knowledge.

Human psychology is the study of the mind and behavior. Two themes will leap out at you as we unfold its secrets: 1) how alcohol and drugs catapult our psychological processes far outside their normal limits of function, and 2) how these processes in our brain become dysfunctional, working to stymie our quest for sobriety and derail our progress once sober. That is why understanding the psychology of our substance-stained minds will help us to gain the upper hand in our sobriety… and allow us to better help others. These brain and mind processes occur unconsciously, and we are perilously unaware of them until we learn what they are and what they do to us. Only then can we defend ourselves from their effects. This enlightens the self-awareness that we need to benefit maximally from the Twelve Steps or any other program of recovery.

I consider the Big Book of Alcoholics Anonymous to be a medical textbook and a manual of psychological therapy, among many other things. As you learn about your brain and mind you will discover for yourself something miraculous: the Twelve Step program of recovery specifically recognizes and addresses all the aspects of brain physiology, genetics, and human psychology that are at work in alcoholism and addiction, even though this program was developed many years before any of this science was known. This 1930s era program stands unchanged more than 80 years on and remains just as valid now despite all the advances in science and medicine and all the changes to our society over the last 80-some years. And it stands true and validated by that science! I can safely say that there is no other medical or therapy text that can make the same claim. Simply amazing.

This information in this book will help the alcoholic or addict in recovery, and help the sponsor to have a deeper insight into our disease. However, it will also help those who strive to help us, or at least understand us. Loved ones, teachers, clergy, professionals who treat alcoholics, all will gain insight into our mist-shrouded alcoholic-addict minds, to all our benefit. Certainly, it will put a stop to that tired question we all hate: "Why don't you just stop?!?" (That alone makes giving this book to your loved ones worthwhile!) As a former doctor and therapist, an addict and alcoholic in recovery, and a husband and father I come from many perspectives, and I have a message for many audiences. Indeed, I hope to inspire healthcare professionals to add to their skill set some techniques unique to the Twelve Step program but, moreover, I wish to pass on a pearl of wisdom that I wish had been given to me long ago: give a Big Book to all your alcoholic and addict patients – it may save their lives (and it will make you look good as a therapist)!

There are those who find themselves drinking or using drugs – or gambling or doing some other addictive behavior – too much and are able to shake themselves off, walk away from it, and never look back. Kudos to them, I wish I was one of them. But I'm not. I tried countless times to be like them, but I failed time and again. I needed help.

I was a practicing MD who was powerless over alcohol and drugs, and I was a hopeless drunk until I found the Twelve Step program. I have been asked too many times how a medical doctor could end up like that. The answer to that is easy: because I'm human like everybody else. Alcoholism and addiction don't discriminate. They don't respect race, education, job, age, or health situation. Immunity to the bottle or the needle doesn't derive from money, possessions, or quality of life. And they certainly have nothing to do with morality, strength of character, or religious convictions. They can ensnare anybody, anywhere, but once they do we all share a common pathway, famously leading to "jails, institutions, and death." It is not Samuel Colt who makes all men equal, alcoholism-addiction does.

When we are in the throes of slavery to our drug of choice, we all share common behaviors and a common destiny. And it isn't good. We become expert liars, cheats, and thieves. We use and abuse those around us, especially the people who care about us the most. We do things we'd otherwise never dream of doing. People, jobs, accomplishments, security, possessions all start to fall away and we don't care – in fact we welcome it because it makes our drinking or using easier, less scrutinized. We keep tumbling further and further until the process is arrested. For some that is early on, before too much is lost; for others it is long after everything is gone and homelessness and destitution and death are the result. If we slide down that path far enough that is where it leads, no matter how lofty our starting point. However, there is great news….

We do recover! Most struggle a long time, usually years, trying every conceivable way to wrestle free from the tentacles of addiction. We dry out, for a while, but relapse over and over again. But there is one common thread in these attempts: we cling the belief that we can do it. We fail multiple times, but somehow we won't accept that. We will learn in the pages that follow why this is so. The Twelve Step program of recovery works, but not for everyone. But I will say this: among people who truly admit their powerlessness and surrender themselves to the program and make it a part of their daily lives the track record is excellent for as long as the principles remain a part of their daily lives. Extensive research funded by the U.S. National Institute of Health since 2005 has firmly established the Twelve Step program as – by far – the most effective of all known treatments for substance addiction. As we learn the science and psychology behind our disease in this book, we will see how we can use that information to help us in our recovery. This information will bolster our recovery, whether we are Twelve Steppers or not.

During my 15 years of medical and psychotherapy practice I had interacted professionally with many alcoholics-addicts and their families. Because I had so much experience, I thought myself an expert on the subject. However, my arrogant naïveté was revealed only after I was myself to hell and back. I have learned through my own experience, as someone who thought he understood alcoholism and addiction, that only an alcoholic truly understands an alcoholic. Same with addicts. You can read about it all you want, but only an alcoholic-addict can truly call out another alcoholic-addict on their bullshit. And if you do want to read about the subject and understand, put down that textbook and read the Big Book of Alcoholics Anonymous. Really.

As a doctor I have been dazzled by the power of the Twelve Step program to rescue people from the downward spiral of alcoholism-addiction and change their lives, to rescue them from their insanity. More so because I experienced this miracle myself, after all else failed and I thought my only remaining option was death. A hard death. Amazed as I was by how well this worked for me, as a scientist I had to know how and why this simple program produced such a profound change in me. So, I set forth to delve into everything I could find in the Twelve Step and recovery literature, the scientific and medical literature, as well as my own training and experience during my time as a doctor and psychotherapist. The way that science, medicine and the Twelve Step program are so deftly woven together is absolutely breathtaking. The depth of the program is far more profound than what most people realize.

We will see how the Twelve Steps are actually a form of psychotherapy, in my opinion the superior form of psychotherapy for alcoholism and addiction, and how this therapy identifies and addresses everything at work in our disease. I will show that you the alcoholic or addict in recovery is a qualified psychotherapist – any of us who is reaching out to or sponsoring another through the Steps is actually performing this very high-end form of psychotherapy, and doing it well. The Twelve Step program teaches us how to do that, and there are things about us as recovering alcoholics and addicts that make us the right "specialists" to deliver this therapy. When we do our Twelfth Step work, we are performing solid psychotherapy techniques, we probably just don't realize it at the time.

A word about terminology. I view addiction and alcoholism as one and the same. After all, we alcoholics are addicted to the drug alcohol, which is in fact a mind-altering drug. The science of alcohol and drugs is the same, so the information presented in this book applies to any mind-altering substance, and it also applies to addictive behaviors, including sex, gambling, over-eating, and others. For the sake of inclusiveness, I often use the term "alcoholic-addict" to refer to "us." The idea is to include both alcoholics and addicts in the term, for the purpose of being all-embracing for anybody who wishes to help themselves or someone else, no matter what the nature of their problem. Sometimes I use just the word "addiction" to refer to addiction to any substance or behavior. Given the wide acceptance of the "disease model" of alcoholism and addiction – which I agree with – I frequently refer to these as "our disease." There are times that I refer to drugs and alcohol collectively as "substances." The semantics here are awkward, and I needed to find a compromise (I hope) we can all live with. You may be an alcoholic or you may be an addict, or both, but please read the term as it applies to you. I hope I am not upsetting anyone's sensitivities with this terminology. We are all brothers and sisters in recovery, and we should have no room in our hearts for outdated stigmata of society.

[6]

I also use the terms "sober" and "sobriety" to refer to the absence of using alcohol or any other substance. Please read any term I use into your situation, whether it be alcoholism, drug addiction, or addiction to behaviors. I am here to help, not to offend. We alcoholics and addicts are among the most hard-boiled of fault-finders to ever crawl upon this earth – me included – and we would do well to part company with that tendency so we can learn some great stuff about ourselves as we read. And have some fun while we're at it.

I have learned that many alcoholics are "cross-addicted:" addicted to other drugs and behaviors in addition to alcohol. Many of us get to the point where our "drug of choice" (pardon the cliché) isn't having as much effect as it once did, and we need something else to bolster it. Or, we seek to mix the effects of one with the other. This has important ramifications. Alcoholics Anonymous has traditionally been for alcoholics, sometimes explicitly to the exclusion of other addictions. I always tell people: if you are addicted to other drugs or addictive behaviors, just go to A.A. meetings and say "I'm an alcoholic" instead of "I'm an addict" – you will certainly find people who share your specific addictions and experiences in the rooms of A.A. There are Twelve Step programs for other addictions: Narcotics Anonymous, Cocaine Anonymous, Over-eaters Anonymous, Sex Addicts Anonymous, and numerous others. Certainly, we can attend different kinds of meetings – many people do – the point is to find what works for us and go with it. All that matters is that we find what we need to achieve life-long sobriety.

In this book I explain what makes us tick as alcoholics and addicts. I do this in regular everyday language, only using technical terms if I think they help explain a concept, or if they are terms that have made their way into everyday conversation. I always make sure you will understand exactly what they mean.

I will use the science to explain the basis of some effects that are widely known about by people in recovery: the "insanity" of alcoholism-addiction, the "pink cloud" effect, relapse dreams, hostage-taking, co-dependency, and the obsession of alcoholism. I will show how the A.A. slogans are much wiser than people may realize, with their tentacles reaching deep into the most up-to-date science. You'll be able to really blow them away next time you are asked to interpret the slogans at a Twelve Step meeting!

We will also look at some deeper issues such as what it means to "deal with" past traumas, including mental, physical, or sexual abuse, and how this is crucial in defeating our substance's death-grip on us. We will explore the weird interactions between recovery from alcohol or drugs and romantic relationships.

Not a believer of the Twelve Steps? That's OK, the information presented in this book will fascinate you and increase your knowledge of yourself and others. Awareness of the inner processes that make us alcoholics and addicts is going to strengthen your ability to recover and improve yourself regardless of how you put it to use.

We will spend some time discussing the powerful interlacing of addictions and mental illness, and examine why they are so closely associated. Mental health and addictions are inextricably tangled, and this is pitifully under-recognized and under-treated. The two fit so well together that there often arises the chicken-and-the-egg paradox: which came first, the mental health issue or the addiction? Each can cause the other, and neither can be properly addressed and relieved without recognizing and addressing the other. These are fascinating and important questions that we will answer over the pages that follow.

The knowledge you gain from this book will help you get much more from the Steps and from your recovery, and to understand yourself much better than otherwise possible. It will also help you to see the psychological benefits from many aspects of the program that you might not otherwise have recognized. You will be much better equipped to help others after reading this book.

Incidentally, anyone who is interested in a comprehensive guide to going through the 12 Steps might wish to check out my book *A Trip Through the 12 Steps with a Doctor and Therapist*. This book combines the latest science of addictions and cutting-edge counseling techniques with the traditional 12 Step literature, with a view to helping you to optimize the healing experience of the 12 Steps. It is not meant to replace a sponsor or the 12 Step literature, but to provide a deeper level of insight for those going through the Steps or those who are helping others go through the Steps. *A Trip Through the 12 Steps with a Doctor and Therapist* is available on amazon.com. I hear it's a good read!

For anyone who is interested, my "story" appears in the epilogue. You may find it helpful, maybe even interesting, and I am happy to share with you.

You are about to embark on a learning experience that will make you understand yourself and others. The information is sometimes alarming, but always awe-inspiring. This book is about making the stranger-than-fiction marvels and elegant beauty of science and medicine accessible and useful for everyone. Enjoy!

# One

## Our Brain in Alcoholism and Addiction

The human brain is a fascinating contraption. It has justifiably been described as the most complex object in the universe. It is a collection of 86 billion nerve cells of many different types that work together in ways that are still scarcely understood. As wonderful as it is, and although it weighs a mere 3.3 lbs and comprises only 2% of our body mass, alcohol or other drugs can manipulate it into shattering our lives. This most formidable of machines – capable of the most wondrous of achievements – becomes utterly bamboozled by what we call alcoholism and addiction. We need to understand our brain to know how and why this happens. But, this is not an easy task. In his New York Times column Harold M. Schmeck Jr. aptly observed: *the ultimate goal is to understand the human brain – that incredible three-pound package of tissue that can imagine the farthest reaches of the universe and the ultimate core of the atom but cannot fathom its own functioning.*

But, take heart. In April 2013, President Barack Obama announced a scientific campaign, the BRAIN Initiative, short for Brain Research through Advancing Innovative Neurotechnologies. Funded $100-million-plus, this campaign aims to develop new technologies that will produce a dynamic picture of the human brain, from the level of individual cells to complex circuits. I am certain that this research will shed new light on understanding our disease, ultimately leading to new therapies. Let's hope so.

Before we learn about the brain's involvement in alcoholism and addiction, let's get to know our brain – and thus ourselves – a little better.

[10]

The main difference between human and animal brains is that humans have more brain cells – also known as *neurons* – per unit volume than other animals, and that is accomplished by making folds in the outer layer – the *cerebral cortex*. These folds form hills and valleys, which give our brain its well-known outer appearance. The more complex a brain, the more hills and valleys it has. Other intelligent animals, such as monkeys and dolphins, also have some folds in their cortex, whereas mice have smooth brains.

Size isn't necessarily everything when it comes to brains. The Neanderthal "cave-people" had brains that were 10% larger than ours. Sperm whale brains are six times larger than ours. However, our brains are the largest of all animals when compared to body size. We also have the largest frontal lobes of any animal, which is the part associated with higher-level functions such as reasoning, planning, judgement, language, memory, and abstract thought.

The human brain weighs 3.3 lbs. (half of what our skin weighs), making up 2% of our body weight. It contains 86 billion neurons – the gray matter – and billions of nerve fibers – the white matter. Each of the 86 billion neurons has up to 10,000 connections to other neurons. A piece of brain the size of a grain of sand contains 100,000 neurons and 1 billion interconnections. There are as many as 10,000 different types of neurons in the brain. It's a mixed-up multifarious motley multiplex mosaic mess of miscellaneous mingled multiform brain cells, yet its organization and trillions of inter-connections are harmonious and sophisticated beyond measure; its abilities boundlessly greater than the sum of its parts. The entire body is there to support it, and it alone is responsible for all humankind's actions and interactions, society, history, and accomplishments.

Even though our brain makes up only 2% of our body-weight it uses 20% of our total energy and oxygen intake. It's composed of 73% water, and all it takes is 2% dehydration to disable its function. The brain is the fattiest organ in the body, being 60% fat. A quarter of all the cholesterol in our body is contained in the brain, which needs it: without enough cholesterol, brain cells die. (I suppose that qualifies cheeseburgers as brain food.)

The brain works by transmitting information between neurons, which is why there are so many inter-connections. None of the brain cells actually touch. There is a gap between them, and they communicate by releasing various chemicals across the gap to transmit messages between them. These message chemicals are known as *neurotransmitters*. Each of the many different neurotransmitters means different things to different brain cells at different times and in different amounts. The sending brain cell produces and releases the neurotransmitter, and the receiving cell picks up these signals on *receptors*, which recognize the signal.

Brain information moves between 1 and 268 miles per hour. More than 100,000 chemicals reactions take place in our brain every second. Our brain generates between 12 and 25 watts of electricity, enough to power a low-wattage light bulb. (Too many obvious jokes, so I'll leave it alone.) Only five minutes without oxygen can cause brain damage. Brain cells will digest themselves as a last ditch source of energy to ward off starvation, one of the reasons that starvation dieting is no longer used as a weight-loss technique. It's good to lose weight by digesting fat cells, but doing it by digesting brain cells is not so good.

We believe that our brain generates 50,000 thoughts per day, and that about 70% of these thoughts are "negative." Even though we have come a long way in terms of knowledge and technology, humankind is not getting smarter. Since the 1800s the average IQ has gone down more than 13 points. Our average attention span is also getting shorter, having gone from 12 seconds to 8 seconds in the last 20 years – less than the 9-second attention span of a goldfish. (One wonders if the rise of the video game had anything to do with this.)

It isn't until the age of 25 that our brain reaches full maturity, although our brain doesn't grow much after birth. The belief that we use only 10% of our brain is wrong; we actually use most of our brain most of the time, even during sleep. Our brain's storage capacity is virtually unlimited; it doesn't get "used up" like computer memory. While we are drunk our brain is incapable of forming memories, but is otherwise capable of performing purposeful tasks reasonably well, which explains alcoholic "blackouts." We don't forget what we've done, we just don't record any of it in memory. This is why, no matter how hard we try, we can't remember what we did during a blackout. Memory plays a huge role in addiction and recovery, and we'll be discussing this important issue in a later chapter.

There are a couple of things that threw me a curve when I was first exposed to brain surgery as a medical student. The first thing was that the human brain is not solid; it's soft and jelly-like, with the consistency of warm Jell-O (sorry: as a rule, I try NOT to use food when describing anatomy). When it's exposed to air it quickly softens, so there is an urgency to get the surgery done and get the skull closed up before the brain turns to goo. The other thing was that although the brain is full of nerve cells, it has no pain receptors and therefore feels no pain. Because of this it's possible to perform brain surgery while the patient is awake.

Now that we know more than we probably wanted to know about the brain, let's talk about what happens when it collides with alcohol and drugs.

\*

We interact with the world around us – learn, store memories, interpret senses, communicate, plan, make decisions, engage thought processes, and so on – by the connections that we form between neurons in our brain. We spoke earlier about how each brain cell has up to 10,000 connections to other brain cells. When brain cells connect in a series, we call that series of connections a *pathway*. When the series of brain cells in a pathway send a signal along that pathway, we say that the pathway *fires*. When we learn something, new neuron connections forming a pathway are laid down, and these pathways become our memory. When we access that memory, the series of neurons that form that pathway fire, and we recall the memory. We will discuss how these pathways are formed and what their effects are when we discuss the surprisingly powerful effect of memory and learning on addiction and recovery in an upcoming chapter.

The most long-lasting changes that occur in the brain from substance addiction are the pathways that form as the addiction develops. Because most addicts and alcoholics spend a long time – usually years – in their substance use and related thought processes and behaviors, the associated pathways become very firmly cemented in the brain.

The more a brain pathway is used, the stronger that pathway becomes. A brain pathway is like a path through a cornfield that becomes more and more

[13]

worn the more it is used. Like a well-worn path through a cornfield, the more a brain pathway is used the easier it is to find and follow it in the future. This is why we study something, repeating it over and over; it becomes more entrenched in our memory and we can access the information more easily on a test. Therefore, this tendency for well-used pathways to become more prominent and dominant is good, right? Sure, but it can be deadly when alcohol or drug use starts using this process to form an addiction. Because we end up using our substance multiple times, the brain pathways involved become firmly entrenched in our brain. We form pathways associated with having cravings, answering those cravings, and all the behaviors around using our substance. Like a well-used pathway through a cornfield, these addiction-related mental pathways become prominent and therefore likely to be used again in the future. And, like a path through a cornfield, these prominent pathways take a long time to fade away when we stop using them.

One of the reasons that alcohol and drug addiction is considered a disease is because it manipulates our brain to keep itself going and growing, and to prevent us from eradicating it. Nowhere is this more evident than in the uncanny way it manipulates our memory formation so as to warp reality and logic in order to overpower all our efforts to break away from our substance use and maintain sobriety. We will discuss this extraordinary phenomenon in the chapters that follow.

We mentioned earlier that our brain doesn't finish maturing until about age 25. This has important ramifications when it comes to addictions. Pathways that are laid down in the developing brain tend to become permanent, kind of like tracing a line in wet cement with your finger. Like a line in hardening cement, these pathways become a part of the developing brain. Because of this, people whose brain hasn't finished maturing can develop especially deeply imprinted mental pathways related to substance use. This is why early onset of addiction is especially ominous. Even the fetal brain develops pathways related to substance use when the pregnant mother uses substances. The child is born with addiction pathways already embedded. This is, of course, a significant risk factor for development of addictions later in life, often not so far in the future.

Separate brain pathways that tend to fire together with a stimulus become more and more strongly associated with repeated exposure to that stimulus.

So, for example, if we are exposed to a particular sight, sound, feeling, or smell whenever we drink or use drugs, any future exposure to that sight, sound, feeling, or smell will also trigger the brain pathway associated with drinking or using. Because this association between the trigger (the sight, sound, feeling, or smell) and the behavior (drinking or using) is repeated time and time again over years, the link between pathways becomes deeply cemented, and we can be susceptible to these stimuli triggering us to drink or use even many years into sobriety. That is precisely why we need to find new people, places, and things in recovery... so that we can avoid these pathway triggers.

There is yet another aspect of brain function that can cause addiction problems. The more a particular brain pathway is fired, the easier it is to fire the same pathway in the future. This means that it takes less and less to stimulate the pathways that result in drinking or using behavior as we progress further into our addiction. And these "hair-trigger" pathways remains super-easy to fire for a long time after. This is known in brain science as *long-term potentiation (LTP)*.

This LTP process is how we create long-term memories. The more we access a memory, the less effort it takes to access it again in the future, and the more deeply and permanently embedded the memory becomes in our brain. That's great when we are trying to create useful long-term memories, such as remembering how to start our car, but it's exactly the reason that we remain at high risk for relapse if we activate these drinking or using pathways even many years into recovery. These pathways are so sensitive that one single drink or drug can put us right back where we were even after many years of sobriety. Alcoholism-addiction is so cunning a disease that it is able to manipulate our thought processes into denial of our sensitivity to relapse, as we will see a little later on. Scary, isn't it?

*

We have discussed how the brain does its work by passing information and instructions in intricate pathways of interconnected neurons. Neurons pass information and instructions between them by using chemicals called

[15]

neurotransmitters: the sending neuron emits the neurotransmitter and the receiving neuron receives it, and then passes the signal along to the next neuron in the pathway in exactly the same way. Thus the message is passed along the sequence of neurons that form the pathway.

There are many different neurotransmitters, and they all have various functions. Of course, if the neurotransmitters get knocked off balance for any reason the messages will get mixed up and it will affect brain function and lead to many different problems and disorders. These include Alzheimer's disease, Parkinson's disease, depression, schizophrenia, and so on. Addiction and alcoholism are also included on the list. Alzheimer's disease causes specific neurotransmitter disruptions that cause the specific symptoms of Alzheimer's disease. Likewise, alcoholism-addiction causes specific neurotransmitter disruptions that likewise cause the specific symptoms of alcoholism-addiction. By the time you have finished reading this book you will be very familiar with all the brain processes that get disrupted and why they cause all the symptoms of our disease. You will also learn how these same processes can interfere with our recovery even many years after the last drink or drug. We will tie this in to the Twelve Step program to show how this ingenious program addresses **all** of these processes and gives us the tools we need to defeat them.

As I pointed out in the introduction to this book, addiction and alcoholism are, from the point of view of the science involved, one and the same. After all, alcoholism is an addiction to the drug ethyl alcohol. All drugs of addiction have slightly different characteristics, and alcohol is, strictly speaking, another one of these drugs. When we look at how these drugs affect the brain and elicit the disease of addiction, it emphasizes this point. Although they all have differing pathways to get there, the neurotransmitter dopamine is the common end-point for alcohol and other drugs of addiction, as well as for addictive behaviors. Dopamine has been implicated in addictive behavior in both animal and human studies, so we are sure it's the culprit. It is responsible for the euphoria that is brought on by these drugs, which provides positive reinforcement for continued use of these drugs. Conversely, removal of the drug causes reduced production and release of dopamine in the brain, which causes a low mood, and low feelings, which contribute to seeking the drug. Thus, there is positive and negative reinforcement involved in the drug seeking behavior. This reinforcement, positive and negative, is a form of learning, and we will learn all about its nefarious role in addiction and recovery in an up-coming chapter.

During normal brain functions, the dopamine system rewards our natural behaviors: the elation we feel when we accomplish something important, for example. This reward system is meant to ensure that we will seek out and perform activities that we need to do to live, thrive, and reproduce, by rewarding us with feelings of pleasure when we accomplish these activities. Whenever this reward occurs, the brain remembers the activity that produced the reward and we are driven to perform this activity again. The perfect example is the pleasure we feel from a good meal. The memory of the pleasure and relief we felt drives us to seek out food again when we are hungry. In this way we are driven to carry out a behavior necessary for our survival: eating. In normal life, rewards usually come only with time and effort. Substances of abuse give us a much bigger and faster burst of reward without all the work involved, providing a shortcut, flooding the brain with dopamine and other neurotransmitters.

The brain is not naturally exposed to these artificially huge substance-induced bursts of dopamine, so it compensates, trying to get things back to normal, a process known as *homeostasis*. The brain reduces the number of receptors that are stimulated by dopamine release, and we become sensitized to dopamine, so that the good feelings from its release are reduced. Then the brain starts to "down-regulate" production of dopamine in order to further compensate for the repeatedly high levels produced by the addictive substances. As a result we need more and more of the drug to get the same effect as we continue on in our alcoholism-addiction. This is what is known as *tolerance*. I have always found it an odd quirk of society that many cultures around the world revere tolerance to alcohol or drugs: people who have a high tolerance for drinking or using are considered to be cool. Hmmm.

As if this tolerance thing wasn't bad enough, the brain compensation results in lower than normal levels of dopamine when the substance of abuse is not present. When we are not "high" or "drunk" our baseline dopamine levels are now much lower than in a non-drinker/user, and we feel depressed, lifeless, lacking energy, and things that normally produce pleasure no longer do so. We are now the opposite of rewarded. We no longer feel any reward

[17]

for eating, accomplishing tasks, or even finding a fulfilling relationship. We need the drug just to feel normal, let alone "high." These changes become permanent after a while, which partly explains our life-long vulnerability to relapse after the substance use has stopped. Thus, the Twelve Step premise that we are alcoholic-addicts for life and can never drink or use again has merit, as demonstrated by the brain science.

This is how substances of addiction insert themselves into the brain's communication system – the neurotransmitters – and interfere with the way neurons normally communicate. Anything we put in our bodies that does this is referred to as being *psychoactive*. All substances of addiction are psychoactive, including anabolic steroids. Some drugs, such as marijuana and heroin, have a chemical structure that mimics that of a natural neurotransmitter. This "fools" receptors and allows the drugs to activate the neurons. Although these drugs mimic the brain's own chemicals, they don't activate neurons in the same way as a natural neurotransmitter, and they lead to abnormal messages being transmitted through the network. Other drugs, such as amphetamines or cocaine, cause the neurons to release abnormally large amounts of natural neurotransmitters or prevent their normal break-down. This disruption produces a greatly amplified message, ultimately disrupting communication channels and producing symptoms consistent with these high levels of neurotransmitters.

Alcohol artificially stimulates the receptors for the neurotransmitter GABA, whose job is to inhibit brain cell function and slow things down when we are too excited. This is why we get so sedated and slow and slurred when we are drinking. This is also why we feel so jittery and excitable and risk having a seizure when we withdraw from chronic alcohol use. Alcohol also stimulates receptors that are involved in depression – most notably those of the neurotransmitter serotonin – leaving them lacking in stimulation after the alcohol wears off. This is part of the reason alcohol is called a depressant, but we'll look at this more closely in the chapter on mental health and alcoholism-addiction. Regardless of their mode of action, all substances of addiction, by their various pathways, have the end result of flooding the brain's reward system with dopamine.

Because these substances stimulate the natural reward system, albeit to a much higher degree – up to 10 times the amount produced by sex – and much more rapidly and longer lasting, we are driven to seek them out again when the reward effect wears off. When they cause the brain to overproduce dopamine (or to prevent its break-down) the overstimulated reward system produces the euphoric effects that we call a "high" or "being drunk". Naturally, we are driven to repeat this behavior that produces the euphoria, and this is what we call addiction.

*

Although we have so far mostly limited our discussion to the neurotransmitter dopamine, because that is the one most responsible for our disease, addictive substances also affect many other neurotransmitters, many of which are involved in crucial brain functions. In medicine, we refer to this as being *receptor dirty*, referring to the fact that a drug doesn't cleanly limit its actions to just one neurotransmitter receptor. The same process of tolerance that leads to chronically low levels of dopamine in the addict's brain occurs with other neurotransmitters resulting in profound changes in brain circuits and their function, with potentially severe compromises in crucial functions of the brain. These changes lead to some degree of impairment in cognitive function, which I referred to earlier as our higher brain functions. This means that our memory, judgement, intelligence, learning, spatial perception, and so on all experience some degree of impairment. It is common knowledge that drinking and drugging "fry your brain", kill brain cells, and can affect your intelligence. I am reminded of the old Public Service Announcement TV ads that showed an egg frying in a pan with the caption "this is your brain on drugs." Unfortunately, some of the damage from these effects of drugs and alcohol appear to be largely permanent.

Critically, the neurotransmitters that cause depression, anxiety, and other mental health problems are also affected, which explains why there is such a staggeringly high degree of similarity and interaction between mental health issues and addiction. We will unravel this bewitching and often ignored issue later in this book.

In addition to its role in the reward system, the neurotransmitter dopamine is involved in a number of other brain processes, including those that regulate movement, emotion, motivation, and, oddly enough, screening our thoughts. Because of this, imbalances in dopamine, such as the highs and lows brought on by addictive substances, can have other serious consequences. High levels of dopamine cause the symptom of *psychosis*, which is defined as a loss of touch with reality. The high dopamine interferes with our brain's system for screening subconscious thoughts before they are allowed through to our consciousness, so thoughts that would normally be rejected as unreal are allowed through. The result is psychosis. Symptoms of psychosis include hearing things (auditory hallucinations) including hearing voices that give compelling instructions, seeing things that aren't there (visual hallucinations), paranoia, ideas of reference (believing that people on TV and the radio are talking about us), catatonia (holding absolutely still in statue-like poses for prolonged periods of time), and general weird behavior. Unfortunately, violent behavior is common, especially if there is paranoia. Since drugs of abuse cause elevated dopamine levels it is not at all surprising that psychotic symptoms are a feature of being under their influence. This is also why violent behavior is so commonplace. Unfortunately, many drugs (most notable marijuana and MDMA, or ecstasy) can cause permanent psychosis, which is known as the psychiatric disease schizophrenia.

Low levels of dopamine is the cause of Parkinson's Disease, so the lower than normal levels of dopamine that occur when we withdraw from drugs of abuse is the reason that we experience shaking and unsteadiness on our feet. Dopamine is involved in regulating emotions, and the effects are easy to see in the weird and unpredictable emotions displayed by many addicts and alcoholics.

*

There is no way we are going to be experts on our pickled brain without first talking about "wet brain," so let's do that now. Wet brain refers to an alcohol-induced syndrome called Wernicke-Korsakoff syndrome (WKS). Wernicke-Korsakoff syndrome is actually a combination of two separate conditions: Wernicke's encephalopathy and Korsakoff psychosis (poor Dr. Korsakoff... it's a dubious honor to have a psychosis named after you). It's possible for the alcoholic to develop either Korsakoff psychosis or Wernicke's encephalopathy independently, but they share a common cause and therefore usually end up striking together. Wet brain, WKS, is almost exclusively seen in alcoholics, but isn't directly caused by alcohol. It's actually a disease of malnutrition, specifically the deficiency of vitamin $B_1$ – thiamine – that often occurs in the "advanced" alcoholic.

As the alcoholic becomes more and more destitute the bits of money that do come along end up going into alcohol instead of food. The inflamed stomach, liver, and pancreas – and the associated vomiting – result in poor absorption of any food that does come along. Thiamine is a vitamin, which means that our body can't produce it, so it must come from food. So the available supply runs out. Lack of thiamine interferes with delivery of proper nutrition of the brain. As we discussed earlier, the brain uses 20% of our body's total energy and when it's not properly fed it will start to digest itself. This is exactly what happens, and the brain progressively withers and we get WKS.

Sadly, only 20% of cases of WKS are identified before death, so no treatment is provided. This is because most people who develop WKS are chronic daily drunks, so their symptoms are just assumed to be from being drunk. As well, many of them are long estranged from their family and friends, even homeless, so there may not be anyone around who cares enough to notice. Their disheveled appearance and strange, psychotic behavior – such as staggering around repeating weird statements – scares people and they tend to be avoided and shunned. This failure in diagnosis of WKS and thus treatment of the disease leads to death in 20% of cases, while 75% are left with permanent brain damage. About 25% require long-term institutionalization in order to receive effective care, but many never get this care. Instead, their behavior and socially unacceptable demeanor lands them in jail and the local Emergency Room, but their fate is usually the street.

I recently saw a reality-TV show about jails, and one of the individuals they featured on the show was a die-hard alcoholic who "boasted" over 1,080 jail stints. He was picked for the show because of his weird and rowdy behavior on camera, as well as his clownish appearance. I quickly recognized

[21]

that he was suffering from WKS, and therein lay his entertainment value for the cameras. The show gave some background on him, and he was once a very attractive, employed man with a family. This could have been any one of us, if alcohol had maintained its dominion over us long enough.

Usually the symptoms of Wernicke's appear first. These are typically from three main categories: 1) changes in mental state (confusion, lack of interest in anything, inability to concentrate, and lack of awareness of the immediate situation), 2) visual changes (rapid eye movements, partial paralysis of eye movements, reduced vision), and 3) unsteadiness standing and walking. Left untreated, Wernicke's leads to coma or death. These symptoms come on suddenly, usually starting with the individual appearing confused. This can be hard to diagnose in a person who is habitually intoxicated, because they tend to be alone by this point in their drinking career, and their confusion is easily confused with drunkenness. Unlike drunken confusion this confusion is constant, even when the individual hasn't been drinking.

Later, the ominous symptoms of Korsakoff psychosis appear. As we discussed earlier, psychosis is a loss of touch with reality, so the symptoms of Korsakoff's psychosis are: hallucinations, memory loss, confabulation (making up stories to compensate for the memory loss), inability to form new memories, and nonsensical speech. Initially only the ability to form new memories will be impaired.

You may have seen someone with WKS. These unfortunates are usually dismissed as "crazy drunks." They are usually dishevelled and unkempt, bottomed-out drunks by this point. They appear thin and poorly nourished. Their eyes vibrate and often don't line up properly. They appear to be in another world, and it is difficult to get and hold their attention, although they will follow simple commands. They talk to themselves, often repeating the same random phrase. They stagger when walking and fall easily. They are the extreme endorsement of the truth that no one ever drank themselves smart, successful, or happy.

The onset of Wernicke's encephalopathy is a medical emergency. If treated promptly, it may be possible to prevent the development of Korsakoff's syndrome and therefore prevent it from developing into full-blown WKS. At the very least treatment can reduce its severity. Treatment can also reduce the progression of the damage if there's already WKS, but will not completely reverse existing deficits. For such a devastating and deadly disease, treatment is cheap and easy: thiamine given through intravenous once a day for three days. That's what makes it so sad to see cases where it has gone untreated.

Treatment is not guaranteed to be effective and WKS will continue to be present, at least partially, in 80% of patients. However, it's also important to continue supplementing with thiamine until a normal diet is in place, but many of these unfortunate people end up back out on the street picking up where they left off. Therefore, in order to reduce the risk of developing WKS it is important to address the alcohol addiction that led to its onset. Failing this, some prevention of progression of the disease may be achieved by taking a thiamine tablet once a day, which may be difficult to accomplish with those who continue drinking. Untreated, these people's brain function usually deteriorates to the point of coma, then death.

What about those with WKS who do manage to find sobriety? It depends on how soon in the process the drinking is stopped and the thiamine deficiency is treated. Most of those who do find their way into recovery will be able to regain much of the functioning that was lost to WKS. Some will have to lingering effects, but should be able to adapt and find a better life away from alcohol. The amnesia from Korsakoff psychosis seems particularly permanent, and 80% of these people will always have problems with forming new memories. No matter what, finding sobriety is by far the best thing for them. Now we know all about "wet brain." Luckily, we usually don't see much of it around, unless we work in the healthcare field.

If you want to learn more about WKS, there are a number of credible websites that have non-commercially-biased information about it in everyday language. I recommend the Mayo clinic website.

\*

Even though the liver and brain are not located close to each other – our liver is tucked under our right ribcage – an advanced liver disease known as alcoholic cirrhosis also affects the brain. The diseased liver produces toxic

[23]

substances that travel in the blood and poison the brain, resulting in a condition known as *hepatic encephalopathy*. (As you can see, one of the toughest parts of medical school is the spelling tests).

This brain impairment occurs in 70% of people with cirrhosis. The effects are barely noticeable in half and debilitating in the other half. Fortunately, it resolves with treatment, which is done by reducing the toxic substances being produced by the liver. This is easily done with very inexpensive medications.

In terms of symptoms, these people look sick from their cirrhosis. They are usually jaundiced (yellow skin and eyes), with swollen bellies from a big liver and abdominal fluid (ascites), with swollen legs, and an overall sickly appearance. The brain effects make them forgetful, confused, and irritable. Oddly enough, they typically get a reversed sleep-wake cycle, where they are up all night and sleep all day. They often develop a "liver-flap," which is a jerky, flapping, uncontrollable movement of the limbs. A peculiar smell known as *foetor hepaticus* (again, with the spelling) is often present. It's difficult to describe a smell, but the fact that it's also known as "breath of the dead" should tell you that it's not pleasant (to me it's a fruity-rotten eggs-feces smell). As the brain becomes more poisoned these sick people become more and more forgetful and confused, experience personality changes, and are increasingly sleepy. This sleepiness will eventually progress to a coma.

Luckily, hepatic encephalopathy is easily treated, but the important thing is to treat the cirrhosis that caused it, otherwise it will come back. We are blessed that the liver is a forgiving organ, and it usually returns to health once we stop battering it with alcohol, as long as it's not too far gone. When I was an intern, the hospital where I was working was collecting data on cirrhosis, and they followed men with late-stage cirrhosis who were told that if they continued drinking they would be dead within six months but they would survive if they stopped. They found that 82% of these men continued drinking until their death; most died within 2-3 months. We must never forget that we are dealing with a deadly disease.

\*

Now, an important question: lots of people try drugs, and most people drink alcohol at some point in their life, so why do some people become addicted while others don't? Does the way our brain works provide a clue?

The first time anyone tries alcohol or another drug, it's a voluntary choice. We may be coerced, or even tricked into it, but in most cases it's by choice. We might get drunk or high, have a good or a bad experience, and the next day we carry on with our lives until the next time we choose to do it again. But in some people, at some point a switch gets flipped within the brain and the decision to use is no longer voluntary. After initial exposure, no one gets to decide how their brain will react to drugs or alcohol. So why do some people develop addiction, while others don't? The answer lies partly in the brain.

As we've already discussed, what we call tolerance develops because as our addiction progresses, dopamine has less impact on the brain's reward center. We find that our substance of abuse no longer gives us much pleasure, and we have to take more of it to obtain the same dopamine "high." It is at this point, that the obsession and compulsion that is alcoholism-addiction takes control. We will be discussing this villainous "obsession" and its evil buddy "compulsion" in detail later in this book, but we can see now how it takes over. The pleasure associated with an addictive drug or behavior subsides – yet the memory of the high becomes overpowering (the obsession) and great anxiety over the need to recreate the high (the compulsion) take over, driving us to go after it. The normal thought processes, logic, needs, motivations, and desires of the brain become derailed – the brain is now addicted.

It is not the desire for the experience of pleasure from an addictive substance or activity alone that makes us addicted. Otherwise, we would all be addicted: everybody wants to experience something pleasurable. Dopamine does more than give us the sensation of pleasure; it is also involved in learning and memory. As we will discuss in greater detail later in this book, learning and memory are key elements in the transition from enjoying something to becoming addicted to it. Our genes – our DNA that we inherit and which affect who and what we are – play a major role in deciding which of us is susceptible to this process and possess the correct brain wiring for it to occur to such a degree that it tips the scales over to the point where

[25]

addiction occurs. That is why a family history of addiction and mental health problems are risk factors for addiction. Most of the genes involved in making someone prone to addiction are genes that act on the brain. We discuss this more in the next chapter. As well, our life experiences and environment play a major role in tipping the scales. That is why things such as poor nutrition, exposure to abuse, parental drug use, our friends, our neighborhood, poverty, life stressors, and so on are risk factors for addiction.

We can see, then, that we can't just isolate brain function alone as being responsible for our disease. It's our brain function, together with our genetic make-up, our environment and experiences, our memory and learning, our mind processes (our psychology) that all come together in the process of developing addiction. We must look at all those aspects together in order to find out why we are addicts and others are not – and what we can do about it. That is why this book covers all of these inseparable topics all under one roof. They are all hopelessly intertwined. For example, as we will discuss in the chapter on psychology, our natural instincts and behaviors play a major role in addiction. Naturally, our behavior and instincts come from our brain, so these two factors affect each other.

*

As I mentioned earlier, the human brain continues to grow and develop until we are in our mid-twenties. We know that a brain that is still changing and maturing is particularly vulnerable to the effects of alcohol and drugs, and the changes they can bring on are all the more likely to be permanent. So, the younger the brain the more susceptible a person is to alcoholism-addiction. Given that the age of exposure to alcohol and drugs is getting progressively younger, the role of the brain in our disease is also growing, as the substance-interrupted brain development becomes more and more common. In the next chapter we will discuss the effects of genetics on addiction and answer the question: my parents were alcoholics, does that mean I will become one, and does that mean that my children will end up alkies too? It turns out that the genes that influence susceptibility to alcoholism-addiction do so by influencing brain development, so the genetics of addiction and brain involvement in our disease are very closely tied together.

Looking to the future, perhaps one day a treatment that stabilizes dopamine levels in the brain will be discovered and will lead to a prevention or cure for alcoholism-addiction. However, at this point we don't seem to be anywhere close to that dream despite all that we have learned. And, I doubt we will be for a very long time. I keep a very close eye on current research and developments in medicine, with an especially keen eye on developments in addictions treatments, and I can say that there doesn't seem to be anything in the works that would give hope to this happening anytime soon. There are always new catch-words being thrown around, but unfortunately that is all they have panned out to be. One such catch-word is *neuroplasticity*, which is simply a word that means that the brain can be changed. The concept is that the brain can be taught to no longer be addicted. Don't let the fancy name fool you, this is a very old concept, which is the basis of treatment approaches that have not proven effective in treatment of addiction, namely Cognitive therapy, Behavioral therapy, and (of course) Cognitive-behavioral therapy (CBT). Taking advantage of neuroplasticity is an important part of a program of recovery from addiction – as it is in the Twelve Step program – but not when it forms the sole basis of the plan of recovery. That will be made clear in the chapter on psychotherapy in this book. If we look at the state of medical treatment for addiction as it existed in, say, 1935 (A.A. devotees will know that I didn't pick this date randomly), it has advanced very little since then.

Even though our developing knowledge about the brain's role in alcoholism-addiction hasn't yet led us to a cure, we must keep working toward exactly that goal. However, there is another reason that working out the brain pathways in our disease is important: it helps us to work out the genetics of addiction. That is the subject of our next chapter.

# Two

## The Genetics of Alcoholism and Addiction

Genetics are an amazing contrivance, whose genius and complexity of engineering bear witness, I think, to the existence of an engineer of astronomical abilities, something you might call a higher power. Imagine the concept: within each of us is a complete blueprint, so massive that only a tiny percentage of its information is needed to construct every aspect of us, yet so tiny that one million copies of it would fit in the period at the end of this sentence, and this blueprint lays out how every little bit of us, from the smallest chemical reaction right up to how tall we will be, is to be constructed. Not only is every detail of us recorded, but also the exact recipe for all the trillions of different things that have to happen and come together perfectly to make each detail a reality. What's more, this whole blueprint is a record of our legacy, giving us pieces of our ancestors going back tens of thousands of years so perfectly that we can even identify exact DNA from our "cave-man" early human ancestors and Neanderthal man. The plan for all of humanity to come was contained within Adam and Eve, and is still within each of us.

Impressed? There's more! A separate but identical copy of that blueprint is contained in (almost) every single one of the 37 trillion microscopic cells that make up our body, so that the sperm and the egg that fatefully meet each brings a representation of ourselves and our ancestors. And then, there is a mechanism whereby at conception the blueprint from each parent is randomly and thoroughly mixed and combined, so that an unpredictable mix of the

[28]

genetic blueprint of each parent and his or her ancestors is beautifully laid out in this new miracle that will develop into a brand new person.

So, what exactly is a gene? A gene is a collection of DNA, and DNA is a chain of four different chemicals, and the sequence in which these chemicals occur varies and provides a code. This DNA code spells out the instructions for constructing a person, similar to the way in which letters of the alphabet appear in a certain order to form words and sentences. It's an efficient way to store data: 2 grams of DNA could hold all the digitally stored information in the world. A grouping of DNA that together form a coherent set of instructions is called a gene. In humans, genes vary in size from a few hundred pieces of DNA to more than 2 million. The Human Genome Project has estimated that we have between 20,000 and 25,000 genes. Each one of us has two copies of each gene, one inherited from each parent. The differences in our genes determine each person's unique features.

We have A LOT of DNA. If we laid out all the DNA contained in our body it would stretch 10 billion miles, from here to Pluto and back. All this DNA, contained in these thousands of genes, is balled up and stored in bundles that are known as chromosomes. However, the sheer amount of DNA we possess doesn't mean we are complicated – there is a single-celled organism, among the simplest of all living things, that has more than 200 times the amount of DNA that we do. In fact, we don't even use much of our DNA, only 2% of it. The other 98% is what we call "junk DNA" because it doesn't seem to have any uses. I am skeptical about that, because I think we will one day find out that a lot of it does have a purpose. We do know that much of it, though, is composed of deactivated genes that were once useful for our non-human ancestors – genes for making a tail, for example. One spooky thing about our "junk" DNA is that a lot of it is "parasitic" DNA left behind by viruses that have entered their genes into ours in order to slyly use our cells to replicate themselves. Because viruses do this, they are being looked at as a way to insert new genes in gene therapy.

There is a commonality among all life forms on earth when it comes to our DNA, as we share 98% of our genes with chimpanzees, 90% with mice, and even 21% with worms. Among humans 99.9% of all our genes are the same, so all the differences inside and out among us come from a tiny percentage of our genes. We are far more alike than we are different. We

[29]

would be well served to remember that next time we see one group of humans in conflict with another over their "differences."

*

There are two things that decide who we are as people: one is our genetics and the other is our environment. By environment I mean everything that happens to us after we are born: what kind of parenting we receive, what kind of home we grow up in, our diet, our friends, our education, our life experiences, and so on. This is the "nature vs. nurture" you may have heard about, where "nature" refers to our inherited genetic make-up, and "nurture" refers to our environment that affects our development. Just how much each is involved in certain traits that we have is always being debated. Sometimes, it's clear: our eye colour is 100% nature – determined by our genetics. But usually it's not so clear: if we develop cancer some of it is because of our genetics and some of it is because of things from our environment. One of my instructors in medical school used to say: "Your genetics load the gun. Your lifestyle pulls the trigger."

When it comes to alcoholism and addiction it is definitely a combination of our nature and nurture. We know that 40 to 60% of our disease comes from our genetic predisposition, so the remaining 40 to 60% comes from our life experiences. That means that even someone who is not genetically susceptible to becoming addicted to a substance or behavior can still do so. This is especially so if they grow up in an abusive home, experience traumatic events, are exposed to drugs and alcohol from an early age, and are financially disadvantaged. Or, someone who is genetically susceptible may never suffer the disease, especially if they lead a life that is more nurturing and isolated from negative influences and experiences. We must remember that although our genetics and environment play a huge role in who we are, we also have free will. **Our genetics are not our destiny** (repeat that three times!). The lesson here is that possessing genes that predispose us to addiction does not necessarily mean that we will become addicted, and not possessing these genes doesn't necessarily mean that we are safe from it.

This is a life-and-death message, because we must not allow our knowledge of our "addictive" genes to become a self-fulfilling prophesy. When the genetic predisposition to alcoholism-addiction was announced to the world via the popular media, as a doctor I immediately recognized that this would prove to be harmful information for many individuals unless it was given in context, which it wasn't. Without the context that we are discussing in this chapter, this information could lead the children of an alcoholic-addict to become convinced that they will necessarily share their parent's destiny, which could lead to it becoming a self-fulfilling prophesy, a foregone conclusion. As well, they might believe that their genetics make them untreatable, which may tragically prevent them from seeking help or from believing in their ability to achieve sobriety.

The other fear I had was that this information would enable alcoholics to affix blame for their disease on their alcoholic parent and their genes, which can very much impair their ability to find recovery. It is true that many of us have been dealt a bad hand by our parents and our genes – which is something that we cannot control or change – so we can easily be focussed on blaming those things. This distracts us from focussing on our own role in our disease – which we can change – and therefore distracts us from an achievable solution to our problem. As well, it causes resentment toward the parent (and the universe) to grow, which in itself can cause us to drink or use. Readers who are involved in the Twelve Step program will recognize the inherent dangers here. As a doctor and psychotherapist I could see the dangers here in that the information gives alcoholics an "external locus of control" for our disease, which is a major impediment to getting anywhere with the psychological problems around the addiction. We will become very familiar with the simple concept of "external locus of control" and its devastating involvement in our addiction and our life problems in an up-coming chapter.

Another danger involved in the information about how genetics are involved in alcoholism-addiction is that many people who are addicted to alcohol or other drugs or addictive behaviors carry a lot of guilt over the fact that they may have passed these genes on to their children. This guilt is unfounded for a couple of reasons. First of all because we are no more at fault for being born with genes for addiction than we are for the genes for our eye colour or for how big our nose is. Secondly, there is no way for any of us to know if we were born with these genes or not. We can't go see our doctor and ask for genetic testing for addiction. Any one of us and our parents could have ended up with addictions issues even without the addiction genes. Maybe one day genetic testing for that will be available, but it's unlikely because there is no single "alcoholism-addiction gene." There are dozens, if not hundreds, of different genes that all come together in different combinations to contribute to that chain of characteristics that give rise to susceptibility to addiction. As well, our kids' genes are a combination of our own genes and the other parent's genes, so there is no way to know what combination that our kids ended up with when it comes to the genes involved in addictive tendencies.

This guilt that people with alcoholism-addiction problems feel over passing this genetic legacy on to their children is actually quite a dangerous thing. Guilt is a major factor in causing people to develop mental health and alcoholism-addiction, and can be a major impediment in treating these problems. Since this guilt is unfounded and illogical, as guilt often is, it is truly a shame that it happens so commonly. But it does. I really hope that it doesn't cause people to decide not to have children, but it probably has done so for some.

If you are a person who feels guilt over thoughts of passing on your "bad" genes to your kids take heart: your "genetically enhanced" (I say that tongue-in-cheek, of course) addictive behaviors will give you an edge as a parent that can counter-act anything negative that you have passed on to your kids. We will address this directly, but first let's learn a little more about genetics and alcoholism-addiction, and then at the end of the chapter we'll talk about some practical things we can do to counter-act any negative genes we may or may not have.

*

The genetics of alcoholism-addiction – how susceptibility to it is influenced by inheritance – has become a hot topic, particularly since it became public knowledge that our disease tends to run in families. Because it's so important, let's once again make one thing clear: possessing genes that predispose us to addiction does not mean we will become addicted. What is at stake here is a genetic predisposition to alcoholism-addiction, not a genetic guarantee of it. In other words, some people are genetically more vulnerable to alcoholism-addiction than are others. Who we are and what we are is determined by much more than just pure genetics, especially when it comes to mental and behavioral processes. Obviously, our life experiences – our environment – affects us a great deal. The fact that many people with a strong family history of alcoholism-addiction (genetic vulnerability) do not become alcoholic-addicts, while many people with little or no family history (low genetic vulnerability) do, illustrates this point. There are far too many moving parts here to be able to make any rules.

Some genes directly control an obvious physical trait. An example is the gene that is responsible for the dreadful disease Cystic Fibrosis, where a single gene causes the disease. However, most of our physical traits are controlled by a complex collection of entirely separate genes that are themselves in turn influenced by other unrelated genes. Because of this, something that would seem simple like the genetics of eye color or hair color is actually very complex. The number of genes that interact to determine eye colour are so complex that we still do not fully understand them, and we definitely can't predict eye colour. The genetics of alcoholism-addiction are similarly very complex, because there are a number of different physical factors that can affect it, each with its own complex genetic controls, and we don't even fully understand exactly what all these factors are and how they work, let alone their genetic background.

While the search for these genes and the physical factors they control goes on, we are mostly limited to analyzing statistically how alcoholism-addiction runs in families and by comparing identical twins where one or more of the twins is an alcoholic-addict. These studies are complicated by the fact that alcoholics and addicts tend to be very unreliable in terms of participating in medical studies (and anything else, for that matter).

However, some progress has been made. Specifically, we believe that the size of the part of the brain that is involved in alcoholism-addiction (where we find the dopamine) seems to be a factor, so we are searching for the genes that control the size of this part of the brain. As well, we are searching for the

[33]

genes that affect how much dopamine we produce, our reaction to dopamine, and other biochemical processes known to be involved in our disease. To further complicate things, the genetics of other traits that influence whether or not we are susceptible to addictive behavior, such as the genetics of certain mental health disorders, also become involved.

*

Let's take a closer look at how much our genetics influence our alcoholism-addiction. Earlier I mentioned that genetics account for between 40 and 60% of our addictive tendency, but there's more to those figures than meets the eye. The National Council on Alcoholism and Drug Dependence – NCADD – says on its website that genetics make up 50% of the risk for alcohol and drug dependence.[1] The National Institute of Health (NIH) website cites an article that gives figures for the heritability of addictions to specific substances.[2] These range from 39% for hallucinogens to a whopping 72% for cocaine. I would be very careful with these figures, because there is not and may not ever be a way to separate genetic and environmental factors in the statistics. To illustrate, let's look at cocaine (we'll just look, we won't touch).

A baby born to a cocaine-addicted mother who was using during pregnancy will be born addicted to cocaine. When I was an intern working in a Neonatal Intensive Care Unit, most of our tiny newborn patients were born addicted to cocaine and we were helping them survive the withdrawal effects. The brain changes that occur in the addict are therefore already in place in such a child from the start of life, so, sadly, the child will be very vulnerable to addiction later in life. That is because the child has already been addicted to the drug, and not because of genetics. Fortunately, these children are removed from the care of their mothers until such time as the mother is in recovery and fit for parenting. This illustrates how a child of a cocaine-addicted mother is born predisposed to being an addict later in life for reasons that have nothing to do with genetics. The mother might have "addiction" genes, but we can't separate out how much of her child's susceptibility came from the genes and how much came from being exposed to cocaine in the uterus. So, this is why the statistic for genetic cocaine addiction predisposition is so high at 72%. In other words, we can't separate out how much this was nature (addiction genes) and how much was nurture (exposure to cocaine during brain development in the womb). And there's another aspect that further confounds our ability to sort out how much genetics affect addiction. Let's keep using the example of cocaine addiction.

Sadly, despite the best efforts of our Social Services many children end up being raised in homes of active cocaine addicts. It's safe to say that very few actively addicted couples remain together to raise a child, and even if they do their relationship and home life will likely be unstable and non-nurturing. So, the child will likely be raised in a home with a mother with multiple short, volatile relationships, the child will receive very poor parenting, very poor nutrition, and will grow up in a home where drugs are always available, close at hand. The child may be physically, mentally, even sexually abused. All these "nurture" factors come together to make the child extremely high risk for developing alcoholism and addiction. All this has to do with environmental factors, nurture, and not necessarily genetics, nature, although "bad" genetics, if present, will add to the risk.

In the example I just gave, if the child ends up an addict at some point then statistically it could be said that it was genetically predisposed to addiction, and therefore became an addict. But in reality environmental factors played a huge role. How much was this due to genetics, and how much was due to the environment, being born addicted, raised in an abusive home, poor nutrition, a lack of a positive role model, and easy access to drugs and paraphernalia? I don't think science will ever be able to know for sure.

\*

How do genes affect whether or not we will become addicted when we take a drink or drug? In the previous chapter we talked about neurotransmitters, the brain chemicals that brain cells use to pass messages and instructions. The sensitivity of our brain to these neurotransmitters is genetically determined. Our genes accomplish this by controlling the number of receptors and transporters for each of these neurotransmitters, as well as the amount of production of the neurotransmitters themselves. We discussed the importance of the specific neurotransmitter dopamine, the "feel-good" brain chemical used to reward us for good behaviors. We know that when our dopamine levels are low we feel the opposite of good: we feel lifeless, slow, and bored. There is one gene in particular that has been identified that causes dopamine to be broken down more quickly by the brain, resulting in chronic low levels. In order to compensate for the low levels of dopamine, the people who possess this gene are known to be subconsciously driven to seek out behaviors that increase dopamine levels. That means they tend to be "thrill-seekers", risk-takers, adventurous – looking for excitement to stimulate dopamine release. Unfortunately, addictive behaviors that release dopamine, such as gambling, compulsive shopping, sex, and so on also become sought after. And, as you have probably guessed, these people are likely to pursue daily alcohol or drug use to further overcome their dopamine shortage. So, this could be considered an "addiction gene." Just one of many.

Today I saw a news article about a young woman in a nearby city who was rescued from the hook dangling from a huge construction crane, 12 stories in the air. During the night she climbed up the crane and then slid down the cable and perched on the hook, swaying in the wind high in the skyline. Police said they were unable to determine a motive, but her friends said that she does this kind of thing all the time. I'm willing to bet that she has the dopamine receptor gene defect that we just talked about. She's a genetic thrill-seeker. It would be interesting to know if she is or will be addicted to substance use.

There are so many ways that genes can make us susceptible to addiction to substances or behaviors that we may never identify them all. It is reasonable to say that the more of these genes a person has, the more likely they are to become addicted. However, in the end it is the nurture, the environmental influences on the person, that push the person over the edge. Remember: genetics load the gun, but it is lifestyle that pulls the trigger.

As we will discuss later in this book, mental health disorders and addiction share many genes. Given that both are all about brain structure and neurotransmitter function, that is hardly surprising. That is precisely why there is such a huge overlap in addictions and mental health problems: depression, anxiety, bipolar disorder, and so on. More on this in chapter 8.

[36]

\*

Now that we are identifying some of these alcoholism-addiction genes, can we do anything to rid ourselves of them? There is a lot of intense research going on looking into gene therapy, seeking to be able to remove undesirable genes and replace them with better functioning ones, de-activating harmful genes, or putting in genes that are not natural to us but which would help us in some way. It's not easy to put a gene into our chromosomes, and we have turned to using viruses to help us do that. Viruses operate by inserting their DNA into our genes and fooling our bodies into making lots of baby viruses. Now – with ironic pay-back – we are inserting our therapeutic DNA into viruses to fool them into inserting it into our genes. It is double pleasure to deceive the deceiver. However, even if we successfully place DNA into our genes, there is no guarantee the body will recognize it and use it. Nevertheless, the research has had promising results, including for Cystic Fibrosis, the single-gene disease I mentioned earlier. Still, our dogged pursuit of gene therapy still has a long way to go before it can be safe and effective. And, there's a major barrier to its eventual use that has nothing to do with science: gene therapy walks a knife-edge between medical miracle… and ethical disaster.

In the future it will be possible to use gene therapy to modify our genetic profile, with a view to "improving" our health, physical and mental abilities, and life expectancy. Like genetic cloning, gene therapy can easily be taken too far, which makes it an issue of great ethical debate. Because gene therapy involves making changes to the body's set of basic instructions, it raises many unique ethical concerns. Consider how you would answer these questions: who decides which traits are normal and which need to be changed? Will the high costs of gene therapy make it available only to the wealthy? Could the widespread use of gene therapy make society less accepting of people who are different, or "less perfect"? Should people be allowed to use gene therapy to enhance non-illness traits such as height, intelligence, or athletic ability? Could gene therapy be abused to make people "super" for tasks such as warfare, crime, or professional fighting (with traits such as improved night-vision, larger muscle size, faster reflexes, more resistance to pain)? What effects will genetic manipulation have on our offspring?

The only reason I bring up the ethics of gene therapy here is to illustrate that just because a technology comes along doesn't mean it will end up in use. Genetic cloning has been banned in many countries. The U.S. government will not fund certain aspects of gene therapy research, and there are many groups that are emphatically opposed to genetic manipulation of any kind. Even genetic engineering of our food is loaded with debate. Gene therapy is a long way from becoming a standard treatment. Alcoholism and addiction are not a single-gene disease like Cystic Fibrosis, so the many genes involved make gene therapy even that much further out of reach for us. So we shouldn't expect anytime soon to walk into our doctor's office and get a shot that will take away that 40 to 60% of our vulnerability to alcoholism-addiction. But don't worry: there's much we can do without gene therapy.

*

Now that we've talked about what we can't do about our genetics, let's brighten our horizons by looking at what we can do. If we have an inkling that we have given our children the genes that will make them more susceptible to our disease it pains us very much to know that we may have "caused" our children to face the misery we have faced. Although there is not yet any widely available genetic testing for this – it's still in the research stages and probably will be for many years – probably the best indicator that there may be something going on genetically is if alcoholism-addiction issues are strong in our family. In my own case, I know very little about my father's family, but I do know that my father and his father both died of complications of chronic alcoholism. So, it's a good bet that there's something genetic going on there. However, there is no history of alcoholism or other addictions whatsoever in my extended family on my mother's side. I got my genes from both sides of the family, so who knows what I have genetically. As well, I have one sibling, my older sister, and she has never had any problems with addictions of any kind, while I have struggled with drugs and alcohol. Look

[38]

at your own situation, and see what you think your genetic make-up might be. When it comes down to life it really doesn't matter, because if we become an alcoholic or addict what matters is getting us better, not whether or not our genes were to blame. However, having said that, if we think there may be some alcoholism-addiction genetics in our family, a little extra vigilance and education in our children's lives may be warranted.

Despite ten years of medical training and fifteen years of practice, I really knew very little about alcoholism and other addictions until I lived the experience myself. I found my sobriety in A.A., and that program has schooled me about addictions and recovery in a way that will serve to more than off-set any "bad" genetics that I have passed on to my kids. I have heard and read the stories of many other addicts and alcoholics in A.A. and these stories, together with my own experiences, make me highly tuned to picking up when someone else is headed for the bottle or the needle. As well, I have heard several female speakers' stories about their experiences when they were using drugs and alcohol as 12 and 13 year-olds, something that has given me some insight into watching for problems with my own 12 year-old daughter. So, in a very real way, my disease has made me far more capable of dealing with it if it pokes its ugly head into my children's lives. That offsets any "bad" genes I may or may not have passed on to them.

Likewise, my ability to provide care and advice to patients – and their families – who struggle with addictive substances and behaviors would now be far above what it had been prior to my own misadventures in addiction and alcoholism. Perhaps most notably, I am nearly bulletproof to the lying that forms a core symptom of our disease. In medical school I was taught to take the amount an alcoholic claims to be drinking and double it. Now I laugh at that nugget of attempted medical shrewdness. It's a monumental nod to our epic skills as liars that we alcoholics have succeeded in fooling the medical establishment so well. We alcoholics and addicts invented deceit. Now the only reason I even ask them how much they drink is so that I can get a feeling for exactly how deeply they are trying to deceive me. Then I check with their family for a more realistic answer. And then I double that.

My own recovery and all that I have learned about recovery and personal growth from the Twelve Steps have made me very well-equipped to become involved in my own kids' lives when it comes to substance use and abuse. I know I can speak to them about the subject. I haven't yet decided when and how much I will share my own experiences with them, but I know that by living my life sober and free from addiction – that cruellest of prisons – I can speak volumes without saying a word. Good genes or bad genes, as parents we must never forget that our children will one day follow our example, not our advice. We can't stop the gun from being loaded by the genes we passed on to our children, but we can do much to prevent the trigger from being pulled. We should rightfully feel great comfort in that.

# Three

## Our Memory and Our Disease

*When I was younger, I could remember anything, whether it happened or not.* As usual, Mark Twain's jest is wrapped in truth: our memory is a marvelous but treacherously deceptive process. If data on our computers were subject to large errors in being saved to memory, tainted by other data while stored, and then further distorted when called up, we wouldn't rely on our computers. But this is exactly what happens with our brain's memory processes, so how much should we rely on our memory?

The biological purpose of our memory is to use past experiences to guide future actions. That's scary for an alcoholic-addict in recovery, particularly if our substance use encompassed a large part of our life – we don't want those past experiences to guide our future actions. Will our memories guide us back to where we were, or can they lead us toward a future of sobriety and life? Unfortunately, the latter won't happen on its own. As is the case with all our higher brain functions, our memory processes are commandeered by alcohol and drugs and brutally used against us. To counter this process, we need to know how our memory works. Then we can understand how to prevent disaster and make our memory work for **us**... and not for the bottle or needle.

The fact that our memory is so subject to corruption is baffling, because – biologically – accurate, unadulterated memories would serve us better. But, we are forced to deal with our memory as it is. There is one aspect of our memory recall that has a particularly great impact on our ability to stay in sobriety: that is the tendency to remember the good parts of past events, no matter how crappy the events were at the time. Our memory is not like a photograph: it can be altered by many influences. Not least of these corrupting influences is the alcohol and drugs that intoxicate our brain.

Memories are impressions of events, our impressions. Psychologists refer to our process of forming memories as self-referent encoding, which means that as we form memories, we elaborate on the facts, interpreting them based on our brain's needs and wants and our own perspective. Because of this, our memories are not like video recorders, recording every detail perfectly, they are patchy at best, heavily biased by our own slant. When we record our memories of drinking or using we are experiencing a dopamine surge, and we have just experienced the rush of having our obsession satisfied. Our brain will record the good feelings we are having at the time and interpret everything going on around us and what is on our mind as positive. No matter how miserable our life has become in our addiction, the memory of the event of that drink or drug will be stored as a positive memory.

Similarly, we are prey to retrieval biases, where our recall of events is heavily colored by our impressions, wants and needs at the time of recall. When our lives are owned by a substance we feel crushing guilt over our wayward ways and our mind reduces this guilt by altering truth and logic about our actions. This is called *cognitive dissonance*. We will get to know this crucial aspect of our mind's function very well in the up-coming chapters, but for now I'll explain. Our mind needs to see ourselves as basically good, and our bad behavior contradicts that, so our mind feels pain over this contradiction. This psychological pain is what we know as guilt, regret, self-loathing, and shame. While we are actively drinking or using – and also when we achieve sobriety – our mind's natural drive to reduce our psychological pain over what we have done pushes us to substantiate our actions by rationalization, by lying to itself. So, our mind supresses our memories of the bad and promotes the memories of the "good" as an excuse for our behavior: we were only pursuing something good. This rationalization also leads us to blame others: "you'd drink too if you had my wife!" This is a big part of the "stinking thinking" that we speak of in recovery. Our mind is geared to recall memories of our drinking or using that are, to us, pleasant. Our disease takes full advantage of our mind's natural weakness for retrieval bias. But take heart: we can turn around this weakness of our memory's natural process and make it our strength.

*

Let's look at the science of how human memory works, and see why memory can drive us to drink or use. Then we can wrest it free from the grasp of our intoxicants and turn it around on them. This is information that can help us win our personal inner war against alcohol and drugs. As George Carlin said, *just because we got the monkey is of our back doesn't mean the circus has left town.* For those who are inclined to help others with their pursuit of sobriety, this is knowledge we can pass on to those we wish to help, with great effect. For you Twelve Steppers, that means this information will up your game as a sponsor and in working your Twelfth Step.

It is commonly thought that the most compelling pleasant memory of our substance use is the act of being high, or drunk. But that's not so. The memory most responsible for the drive to get our next drink or drug is one that we are not even aware of. It's the subconscious memory of the immense psychological relief we felt when the terrible anxiety of our obsession was satisfied when we answered the compulsion to obtain the next installment of our poison potion. That means that our mind best remembers the relief we got by stopping off at the liquor store or the dealer and not the high we got after.

Regardless of which memory is the biggest bully, our mind finds several kinds of pleasant memories: the soothing deliverance from the anxiety caused by our obsession when we are finally able to get that next fix, the feeling of the high from our chemical fix, the perceived fun of being socially disinhibited around other people, and the momentary perceived relief from all our stressors. We also have unpleasant memories: the deathly ill hang-overs, the shame and guilt of our actions, the loss of family, friends, and possessions, and the frustrating inability to stop. As we just discussed, our mind is geared to suppressing the negative memories and emphasize the good ones so as to rationalize our bad behavior. So it is these pleasant memories that dominate us, and drive us back to drink, and the bad memories that could

[43]

keep us from repeating our mistakes are suppressed. But, it's not just memory recall that our disease kidnaps, it's also memory formation.

When we form a memory of an event, the stronger our attention is directed at that event, the stronger the memory. For example, a groom who tries to recall what a certain guest was wearing at his wedding may not be able to, but he will definitely recall how his bride looked. That is because his attention was highly focussed on his new wife, but only peripherally focussed on his guest (hopefully so, for the sake of his marriage). So, the memory of what he focussed on most at his wedding will be the strongest. It is the same for our memories of drinking or using. When we are obsessed with getting a drink or drug all of our attention is focussed on that drink or drug. It's all we can think about, which is why it's called an obsession. So the memories around the pleasant feelings of getting that drink or drug and the effects of it are recorded very well in our memory. When we are sick and distressed the next day, we try our best to sleep it off, and most likely have already focussed our attention on getting the next fix. Our attention is brought away from the bad by our obsession. The memories of the bad will not be strongly recorded.

The memories of the "pleasantness" of getting a drink or drug will be reinforced by the fact that they are registered over and over again, multiple times. Many alcoholic-addicts have many years of daily drinking or use behind them, so these pleasant memories are going to be very solidly entrenched. Because using substances involves so many senses and behaviors, there are many cues that become linked to our memories of it. The sense of smell is especially powerful as a memory cue, and this is well provided for by our substances. These cues play into a specific type of memory that sharply tests our ability to stay sober: cued memory.

One of the ways that we recall memory is *cued recall*, where a cue triggers recall of a related memory. Unlike forced memories – where we are trying to remember an event – which often takes quite a bit of conscious effort, cued memories occur automatically, without any planning or effort on our part. The cues that bring these memories on can be anything: sounds, smells, tastes, places, visual cues (including people's faces), even emotions. In recovery lingo we call these cues "triggers," because they not only trigger our memory of our intoxicant, a pleasant memory, but they can also trigger us to seek out that intoxicant again. I think any of us in recovery will have experienced cued memories: something that makes us suddenly and unwittingly remember our drinking or using. For many of us, these unwanted and unexpected memory flashes are very uncomfortable and distressing, and they definitely put us at risk for relapse. The Twelve Step program addresses these powerful cued memories by advising us to seek new people, places, and things as part of our plan for recovery. We need to avoid these cues, especially in early recovery. Shortly we will discuss how to tie these cues to bad memories, so they no longer draw us back to our former ways.

\*

The cues in these memories are brought on and reinforced by a process known in psychology as classical conditioning. This is the "Pavlov's dog" effect, where a neutral stimulus – such as the sight of the face of a drinking buddy or a street where our favorite watering hole or our dealer is located – elicits a response, in this case a memory of drinking or using, because in the past it has been paired with our drinking/using. For example, whenever, in our drinking days, we saw that street or that drinking buddy's face we were soon after getting our obsession satisfied and experiencing the euphoria of the alcohol. We associate these things with the "fun" part of drinking or using, our pleasant memories. We do not associate these cues with the bad things, because they are not present when we are sick and hung-over, fighting with our loved ones, being chased by bill collectors. The "good" part of drinking or using – the high, relief of our obsession, and relief from our worries – occurs immediately when we see our cues, but the bad parts – hangover, guilt, withdrawal – occur the next day. We associate the cue with the part that happened right away, not the part that happened the next day. So, whenever we see these things in our sober days, they cue pleasant drinking memories. Any alcoholic or addict will know how insidiously compelling these triggers can be. Classical conditioning is a powerful way that our brain learn, and it is repetition-based. The multiple repetitions of our substance use embeds these learned cues deeply in our mind. Usually for a lifetime.

These are our trigger memories, and the scary thing is that these memories are an unconscious process requiring no effort, so we have no

[45]

control over them. Memory studies have shown that distracting ourselves at the time of recall can slow the recall process, but doesn't stop the memory or reduce its strength. So, reading a book, watching a movie, going for a walk will not derail these cued trigger memories when they occur. Learning is a relatively permanent change in behavior resulting from experience, so this substance-taught learning is no small barrier to recovery. Unless we can undo these learned triggers we will experience them long into our recovery. Now let's find out how to "unlearn" this monkey on our back.

*

A learned association, in this case seeing a face or location that we associate with pleasant drinking/using memories, can naturally diminish when we stop reinforcing the learned association in sobriety. In other words, when we abstain from using or drinking the learned association with our triggers will begin to fade. This is known as *extinction*, but this process is very slow and drawn out if not helped along, because these cues have been learned by the brain over and over again. Even if the learned association does fade, spontaneous recurrence is common. But, they can be unlearned. Our "new people, places, and things" slogan leads us to avoid triggers that may make us drink or use, but it also taps into what science calls *cue-dependent forgetting*, which is the decay of memories when the cues that trigger them are no longer there. There is solid science behind that old slogan.

Another A.A. slogan: "remember when" teaches us to make sure we think of all the misery that our drinking or using brought on, so as to replace the dominant memories of the good times. This deceptively simple slogan brilliantly taps into science's other effective technique for deleting undesired learning. This technique is known as *interference*. Interference is self-explanatory: when one memory (the bad times when we drank or used) gets repeatedly recalled it disrupts another memory (the good times). This effect is magnified if we recall the preferred memory whenever the unwanted memory tries to assert itself. However, this process won't occur on its own, as our mind is still geared toward remembering the good times. So, it takes some work on our part, and we must actively "remember when." Unlike the process

[46]

of extinction, which is slow and incomplete, unlearning harmful memories by interference is powerful and prompt, and can have a robust effect on defeating our alcoholism-addiction.

By far the best way to engage this potent memory interference process is by meditation. Meditation isn't as spooky or other-worldly as it sounds. I have practiced meditation for many years and I learned it as part of the process for getting my black belt in karate. In martial arts the idea behind meditation is that the mind is naturally weak and will go where it wants to go when it wants to. In a combat situation, if you get hit in the nose the pain will be intense and the mind will forget everything else and just focus on the pain. We will bend over, turn our back, and cower, resulting in us getting a really bad beating. Therefore, the idea of meditation is to practice focussing the mind and keeping it focussed, not allowing it to wander. With practice, our mind can become so disciplined that we can keep it from wandering away from where it needs to be focussed.

Initially, the idea is to practice keeping our mind focussed on a thought or an object during a brief meditation, and bringing it back on track whenever it starts to wander off. Given the 8 second attention span of the human mind, this isn't as easy as it sounds. With time and practice we become good at it; our mind becomes disciplined. Then, we start adding distractions while we meditate, making it harder and harder to keep our mind focussed. Eventually, we become so good at it that our mind is disciplined even when we are not meditating. If something happens to us – such as encountering a trigger for our drinking or using – we are able to keep our mind from its usual practice of snapping to an undesirable reaction – such as picking up that first drink or drug.

The ability to keep the mind focussed and prevent its distraction has other useful applications. First of all, if we are in a situation where someone angers us, the weak mind will go right to anger and we may lash out with some rash action we will later regret. The disciplined mind will stay on task, without becoming distracted by the anger, allowing us to process the situation and come up with a measured reaction. Rather than just lashing out in anger, we give a thought-out response. We remain in control of ourselves. We no longer **re**act, we act in a measured and intelligent way. Think of what a wonderful life skill this is!

Going back to my martial arts example, in a combat situation if we get injured we can keep our disciplined mind on ending the fight, either by escaping or by fighting back, because we were able to keep our weak mind from focussing on the pain. Even better, our disciplined mind will help us keep our cool and de-escalate an emotionally-charged situation and avoid a fight to begin with. This is meditation as I learned it, applied to martial arts. The same concept has served me well in recovery, but a much watered-down version is perfect for engaging the extinction method of dispelling the harmful learning that led to our drinking/using triggers.

*

Ready to try some simple meditation? Don't worry, it's not some kind of a secret ancient procedure, and it's not mystical. Meditation is not time consuming, not about having an empty mind, sitting in weird positions, chanting, and it's not religious or other-worldly. In fact, it's about being comfortable, takes only a few minutes or can be done momentarily through the day, involves an active mind, and it's very real and practical. As I mentioned earlier, I learned to meditate as part of my martial arts training and the United States Marine Corps teaches it to their soldiers. Many people enjoy new-found life skills from its benefits, including eliminating drug or alcohol cravings. What could be more practical than that?

We start off in any position we wish, as long as we are comfortable. Sitting on the couch or floor – cross-legged or not – however we are most comfortable. Some people like to meditate laying down, but I don't. Many are surprised by how incredibly relaxed our mind becomes as we meditate, and I have a tendency to drift off to sleep when I meditate laying down. In fact, on nights that I am unable to sleep I will lay down and start meditating on something pleasant and it always puts me to sleep.

I recommend closing eyes, as it is much easier to concentrate and focus the mind with the eyes closed. As we start introducing distractions to our senses in order to challenge and advance our skills, keeping eyes open is one way of doing that. However, I have been meditating a long time and I still prefer keeping my eyes closed.

Breathing is very important for starting our meditation, because we want to send a burst of fresh oxygen to our brain to kick-start it into action. Even though our brain makes up only 2% of our body it uses 25% of all of our oxygen intake. Our brain needs to breath. While we meditate, we breathe in through the nose and out through the mouth. If we keep our back straight and erect it gives our diaphragm – the big dome-shaped muscle between our chest and abdomen – more room to do its job as it contracts to draw fresh life-giving air into our lungs and up to our brain.

We start with three to five deep breaths in through the nose and out through the mouth, but no more than five. We don't want to make ourselves dizzy. Some call these "cleansing breaths." As we meditate we will continue breathing in through the nose and out through the mouth, but we'll just breathe at a normal rate. Meditation has been shown to lower our metabolism; as our mind achieves a state of relaxation our body seems to follow. As our relaxation slows our metabolism our oxygen consumption drops and our breathing will slow and become shallow. So, don't be surprised if you notice this happening.

As a beginning meditator, it takes some practice to get physically and mentally relaxed. It becomes very easy before too long. Once we are in a relaxed state it's time to start our mental exercise.

*

We now focus our mind and all our thoughts, with eyes closed, on dark, empty space. Blackness. Nothingness. Every time our mind starts thinking about something, including what we are doing, we guide it back to focussing solely on the nothingness. This can be done for increasingly longer periods of time. It is important to keep focussing our mind, not allowing it to wander. Our undisciplined mind will keep trying to wander off on its own agenda: to some problem we've been dealing with, something someone said to us, something we forgot to do, what to have for supper, some big task coming up, and so on. That is our challenge: to keep guiding our mind back to the nothingness. Quite often, we will find ourselves thinking about something during meditation and we don't even realize it initially, until after we've been thinking on it for a while. As soon as we realize it, we reign our thoughts in again. It's like our mind is a dog on a leash. Every time it tries to wander off the sidewalk we pull the leash to get it back on the sidewalk. We shorten the leash, and keep pulling it in. After a while, the dog starts staying on the sidewalk. So it is with our mind: with repeated practice it takes less and less effort to keep it focussed on the nothingness, and we rarely have to pull it back in. Our mind is becoming disciplined.

We limit our meditation to this simple exercise until we are very good at it. Initially our meditation should only last 2 to 4 minutes. As we get better we can start extending the time of the meditation. The longer we meditate the more challenging it is to keep our mind reigned in. Only when we can meditate for 5 to 10 minutes with a focussed mind without difficulty can we move on to the next step in developing our skill.

*

Now that we have the trappings of a disciplined mind, let's try a visualization exercise during our meditation. We start out as we did before: positioning, cleansing breaths, clear mind. Once we have achieved our relaxed state, we visualize breathing in cool, blue air. We take in air that is ice-blue: cool and pure, fresh, clean air. The blue air we are inhaling is cool, but also calm and smooth. It comes in through the nose.

When we exhale, we visualize hot, red, bad, toxic air going out through the mouth. It's actually red in color, very warm, dirty, angry air. This red air is turbulent and poisonous. This red, hot air is filled with anger, hate, fear, and guilt. It comes from down deep inside of us, and dissipates into the sky once it's out.

We continue breathing in this cool blue air, in through the nose, and exhaling this hot red air, out through the mouth. We visualize the cool blue air going deep down inside us and swirling around, and pushing out the hot red air, which rushes out of our body and dissipates into the sky. We can feel the cool blue air going throughout our body as it circulates, reaching every part of us, all the way down to our fingers and toes. As it does this it pushes the hot, red air out of every last part of our body.

[50]

As we continue to breathe, we imagine there becoming progressively more blue air deep down in our body, and less and less red air. Gradually, there is less and less red air, and more and more blue air, until finally there is nothing but cool blue air, blue air coming in when we breathe in, our lungs full of cool blue air, and cool blue air coming out through our mouth when we exhale. There is nothing but cool, blue, calm, clean, smooth air in and out. At this point, our mind is relaxed and focussed. We are unaware of our body, and have no thoughts beyond our breathing.

The cool blue air represents peace, serenity, confidence, love, goodwill, cleanliness, health, positivity. As we feel the blue air circulating through our entire body, being distributed by our circulation to every inch of our body, we feel the cool air's effects: we feel peaceful, serene, confident, loving, positive. We keep visualizing this and let it affect our mood. For the rest of our meditation we just keep our mind focussed on the clean, cool blue air coming in and out, reaching every part of our body.

This exercise is an excellent way to practice relaxing and focussing our mind. Once we have practiced this visualization a few times, we can use it to focus our mind and center our mood at the start of a meditation, or use it as the entire meditation for its calming, centering effects. I often start every meditation with this visualization, because it makes me feel like I am purifying my body and emotions.

*

These are just a couple of very simple introductory meditations. In my up-coming book *Science Meets Spirituality* I get much more into basic and advanced meditation skills and how to apply them to our daily life. Now, let's apply the "remember when" principle to our meditation. For me, this is the skill that most contributed to taking away my obsession and cravings for alcohol and drugs. What we are doing is using meditation to replace that learned association between drugs or alcohol and "good" things, and replacing it by an association with the bad things. This is putting the science of memory to full use in our recovery by maximizing the interference learning principle.

[51]

We start out in the same way, getting physically comfortable, and then mentally comfortable and focussed by using either our "nothingness" meditation or our "blue air" meditation. Then, we focus our mind on the hell that our substance use put us through. We meditate on the time and effort and money we had to spend getting and hiding our substance, the things we lost, the people we hurt, the hangovers and withdrawals, the guilt and shame and regret, the wasted days and months and years. Every time our mind wanders off topic we bring it right back. We don't have to spend long at it, just a few minutes every day. Before long we find it easy to call up those memories when our stinking thinking kicks in and we are struck by memories of the good times and left with a desire to relapse.

This speeds up and deepens the process of interference. This advice is not only for newcomers; the further away from the events we get, the more likely we are to remember the good times and forget the bad. So, the further we are into recovery, the more susceptible we are to these memories that can trip us up. As well, meditation doesn't have to be all about bad memories. Some of the other things to meditate on are: the things in life we am grateful for, reflecting on the day to see what we could have done better, reflecting on our defects of character that we can improve on and how they came out in our actions today, and pleasant situations and places that relax our mind.

The other way this meditation can help our immediate recovery is by giving us the mental discipline to snap our mind back to reality anytime our disease causes us to think about picking up drugs or alcohol. If we allow our weak mind to be led down this thought path far enough we may fall. The disciplined mind is easily able to counter-act our disease's attempts to highjack our thoughts.

There are many other ways we can use our meditation to enrich our recovery, and life. These are beyond the scope of this book. For Twelve Steppers, exploring this is part of Step Eleven. I encourage all to learn more about meditation. Watch for my up-coming book!

*

We have seen how our memory can be a fiction, a distortion of what actually happened. We have also seen that our mind has a mechanism for distorting memories, and that our disease of alcoholism-addiction uses that mechanism to manipulate us into remaining its prisoner. As if that isn't bad enough, we have yet another quirk of memory that can trip us up in our recovery: we have a natural tendency to forget information from our past that isn't compatible with how we see ourselves now. Alcoholism and addiction will debase even the most extraordinary of people, and most of us in recovery resemble little the person we had become. In fact, those who have found sobriety through the Twelve Steps experience aspire to a "fundamental change in character," something I experienced personally. Recovery is great! We are enjoying life again, we are finding comfort in our own skin. Every one of our senses is alert and alive. We now see ourselves as happy, useful, productive people, and our mind likes that. This causes our mind to subconsciously forget the unhappy, turbulent, miserable memories from our drinking or using days in yet another ploy to alleviate the psychological pain from how we were then. Our mind revises history – our memories – to make itself feel better. This effect can be cumulative, and our memory becomes more and more distorted by it the further along we are from our substance-soaked days. Again, our "remember when" meditation is the antidote, and this is increasingly important the further along in our recovery that we become. People who "do the work" of recovery – including meditating on "remember when" – can completely negate the effects of this quirk of memory and, coupled with the effect of the interference that we have discussed, no longer live under the thumb of those dominant  false memories. It's about facing up to and owning who we were, now that we've done something about it, rather than just sweeping it away under the carpet, as our mind is wont to do.

Memory science sheds still more light on why the "remember when" slogan is so potent at halting our natural memory processes from derailing our sobriety. I spoke above of interference, where strengthening one memory interferes with the recall of another. There are two types of interference: proactive and retroactive. In proactive interference, strong older memories will interfere with our recall of newer information. This means that these deep-rooted unwanted good memories of our substance use will tend to smother new information we are trying to learn. So, the memories of the

[53]

good-times can repress our efforts at trying to learn to recall the repressed memories of the bad that came with our chemical misadventures. However, the other type of memory interference, retroactive interference, is when stronger new information that we place in our memories will interfere with the recall of the old. When we meditate on the "remember when" our focus on these memories makes them stronger, which engages this retroactive interference process to get our desired effect. We are eliminating these good memories of drinking and using that draw us back to the bottle or needle. For the Twelve Steppers, this is part of your Eleventh Step work, so it's built into your program. The science shows that meditation is not such a hoofy-doofy thing after all. Meditation allows us to dominate those old, unwanted, harmful memories, rather than the other way around. They no longer "own" us.

*

Memory formation is also called learning, and we discussed classical conditioning: a type of learning where a cue – such as a place or person or smell associated with our substance use – will trigger positive thoughts and lead us to crave our substance. There is another type of learning that is also a formidable roadblock to our recovery: this learning is called *operant conditioning*. Here, we learn to associate a behavior with a reward. In our case, when we do what we do to obtain our poison – jump in the car and drive to the liquor store, or a bar, or a drinking buddy's house, or our dealer's house, or the casino – we soon associate it with the rewards we get from our intoxicant: relief from our obsession, euphoria (dopamine release), relief from our stressors. When we are in recovery and something stresses us or we are having cravings, our mind is inclined to recall the memories of the pleasant effect that result from our substance-obtaining behavior, and it tries its best to compel us to do that behavior as it seeks relief from that stressor. This is what happens when people say that something stressful happened and they found themselves almost unconsciously driving to the liquor store. This learning occurs from positive reinforcement, which means that our behavior of obtaining our intoxicant becomes associated with a reward: the pleasant aspect of our drinking or using. There is no negative reinforcement, which would make us learn to avoid that behavior, because the sickness and pain and remorse comes much later – the next morning – and is therefore not associated with the behavior. That is why we must make that association between the substance-seeking behavior and the misery through meditation. Otherwise, our mind will have an on-going reflexive desire to carry out the substance-seeking behavior, and our sobriety is in peril.

Science has identified that emotions can strengthen the formation of memory, and that they can also influence our recall of these memories. Emotionally-charged events are imprinted on our memory strongly. We remember vividly the birth of our children, a house fire, a big argument. Emotions can be one of those cues that brings about a trigger memory. Specifically, the more down you feel, the more likely you are going to remember unpleasant memories. The better you feel, the more likely you are to experience the pleasant memories. This explains why so many people have described life being "too good" as a trigger to relapse. It also explains part of the danger of the "pink cloud" effect that many of us experience in early recovery. (We will investigate the psychological curiosity called the pink cloud effect in the next chapter and again in the chapter on mental health). Again, the learned association (by our meditation) between our substance and the misery it caused can prevent this mental tendency from allowing our addiction to get the edge.

*

So far we have focussed on spontaneous mind-driven memories. The other type of memory, known as recall memory, is when we deliberately try to remember an event in the absence of a stimulus. This type of memory recall is done consciously and requires effort to do. It is easily over-ridden by the unconscious, automatic, effortless trigger memories. Science has shown us this, and we know it to be true from our own experiences: our triggering memories are superior to recall memories because they are more efficient, rapid, and effortless. This works against us finding and maintaining sobriety. Recall memory is our "remember when" memory, and it will be over-powered by our trigger memories until we use our meditation to turn our recall memories into automatic trigger memories, as we have already discussed.

Research has shown that our memory recall can be greatly influenced by new information, and by suggestions that we insert into old memories, if we do this over time. To science, this principle is known as *creative re-imagination*. This process involves creating a different interpretation of our memories in our mind, which can permanently change these memories whenever they pop up in the future. An extreme example of this is *psychogenic amnesia*, where a person can virtually erase a certain memory. This creative re-imagination is what we are doing with our "remember when" meditation technique, again using the science of memory to our advantage. The power of meditation is solidly based in science, and is a key aspect of using the science to maximize our recovery from overpowering addictions. Meditation should be a part of everyone's recovery.

*

Let's take a breath and summarize the way our disease uses our innate memory processes against us in recovery. Pleasant memories are remembered better than unpleasant ones (in fact, our brain has mechanisms for blocking out unpleasant memories), emotionally charged memories are remembered better than boring ones, and unpleasant memories fade much faster than do pleasant ones. So, in the end, we are much more likely to remember the pleasant aspects of our drinking or using, because they are more firmly implanted in our memory, they are likely to come up spontaneously even when they are unwanted, and they can persist much longer than other memories, haunting us many years into our recovery. Science and experience show that our greatest tool for taking this memory advantage away from our disease and seizing it for ourselves is by our "remember when" meditation.

I have been profoundly impressed by the Twelve Step program and how it addresses all the brain biology, genetics, and psychology of alcoholism and addictions. In fact, I feel professionally that it is the most effective form of psychotherapy there is, thus the subject of the up-coming chapter by that name. The problems brought on by our memory are thoroughly addressed by

[56]

the Twelve Step program of recovery, and it amazes me that this program – which seems to be designed around the science of memory – was developed long before what we now know about the workings of human memory was known to science. And these methods are just as valid now as they were when they were developed over 80 years ago. Whether an alcoholic or addict in recovery is using the Twelve Steps or not, ignoring the power of meditation is an opportunity squandered.

When these memories of our substance-using days come up, the danger lies in what our mind will do with them. People aptly say that while they are working their recovery their disease is always out in the parking lot doing push-ups. (I think my disease is also bench-pressing, doing chin-ups, and sit-ups). That expression is about our memory. The danger of these memories of how pleasant it was to be in the company of our drug of choice is that there is a characteristic of our disease which somehow leads us to think that if we capitulate and pick up that first drink or drug, this time it will be different. This time, we'll be able to drink, or use, or gamble responsibly. For readers who have not lived in alcoholism-addiction I will tell you this, and all my fellow drunks and addicts will likely agree: this is crazy thinking! We have all tried countless times to control our use of our substance, over and over again, and have failed every time. That is why we call ourselves powerless over our substance. That is why this thinking is known as "the insanity of alcoholism-addiction." This thinking is simply our mind rationalizing, trying to manipulate us into getting it its dopamine fix. Insane and illogical as it is, it occurs and it pushes many back down a dark and familiar path. We will discuss the insanity of our disease in a chapter dedicated just to that weird and fascinating subject, the bane of all addicts and alcoholics.

The best way to head off this insane thinking is to prevent it from happening by not allowing those pleasant drinking and using memories to continue "owning" us. Our meditation is the very best way to use the science of creative re-imagination to relieve of us these drinking memories, to thereby kick the arms out from under our disease as it's trying to do push-ups. This is what moves us from having a desire to drink, to having thoughts of drinking. I feel solid in my recovery, and sometimes when I drive past the liquor store I have a thought of drinking. It flashes through my mind of how I once turned into that parking lot and went in the store. But it doesn't elicit a desire to drink. My meditation had everything to do with that.

As well, the science of memory tells us that we can change our brain's interpretation of memories by an act of will. This is where hearing and reading other alcoholic-addicts' stories, talking with other alcoholic-addicts, sharing our own stories, and reaching out to other alcoholic-addicts comes in. One of the strengths of the Twelve Step programs is that they provide ample access to all of those things. We talk the talk and walk the walk and pretty soon we no longer see the "pleasant" part of our drinking or using as pleasant. Our mind will believe what we say and follow our actions. They say it is easier to act your way into a new way of thinking than it is to think your way into a new way of acting. The science supports that. Our mind doesn't like to see ourselves as liars, so if we act a certain way our mind will start to believe in the principles behind how we act. Connecting with others in recovery allows us to be honest and unashamed with people who truly get us, and makes sure that we keep our interpretation of our drinking or using days in the correct context. This is also a big part of the reason why hanging out with people who are still actively drinking and using will topple us. These people's mind will push them into positive interpretations of their drug or alcohol use in order to substantiate their harmful actions. Their stories of drinking and using will be fun, their interpretations of its effects in their lives will be falsely positive. They can easily color our memories in the same way, and push us to produce good drinking and using memories in an effort to fit in with the group.

*

As strange as it sounds, it's true that we don't know what our opinion is about something until we make a conscious effort to figure it out. The reason for that is because our minds contain a huge collection of information, scattered all over the place. It looks like a teenager's bedroom up there in our brain. Our memories are not stored in discrete packages like a movie on a Blu-ray disc. They are stored in little bits of information called *engrams*, each containing a feeling, impression, thought, or belief. These memory engrams

[58]

are all disjointed and jumbled in a disorganized fashion all in different places in the cortex of the brain. When we think of something we pull the various little pieces out and loosely put them together. However, this thought will not create an engram of its own with all the information put together unless we think about it a lot – we call this studying. However, if we communicate our thought, our brain has to put all the information together and then organize it in a logical way for us to communicate it. Now it's contained in its own memory engram. This is why students learn so much better when they write out the information they are studying or, even better, explain it to someone else. When we explain something to someone, our mind is forced to pull out all kinds of this disjointed information from multiple different brain pathways and organize it coherently so that we can verbalize it to the other person. In most cases this is the very first time we have ever organized all this information in our minds, no matter how much we have thought about this information in the past. Just thinking about things doesn't do it, because your mind will jump around to these different pieces of information but not organize them together; you have to actually explain it to another person, or write it down as if you were explaining it to another. This is part of the brilliance of the Fourth and Fifth of the Twelve Steps, where we are led to write our thoughts out and then explain it to our sponsor. It's also why it's so important for us to tell our story to someone we trust: our sponsor, a friend in recovery, a counselor, a therapist, or as a speaker at a meeting. If we don't tell our story, we may never organize it and analyze it in our mind. But it has to be the real story.

We alcoholics and addicts naturally tend to avoid talking to others about our past behavior, because it is hurtful to our pride and we don't want to bring others' negative regard upon ourselves. If we do explain it, if we are not truthful and we leave stuff out we will have an organized collection of untrue thoughts, incomplete and filled with lies. This is why therapists get you to explain your story at length. However, as we discuss in the chapter on psychotherapy, we know from clinical studies that people are not honest with their therapist. It is only when we tell our story that we realize what we really are. But we must tell the TRUE story. Only then will we find the self-awareness that allows us to find humility and all the positive things that come with it. We can't address our problems if we can't even admit to them.

Overcoming this untruthfulness that is part of our disease is another of the strengths that I have observed in the Twelve Step program. The program emphasizes sharing, verbalizing our thoughts and experiences, and is a program of rigorous honesty. This honesty actually does occur because we are speaking to people who will not judge us because they share the same experiences, they are being rigorously honest with us, and we are speaking anonymously, just in case we have any lingering reservations. As a doctor I was used to people telling me their deepest darkest secrets, but I have always found alcoholics and addicts to be especially closed. They will make blatant lies to cover up their actions, but this is a fundamental characteristic of their disease. I did it myself. I have found gamblers to be particularly skilled in covering up their disease. But we also lie to ourselves! And that is why telling our story truthfully is absolutely key to our finding recovery. If we don't explain to someone our story – complete with all the shameful and humiliating details – we lose the benefit of confronting the truth of our past. this leaves our disease an opportunity to work in falsehoods that can lead us back to where we were before. We can't learn from history if the history is remembered falsely.

It continues to amaze me how brutally honest people are in the Twelve Step fellowship. As a scientist, I like to sit back and figure out such uncommon things, and I definitely have done so for the fellowship's raw honesty. I will discuss this in detail in the up-coming chapters, but it boils down to this remarkable program having successfully built up a "culture of truth." We see others sharing details of themselves and their lives that would make an onion cry, and we strive to do the same in order to be part of that culture. Fitting in with others is a basic human instinct. Thus, we have a mental drive to be truthful. More on this interesting issue later.

\*

This chapter has been about how our memory can affect our substance use and recovery. Before we close, let's turn it around and mention how our substance use can affect our memory. The extreme example is Wernicke-Korsakoff syndrome (WKS), which we discussed in the first chapter. This alcoholic disease in its advanced stages can wipe out our memories and prevent us from forming new ones. We also discussed in that chapter how people with alcoholic cirrhosis of the liver can suffer confusion and memory loss. Our substance use can affect our memory and brain function in other ways too. The toxic effects of substances of abuse on the brain, the biological strain of repeated intoxication and withdrawal, poor overall nutrition and physical conditioning, head injuries from falls while intoxicated, and withdrawal seizures are a few ways we can mess up our brains and memory. Some substances have been proven to lower IQ and school performance, particularly marijuana.

Now that we've looked into how our brains and our genetics and our memory affect our alcoholism-addiction and sobriety, now let's look at how our psychology – the processes behind our thoughts and behaviors – plays a role. I have always found the science of how and why we think and behave to be fascinating and entertaining, both as a scientist and as a chronic people-watcher. There is no better way to learn about ourselves.

# Four

## Our Psychology and Our Disease

It's weird, but true. Our brain can understand many obscure and abstract things, but has no awareness of its own functions. For we alcoholic-addicts that's a dangerous fact. After all, our brain functions – our thought and learning processes, memory storing and recall, and instinctive behaviors – play a dominant role in our disease. We can, however, develop an awareness of our dysfunctional thoughts and behaviors and memories, and an understanding of how they come about. The field of psychology has been putting together the immense puzzle of the human mind a little piece at a time for many years, and we as alcoholics can benefit immensely from this information. That is what we will do in this chapter.

In this chapter we'll explore the innermost workings of our mind and how they are involved in getting us addicted… and keeping us there. We'll see how to use this information to remove our disease's sadistic grip over these processes, and we'll tie it into the Twelve Steps. Even those who are not Twelve Steppers can use this information for their benefit. These same processes also cause the behaviors that bring life mishaps to non-alcoholic-addicts, so this information – like the Twelve Steps – will help us with much more than just sobriety, it will help us with life.

*

Let's start with what seems like an easy question: what, exactly, is the mind? We can define what it is, and we know what it does... but science is mystified by what it is biologically. The mind is a set of higher brain functions that we call *cognitive faculties* – the ability to think and reason. The mind processes the information we gather with our senses and the information stored in our memory to decide and control our actions and attitudes. The mind is our consciousness, our awareness. However, biologically we really have no idea what makes us think. Virginia Woolf was spot-on when she called the brain "the most unaccountable of machinery." We know that our brain consists of billions of brain cells with trillions of intricate connections, but we cannot explain how a consciousness, an awareness, a mind arises from this biological machine.

Our mind is what makes us different from other animals. It gives us a sentience that even the most complex computers can't even come close to reproducing. Shakespeare recognized that our awareness is what makes us human: I think, therefore I am. What is the essence of a mind? For all we know the mind has no physical basis and just comes down out of the sky. The ancient Egyptians believed that the mind resides in the heart... maybe they were right. Well, actually we do know better simply because things that affect the brain also affect the mind – as any alcoholic or addict knows first-hand. Beyond that, science fails us, which is why the mind has become the domain of the philosopher and not the anatomist. We don't know where in the brain it is or how it works. And there's as many unanswered questions as there are brain cells: do animals have minds or just subconscious instincts? Will humankind ever be able to reproduce an artificial intelligence to match our biological intelligence? Where does our personality fit into our mind?

\*

Unfortunately, our higher brain functions are heavily influenced by our emotions and feelings, and can be badly outsmarted by our primordial mental processes, the instincts left over from our "cave-man" ancestors. These instincts helped our ancient forbearers survive in a world where violence, selfishness, greed, and aggressiveness were needed to obtain sustenance and

[63]

fight off competitors, but these same instincts seldom serve us well in today's world. Unfortunately, these primal instincts come to us automatically, and often prevent us from using our higher brain functions to process information before we react. That is why we often lash out in anger or jealousy and later regret our action, once we have allowed our higher brain functions to process what happened.

Whether we are talking about our primitive instincts or our higher brain functions, we call these mental processes and the behaviors they cause our *psychology*. Addiction to alcohol or drugs impacts and controls our psychology and therefore our actions, turning our mind into a stranger to us. In fact, addiction warps almost all of our psychology in a unique way that keeps our addiction going, and draws us back if we try to stop. Our addicted mind goes places and does things we ordinarily would never consider.

Even in recovery our mind gives us trouble. People who use the Twelve Step program recognize that it is our "defects of character" that drive us to drink or use, and that we must strive to overcome these as a condition of our sobriety. However, many of these character defects are in our nature: they are left-overs from the animal-like instincts and drives that we inherited from our ancient cousins. It is in our nature to be jealous of others. It is in our nature to be aggressive and angry with others. It is in our nature to be selfish and greedy. It is in our nature to want to put others down so as to pump ourselves up. As long as humans have lived in groups – society – we have been striving to put this side of our nature aside. Practicing our addiction fed these unwanted aspects of our nature, bringing them to their worst. So, correcting these things is a fight against our very nature.

However, it is also in our nature to love, to be kind, to share, to forgive and forget. So, it's not like we have to invent feelings or tendencies to replace our character defects, we just have to feed the ones that serve us well, and cage the ones that don't. That we cannot completely suppress our nature, good or bad, is acknowledged. The Twelve Steps tell us that we achieve progress, not perfection. We are only human.

The ability of our disease to corrupt our mental processes is a major theme in our study of alcoholism and addiction. Seeing how it does this can be a major part of our tool-kit for overcoming this disease.

In the previous chapter we learned a way to guide our mind to overcome the defects in our memory processes, so that these defects can no longer be used by our disease to control us. Likewise, we want to understand and assert control over our psychology so that we once again seize dominion over our behavior, wresting control from our offending substance. We want to learn to allow our higher brain functions a chance to work, and not be usurped by our ugly instincts. We do this in order to learn to *act* rather than *react*. Allowing a substance to decide how we react in life hasn't served us well at all.

Our mind controls our actions, but it is our psychology that controls our minds. However, unless we learn about our psychology we have almost no awareness of its actions. So, let's learn about our psychology.

*

Central to the psychology of our chemical misadventures is *cognitive dissonance*. Don't let the horrible term for this part of our psychology frighten you, it's actually a simple concept.

We alcoholics and addicts are acclaimed for our twisted, illogical thinking. This "insanity" amounts to an extreme form of *rationalization*, which is our strongly ingrained nature to substantiate our behavior with plausible reasons, even if these reasons are distorted and untrue. The psychological basis for this bogus justification of our drinking and using behavior is two-fold: first, our inborn drive to always present ourselves in the best possible light to others, and second, because of cognitive dissonance. Cognitive dissonance occurs when the mind knows that our behavior – in this case our substance use and related escapades – isn't proper and conflicts with our entrenched beliefs about how a good person should behave. This inconsistency between our ideas, beliefs, and values and our real-life actions creates dissonance – a great psychological discomfort – which we feel as guilt, remorse, shame, and self-loathing. Our mind knows that the easiest way to stop the psychological discomfort is by stopping the behavior, our drinking or using, but instead our obsession with alcohol or drugs keeps it going. The mind is then forced to try to relieve its discomfort by warping thoughts or interpretations of thoughts and actions to match our hanky-panky with our

[65]

values. Our obsession for our substance forces us to lie, cheat, steal, sneak around, neglect people and responsibilities, lose people and property, avoid work… our actions therefore become more and more out of line with our fixed concept of how a person should behave. As Robin Williams said: "we alcoholics violate our standards quicker than we can lower them." Our disease is a progressive one, and as the behaviors worsen and the list of wrong-doings lengthens, we end up with great psychological pain. This becomes extreme in the alcoholic-addict because as we consummate our cocktail consumption more and more of our behavior becomes exposed to and known about by other people and the guilt and shame and remorse expand to detonation-levels. Our obsession for our substance crushes the mind's desire to stop the substance use and related behaviors, and our compulsion to satisfy our obsession wins out: we keep on drinking or using. The dissonance – the psychological discomfort caused by our actions – builds so much that our mind has to warp reality considerably in order to even try to substantiate what we are doing. Our mind is hard-wired to start to believe our own lies and warped logic in order to relieve this anguish. It is just normal human nature forced to extremes by the toxic behaviors of alcoholism-addiction.

Oddly, the mind doesn't try to reform our beliefs to match our actions, or change our behaviors to match our beliefs, it just lies to itself about what our actions are. However, over time, a person experiencing cognitive dissonance may superficially adjust their beliefs (for example, have you ever noticed that virtually all marijuana legalization activists are marijuana users? They have likely subconsciously adjusted their belief in what is right and wrong to match their marijuana use). As with other mental processes alcoholism-addiction pushes the mental process of cognitive dissonance to extremes.

The peace and serenity that we seek and find in A.A. or any other recovery program is simply the absence of cognitive dissonance.

*

Prominent among the symptoms of our sickness is the relentless remorse, regret, shame, embarrassment, and self-loathing that become the "stone in the

[66]

shoe" of our mind. Morning after morning... awakening disappointed to be alive... physically sick... already obsessed with getting the next drink or drug... heartsick over yet another failure to stop... all the loss... the troubles we have brought on ourselves and others... the horrible things we have done. Then we hear about some of the things we said and did while blacked out. Ouch! More remorse, guilt, and shame get added on. Waking up to realize that we are in a hospital, or somewhere else strange, and have no idea how we got there, or to look out the window to see that our car isn't in the driveway where it should be. Emotions can't be described... tormented?... miserable?... despicable?... wretched?... pathetic? Multiply these feelings by ten if our eyes open to a jail cell. The feeling that life's problems are insurmountable lead us to seek getting drunk and high as the only way to make those horrible feelings go away for a little while. It's little wonder that our feelings of self-worth have long ago left us.

The natural history of alcoholism is that of progression. Luckily, some of us find recovery before we go down the slope entirely, because it invariably ends in the grave. As our addiction progresses we need more of the drug to achieve the same effects, or even just to feel "normal" – the tolerance we discussed in chapter one. This is very expensive. Drugs and alcohol cost a lot of money, and require a lot of time and effort to obtain, use, and then hangover from. As the addiction progresses, many are unable to maintain a job, and income drops or ceases. Eventually, the money dries up. Then, if selling property or possessions is necessary to continue drinking or using, this is done eagerly, without a second thought. After our valuables are all gone, we borrow money from family and friends. It doesn't take long before this, too, dries up, especially once our loved ones clue in to what the money is being used for. We resort to lying to get this money: "I need the money to get my daughter her asthma medications." Then, to support our addiction, we denigrate ourselves to thievery from family and friends. When this comes to light and precautions prevent further theft, we become really desperate. If we are reluctant to resort to crime, withdrawal from our drug will cure that reluctance in short order. Theft, robbery, burglary, forgery, prostitution, dealing drugs, and worse become our new way. One of my friends in recovery is one of the nicest people I know. He is soft-spoken, gentle, giving, and a good friend. I can't imagine him doing something that would harm

[67]

others. Yet, when he was in active addiction he was regularly carrying out burglaries, as the only way he could support his habit. What a paradox: how could such a good and giving person also be a thief? The answer: he is not a thief. He is an addict who was displaying a typical symptom of his sickness.

When we are seeking sobriety or newly in sobriety we are overwhelmed with guilt, remorse, shame, and self-loathing. This is understandable, but it is a major impediment to recovery: we can feel unworthy of recovery. The shameful behavior is but a symptom of our addiction... it all falls under the umbrella of our disease. So, we are not "liars, thieves, and jerks", we are alcoholics and addicts. Our behavior during our addiction is part of that sickness, and it does not define us. We are sick people seeking to get well, not bad people seeking to become good. Our disease is an issue of biology, not an issue of morality.

Simply pointing this out will not alleviate our guilt. That is not the point. The point is to make us realize that we are not fundamentally bad people. As we will discuss shortly, human psychology unfortunately drives us to paradoxically cudgel ourselves over our perceived failures, and exaggerate our successes. The Twelve Steps – as a form of psychotherapy – address the psychology at work here, allowing us to "come to terms" with the pain (I will explain what "coming to terms" with our demons really means in the chapter on psychotherapy). There is no moving forward while the grip of the past holds us back.

The therapy of the Twelve Steps is not only about coming to terms with our wrong-doings. Far from it. It is also about building us into deservedly healthy, confident, and "useful" persons. After all, the ravages of the disease have torn us down to a very dismal view of self. In my drinking and using days I justifiably called myself a "PLF": Pathetic Life Form. That's what I had become. All my usual roles in life – father, husband, doctor, friend, fitness enthusiast, writer – all became replaced by one role: alcoholic-addict. I didn't feel worthy of recovery, of happiness. To escape the power of our substance of abuse and reclaim our roles in life we must feel worthy of it. Besides being important in allowing us to properly function again, accomplishing this change in mind-set also helps our recovery in a more fundamental way.

Many addicts and alcoholics don't feel they deserve to be sober or happy again. They feel unworthy of recovery, unworthy of love. It is said that: "the only person keeping us from our self-worth is ourselves." That is particularly true of us. Fortunately, the Twelve Steps program recognizes this, and a remedy built into the program starts the minute we meet another alcoholic in recovery. One alcoholic reveals how this is done: "I learned in the fellowship that if others could accept me and love me as I was, then I should love myself as I was…" (Came to Believe, page 3). This is the power of the A.A. fellowship in restoring our sense of self-worth after it was trampled for so long. Later on, the Steps recognize self-disparagement as a defect of character that must be acknowledged and removed, as it is a counter-productive psychological tendency of all people, alcoholic or not.

Feelings of inadequacy and unworthiness play a role in making us drink, but they also splatter out into other character defects. They lead us to lie about and exaggerate our accomplishments in order to try to impress others, so as to prop up our deflated self-esteem. They may lead to us to pursuits that are counter-productive and even harmful, such as taking steroids or spending money we don't have. Two guys I went to medical school with went on to become neurosurgeons, which involves a gruelling, punishing 12 years of training after medical school. In both cases, my impression of both these guys was of an utter lack of self-esteem. I am convinced that the biggest reason they chose brain surgery was to prop up their self-respect, as they felt that this was the most prestigious specialty. While it might not be fair of me to say that, I think I make my point: a lack of self-esteem can lead us unhappily through life by the nose. It can control even major life decisions. And it can make us drink or do drugs.

Of course, we must not go too far in recovering our self-regard. After all, false pride, self-seeking, greed, self-importance and envy can also drag us down, and keep us from our full potential. Once again, human nature pushes us in this direction. The tendency to over-exaggerate our accomplishments and perceived acumen and value is an ancient part of our drive to be respected by others, and to impress potential mates. These primitive instincts that drive us so powerfully are character defects that can cause us to relapse, will make us lose the respect of those around us, and will lead to other defects of character, such as intolerance, lying, inconsideration, lust, and so on. Let's take a look at pride, a well-known emotion that takes on weird proportions in our disease.

\*

Pride has brought down many people, but it is also appropriate... properly applied. We should take pride in who we are and what we do, and not in how big our house is, how expensive our car is, or how many toys we have. I like the way it is put in Drop the Rock: "The willingness to work the Sixth Step [removing our character defects] on pride begins by understanding that having healthy pride in our accomplishments in life is fine as long as it is coupled with humility and gratitude" (page 34).

One common land mine that can blast us right off the path to recovery is the inability to accept help. Asking for help is, to some, a sign of weakness. Ironic, considering that the same person would enthusiastically accept "help" in the form of a bottle of Vodka from anybody at all. The insanity of that sentiment of pride coming from a person whose disease has rendered them pathetic is absurd.

I have observed that the pride involved in the minds of alcoholic-addicts is distinct and unusual. For most people, pride is a by-product of accomplishment, possessions, and their feelings of self-worth. In other words, they have something to at least partly back up their pride, over-inflated as it may be. In the practicing alcoholic-addict, the pride is over-inflated, and defensive in nature... with nothing to back it up. Yet, it is powerful enough to prevent us from accepting our powerlessness over alcohol or drugs, and keeps us from accepting help. When we do accept help, we do so only in a non-committal way and remain convinced we can get sober on our own. Unfounded pride, sturdy and unassailable. What's bizarre about this pride is that it exists in a person who has long ago lost any remnants of self-esteem and self-worth. Another paradox. How can this be?

[70]

Strangely, the pride that feeds our disease is driven by low self-esteem. This sickness-induced pride is an instinctive mechanism to help us compensate, to reduce the psychological pain that comes from knowing how wrong our alcoholic-addict behavior is, but being unable to stop it. In order to compensate for our own sorry behavior and our pathetic situation, we will project a fabricated positive view of ourselves on others by inflated demonstrations of pride, and conversely by criticizing and nit-picking others in efforts to cut them down beneath us. We become consumed by being "right" and can't admit when we are wrong, and we can't acknowledge our defects. An extreme example of this is the drunk trying to pick fights with people who even look at him the wrong way. You know you're an alcoholic when you get in a fight at a yard sale, right? Small wonder others find us obnoxious and can't stand to be around us – I think alcoholic-addicts had a role in helping "pride" find its way onto the list of Seven Deadly Sins. We must move from this bizarre, unfounded, dysfunctional pride to a healthy pride based on who we are and how we live our lives. And, perhaps we shouldn't even call it pride, even then. Allow me to explain

Pride is one of the thornier issues in our efforts to remove our character defects as part of finding permanent sobriety. The word has positive and negative connotations. What do you think when you hear the word pride? Is it a positive character trait, or is it a character defect? Merriam-webster.com offers two conflicting definitions, one being that it is "a reasonable or justifiable self-respect," the other being "inordinate self-esteem;" one definition positive, the other negative. Roget's Thesaurus lists "symptoms of pride": arrogance, insolence, ostentation, vanity, vain-glory, condescension, conceit, self-exaltation, self-glorification, self-satisfaction, self-admiration, self-love. No matter what you base your pride on, these are not symptoms that will help you in recovery and succeeding in life. And they certainly won't gain you many friends. So, just using the word "pride" can be unclear, as it can be interpreted in different ways by different people at different times.

Psychologists identify two types of pride: authentic (good) pride vs. hubristic (bad) pride. This has deep clinical implications, because psychotherapists risk making hubristic (arrogant) jerks out of patients who comes to them for help for problems of low self-esteem. They may be handing their patients a dysfunctional defence mechanism, in the form of

[71]

hubristic pride, for their self-esteem issues. We don't want to be likewise tripped up in our quest to rid ourselves of our character defects in our search for that elusive sobriety. So, the question: should we be using the double-meaning word "pride"?

In a Psychology Today article,[1] Dr. John Amodeo suggests substituting the word "dignity". He points out that if we allow our achievements or possessions to define who we are, we set ourselves up for misery, especially when we cling too tightly to these things, as they will pass. He suggests that: "a more genuine and stable self-worth is based upon validating, affirming, and valuing ourselves as we are. Self-worth is a function of living with dignity, which exists apart from any accomplishments." We must not risk tying our self-worth to external sources of gratification. As soon as the things that are defining and holding up our pride fail us, we head down a road that can lead to relapse.

Dr. Amodeo goes on: "In contrast, dignity can live inside us regardless of our successes and failures. We don't have to prove anything to anybody – or even to ourselves. If an enterprise fails, this doesn't mean we are a failure." The crux of his point is this: "We can experience the dignity of living with integrity, regardless of outcome."

To continue using the double-meaning word "pride" can feed our innate nature to exaggerate and lie to bolster our pride and lead right back to those ugly character defects that make us drink or use. So rather than try to qualify what we mean by "pride", why not replace the word with "dignity"? No one will ever misinterpret what we mean by that.

When we live with dignity that comes purely from being who we are, a human being with inestimable value, we don't need to depend on worldly accomplishments to keep our pride afloat. When we do pursue a goal, we do it for the right reasons – because it is fulfilling and meaningful for us – and not because we are trying to impress someone or boast about it or drive a better car to prop up our pride. Let's allow our pride be the result of living with dignity that derives from our integrity. If we relapse and our behavior becomes as despicable and selfish as it was when we were drinking, then our pride will collapse too, as it should.

*

[72]

Pride is human nature, including this hubristic – arrogant, boastful – pride, and we must acknowledge that fact. It is a part of our psychological make-up, so we must be aware of it so that we can control and direct it, rather than allow it to control us. Humility and gratitude are crucial character assets for life, and we need them for recovery. Many people struggle with this balance. But does living with humility mean that we have to allow people to walk all over us? Does expressing humility and charity and tolerance and patience and giving and putting others before ourselves mean that we can't have self-esteem and self-worth? Does it mean that we can't be ambitious and competitive? What if we have a job that requires us to be aggressive and uncompromising? Do we have to quit our jobs to stay sober? Does it mean we can't stand up for ourselves in a dispute? Does it mean that we can't negotiate with someone for a better deal? These are questions we must answer before we walk out the door and face the world sober.

Luckily, when we base our pride on living with dignity through our integrity, it no longer conflicts with humility and gratitude. But, life being life, semantics aren't going to help solve our day-to-day problems as we interact with the world around us – we are going to run into life situations where a little anger and self-assertion are required. For example, imagine that you come out to the mall parking lot and catch somebody about to drive off after backing into your car. Bystanders stand in front of the offending car so that the driver has to get out and confront you. And she might be drunk. Naturally, shock and anger will well up in you. But, the character traits of empathy, forgiveness, love, and tolerance are not violated by you standing up for yourself and making sure that some kind of justice and compensation is made. How you go about this will determine how you are faring with your character defects. Will you let your anger and shock turn into rage and aggression and boil up into angry, spiteful words and even physical aggression? Certainly, human nature will push you hard to do this. Are you going to hurt somebody, emotionally or physically here today? Again, an uphill battle against our instinctual reaction. Or will you recognize these character defects for what they are, and show respect and tolerance and act in a more measured way? Maybe even detach yourself from the situation, if you must, and allow the police to handle the situation. Maybe even appreciate the

[73]

situation, to some small degree, as a good learning experience and practice for your Tenth Step if you practice the A.A. program. Maybe for your Twelfth Step if the driver was drinking. Either way we handle the situation, justice and compensation are obtained, but one way we acted in a manner consistent with who we aim to be in sobriety – respectful, tolerant, restrained, and measured – and the other way we act like the people we were when we were drinking or using – selfish, angry, hurtful, out of control. One way we go home and sleep well, the other way we go home and stew in anger, and then in guilt and shame.

Life is what it is and the Twelve Step program tells us to live life on life's terms. Sometimes life's terms are harsh and can harm us if we are meek. Someone can hold a position of responsibility that requires toughness and assertiveness without violating the principles that we live by in our new life in sobriety. We can still be respectful, empathetic, loving, and tolerant as we go about our duties. Our measured and fair approach to our duties, and the absence of anger, insults, and disrespect in our dealings will win us much more respect from those around us than did our old methods, before we addressed our character defects in our quest for sobriety. To be sure, if our job involves breaking people's kneecaps while collecting gambling debts, or anything else illegal, that is not consistent with life in recovery in the Twelve Steps, and that must be dropped.

The best way to find the balance between humility and assertiveness as we deal with various life situations in a way that is consistent with our new-found principles – necessary for our recovery – is to meditate at the end of the day on any difficult situations that we ran into that day. We review in our mind what happened and how we reacted. Did any of our character defects show their ugly heads in our actions? Did we do harm to someone? Have we been carrying around anger and resentment over the issue all day? If so, what was our role in what happened? No point in allowing someone else's behavior rule our mind and ruin our day, because we have no control over others' behavior. Were we to blame for any part of it? How else could we have reacted and had a better outcome? Is there someone we need to make amends to over this? If we do this with each difficult situation or conflict we run into every day, we will soon start seeing how to react better and more appropriately in future situations, especially since the nature of conflicts and difficult situations tend to repeat themselves. We will soon be pre-wired from experience and lessons learned through our meditation to handle situations better as they happen. Handling life's difficulties becomes easier as we progress. Twelve Steppers will recognize this as our Step Ten work.

This amounts to a priceless life skill for several reasons. First and foremost, it will help us in our recovery, because it will keep us from developing new anger and resentments. The anger and resentments and related character defects that sneak back into our lives are like pebbles in our shoes that will bedevil us until we get them out. These are the things that made us drink and use drugs, and they are the things that make us relapse if we allow them back in. As well, people will notice that we react with self-control, fairness, and respect in charged situations, and that will win us their respect in kind. The real value in this earned respect is not in its effects on our self-esteem, but in inspiring others to behave likewise, and impacting other alcoholics and addicts to want what we have. This may open the door to what really keeps us sober: helping those who still suffer. Further, we all have been in situations where we lashed out in anger verbally or physically without thinking, and later deeply regretted it. Maybe even landed in hot water over it. And doing so always made a difficult situation worse. Practicing our new values and skills – as people do in the Twelve Steps – will help prevent this from happening, and almost certainly the difficult situations will have better outcomes, maybe even positive outcomes, because of it. I have had several would-be enemies become good friends after angry confrontations where my measured reaction caught them off-guard, and totally de-escalated the run-in. This is a life skill that will make us better at everything we do, including our job, parenting, social life, and day-to-day living. And it goes far to help keep us sober and in recovery.

*

Another downfall of our pride is that it causes us to blame everything wrong in our lives on others. That is our nature: our psychology is geared toward protecting our mind from discomfort, no matter how much it has to lie, warp facts, or ignore logic to do so – the psychology of cognitive dissonance at work. It is uncomfortable for our mind to believe that our misfortunes are our own fault. So, we blame others, or even the world at large or God for our woes, and ignore our mistakes and faults that may have contributed to them. Even when it comes to things that truly are someone else's fault, we must fight the urge to burn with resentment, because it is our nature to do just that. The Twelve Step program teaches us that the resentments and anger that build up over this juvenile blame game are the major cause of our drinking or using, and a major cause of relapse once we get sober. As a psychological therapist I have to agree wholeheartedly with this. Blaming others allows our mind to focus helplessly on what we can't do anything about – other people and the world around us – and keeps our focus off what we can do something about – our own behavior. This kills the mind-set that we need to be able to assert control over our lives again, this "internal locus of control" that we will discuss shortly.

Our mind has another way to try to protect us from the psychological discomfort of our troubles: by seeking out coping mechanisms. These are schemes that our mind comes up with to reduce stress (psychological discomfort) by encouraging behavior that will relieve that stress. This is usually done subconsciously, although repeating the coping behaviors may become a conscious process, although not necessarily a voluntary process. The psychologists call these "coping strategies" or "coping skills", but I prefer to call them *coping mechanisms*, because "strategies" implies that they are well thought out, and "skills" implies that they are positive abilities, and neither characteristic is usually present in alcoholics and addicts. They are usually reactive (an immediate reflexive response to a stressor – drinking or using after a stressful situation) although they may be proactive (performed in advance to prevent stress – drinking or using before going into a stressful situation). The psychologists have classified these coping mechanisms into a number of different types, but I like to classify them as either dysfunctional coping mechanisms (harmful), or healthy coping mechanisms. A healthy coping mechanism may be something like exercise, meditation, going to an A.A. meeting, talking things over with a friend. Examples of a dysfunctional coping mechanism may be denial, avoidance/escape, blaming others, procrastination, lashing out, trivializing the problem. Very dysfunctional coping mechanisms can involve seeking the stimulation of our reward pathways in our brain: sex for the sake of sex, over-eating and Bulimia, splurge shopping, drinking or using drugs; or it can be behaviors of self-harm (cutting, Anorexia, suicide).

The Twelve Steps provide an excellent, sound therapy for the psychology that brings us to these dysfunctional coping mechanisms, including our substance use. They lead us through the unnatural process of confronting our discomfort without using a coping mechanism, so that the sources of this discomfort can be directly healed. They then teach us to use healthy coping mechanisms, and provide us with access to some of these. They also teach us the skills to prevent further accumulation of psychological discomfort, crushing our dissonance. As a psychological therapist, I have been singularly impressed with the simple brilliance of how the Twelve Steps accomplish this. More on this in the chapter on psychotherapy.

I know that my drinking and drugging was a coping mechanism, because my biggest trigger was life stressors. I had fallen victim to a peculiarity of human psychology called *learned helplessness*. This describes what happens when we face life stressors that accumulate and overwhelm us to the point that we don't even know where to start to deal with them. We come to the conclusion that there is nothing we can do to stop them, so we just give up. We believe that everything wrong in our life is controlled by people and things outside of ourselves. Then our dissonance – our mental discomfort over our seeming inability to fix everything – causes us to stop trying to work on our problems and instead focus on blaming others. We have learned to be helpless. When that happens, our mind instinctually looks for coping mechanisms to smother the anxiety and pain that comes with our learned helplessness; our mind doesn't care if they are healthy or dysfunctional, it just wants quick relief. Once I was introduced to the Big Book I found comfort and inspiration in reading the story of one alcoholic who shared my trigger: "…I realized that I had to separate my sobriety from everything else that was going on in my life. No matter what happened or didn't happen, I couldn't drink…. The tides of life flow endlessly for better or worse, both good and bad, and I cannot allow my sobriety to become dependent on these ups and downs of living. Sobriety must live a life of its own" (pages 450-1). I read these words when I first came to sobriety, dry only a few days, and the learned helplessness started to evaporate. I knew what I had to do, although I didn't know how. Luckily, the Twelve Step program taught me how to do that.

Learned helplessness is a big problem in our disease, not only because it induces us to drink and use to cope, but also because it gives rise to another major roadblock on our path to recovery. Learned helplessness leads to a psychological effect that must be broken down for us to get better... it is not a roadblock that can be bypassed. This effect is called an *external locus of control*, which describes the state of mind where we are resigned to the belief that outside people and events control our lives. We feel that nothing we can do will affect how our life goes. We start thinking that we drank or used because our spouse is such a tyrant, or because our finances had gone so badly, or because we didn't get that great job we interviewed for. While those stressors surely contributed to the stress that brought us to seek the coping mechanism of the grog or ganja, by resigning ourselves to these outside influences on our lives we are handing over control of ourselves to these circumstances. If this is not corrected, our sobriety will be fine... until the spouse annoys us again, or we suffer financial set-back, or we blow another interview. In fact, we are letting events outside ourselves control our lives; we aren't going to work hard to fix our relationship or our finances or our interview skills unless we believe that control of these situations lies within us. A major focus of psychotherapy is taking our external locus of control and turning it into an *internal locus of control*, where we start living in the knowledge that our own actions can in fact affect our own lives. It is about becoming people who govern our affairs, instead of allowing our affairs to govern us. The Twelve Steps does this quite nicely, as we will discuss further in the chapter on psychotherapy.

*

I have been overwhelmed by how kind-hearted people are in the Twelve Step fellowship. You read the same observation time and time again in people's stories in the recovery literature, that when they go to a meeting the first time they expect to see a bunch of miserable drunks and addicts and instead are surprised to be greeted by a sunny, happy, friendly group. No wonder, because the Twelve Step program is all about identifying and correcting the things that bring us down, particularly defects of character. Humility is a key part of what makes a devotee of the program such a fine person. I think it's important to clarify what humility means, because it is not about being meek and weak and turning the cheek. Unfortunately, we are once again faced with a word with more than one meaning, and it can therefore mean different things to different people; the word "humility" and the word "humiliation" unfortunately come from the same Latin word *humilis*, which essentially means "low". Again, I turn to Roget's Thesaurus, which gives unflattering synonyms for humility (which it defines as "lack of pride"): meekness, lowliness, abasement, submission, resignation. Hardly what we mean when we foster humility in the recovering alcoholic. So, once again, it is very easy to be misled by this word. For us humility is, very simply: acceptance of our defects, and a modest view of our own importance. This is not meekness... quite the opposite. The humility we seek is well explained in Drop the Rock:

"The Twelve Step way of life is humble but not in any way meek. The picture many of us have of a humble person is someone afraid of his or her shadow.... This image of humility is not what is meant in the Program.... The people who have stayed abstinent for some time practice a degree of humility that was foreign to them prior to recovery.

"For those who have made progress in their Program, humility is simply a clear recognition of what and who they are. They have gotten down to their own right size. Humility is understanding that they're worthwhile.... They have a sincere desire to be and become the best they can be. Today we remember that humility is not being meek. It is being our own true selves.... For our definition we will use this idea from Sam Shoemaker: humility = gratitude" (page 57).

\*

[79]

Gratitude.

It's human nature to take what we have for granted, and to covet what we don't have. When we receive something we are soon focussed on obtaining the next thing. There's even a certain dissatisfaction that sets in when we get what we want. It's healthy to want and to set realistic goals and work toward achieving what we want – that helps us succeed in life. However, when wanting something amounts to raw envy and jealousy of those who have what we want, and therefore leaves us resenting them and the world for keeping us from our wants, we usually just fume away without any realistic positive plan of action to obtain what is wanted. This will not help us to succeed in life, it just makes us miserable and resentful. And these resentments are the sidekick of relapse.

Gratitude is an issue of perspective. A little exercise in empathy helps to illustrate this. The next time you see someone who has less than you, imagine yourself in their shoes looking at you and what you have. Maybe it is a homeless person, or someone dying of cancer, or someone who is blind or in a wheelchair. Try seeing yourself from his perspective, and how he could be envious or jealous of you because of what you have. Maybe also resent you for it. Now, does what you have all of a sudden become a little more fulfilling in your eyes? Do you think that the guy in the wheelchair will be able to walk again by burning in resentful envy over you? These people with glaring deficits in their lives have long ago learned to be grateful for what they do have so that they don't spend their lives chained to the green-eyed monster and his friends. We must do the same.

Changing our perspective can, in fact, have a robust effect on our happiness in life. From the Big Book: "When I focus on what's good today, I have a good day, and when I focus on what's bad, I have a bad day. If I focus on a problem, the problem increases; if I focus on the answer, the answer increases" (page 419). We are lucky here... changing our perspective is easy to do. It's a free way to have better days!

Gratitude is a therapeutic emotion. Having gratitude means having an awareness of what is good in our lives, as well as an appreciation for our lives. It is the difference between having a day filled with regret and envy or a day filled with contentedness and appreciation. Anyone who hasn't tried it should do a "gratitude list." This simple exercise – sitting with pen and paper

[80]

and listing what in life we are grateful for – always has a healing impact. First on my list is always that I am sober today. Many people do a gratitude list every time they are feeling down on themselves and experiencing the "poor-me's." Meditating on what we are grateful for helps as well.

Some of the most content people I know are people in recovery who have glaringly little in terms of material treasures. This is because they appreciate the peace and serenity that they have found in the Twelve Step program – not to mention sobriety – and because they have humility and perspective about their situation and place in the world. Their peace comes from acceptance, and gratitude fills them with appreciation. Their program of recovery has taught them that we are a success today if we don't drink or use today. So they feel like a success every day. They have chosen to rid themselves of the unhappy yoke of unsatisfiable envy.

*

Gratitude gives us a perspective of our life based in humility. Humility does not come naturally to the human mind. Humility helps us to find gratitude by allowing us to recognize that everything we have came to us because of what we were capable of working for, and for which we put in the required effort. Maybe some of it came by chance, or maybe we sometimes came up short for our efforts, but humility is about acceptance of who and what we are. Humility also allows us to gauge our own abilities so that we can set our sights on wants that are realistically achievable for us, so that we can make the plans necessary to realize those goals, rather than wasting our time and energy burning with envy. Humility keeps us from allowing our unrealistic wants to "own" us, to occupy our minds, to cloud our thoughts with jealousy and envy and resentment and push out good things that actually help us.

Certainly, humility reins in our "ego," a Freudian term misused to indicate the over-inflated view of ourselves that many people carry around. Ironically, an inflated ego is the consequence of low self-esteem, as we try to counter by acting as much more than we are. We often even come to believe our own act. It is a dysfunctional coping mechanism for the pain we feel at

[81]

not being up to what we wish we could be: in other words, for lacking humility. An inflated ego makes us annoying – even intolerable – to others, which therefore detracts from our ability to function to our potential. I consider ego to be the "anti-Christ" of the crucial character trait of humility.

There is another drawback to an over-inflated sense of self-importance. Psychological research has shown that people with an unwarranted high view of themselves tend to react to failure – which can be anything that contradicts their view of themselves – by lashing out, sometimes with violence. This just adds to the list of dysfunctional behavior brought on by our alcoholic pride and ego. So we need to address this on our journey to recovery.

The odds are stacked heavily against us in the ego-humility wrestling match. Unless we come to the Twelve Steps or some other program of deep introspection and guided self-awareness we may never put any thought into humility. The word is vexed by a connotation in our society that is on par with the word "weakness." Worse still, people associate "ego" with the word "self-confidence." We may spend our entire lives striving for more ego, in the belief it may fix our insecurities and lack of self-confidence. We've probably always seen humility as something to beat, and ego as something to build. We have probably seen people with a great deal of material success and saw their inflated egos as a reason that they are so "successful" while in reality it's the other way around. Most people live their entire life in this elusive backwards pursuit; unless they happen to be alcoholics or addicts in recovery they are never blessed with the therapy of the Twelve Steps or any other character-changing program.

Our culture really does much more to stack the odds against seeing humility as a virtue. Have you ever noticed that the people most admired in our society show very little, if any, humility? Rock stars, movie stars, sports stars, political leaders, corporate CEOs and so on. Even the fictional characters in TV and film are seldom icons of humility. Quite the opposite, they are self-important, glamorized, and aggressive.

In his excellent discussion of humility on the Psychology Today website,[2] Dr. Karl Albrecht offers a definition of humility that I absolutely love. He says humility is a psycho-social quality (I like the inclusion of the word "social") that involves: "1) a sense of emotional autonomy, and 2) freedom from the control of the "competitive reflex," where the competitive reflex is the "visceral impulse to oppose or outdo others." Further: "humility is about emotional neutrality. It involves an experience of growth in which we no longer need to put ourselves above others, but we don't put ourselves below them, either." Importantly, he emphasizes that humility is NOT about letting others push us around or "walk all over" us. It's not about sacrificing our interests or hiding our feelings or avoiding conflict just to please others (although a person rich in humility may choose to do this sometimes). Further, it is the realization and acceptance of the fact that we are not in this world to live up to others' expectations, and others are not in this world to live up to ours.

Dr. Albrecht's article is pure gold. He says: "humility is less a matter of self-restraint and more a matter of self-esteem. The greater your sense of self-worth, the easier it is to appreciate others, to praise them, and to encourage them." We don't need to push others down in order to lift ourselves up. This flies in the face of our society's beliefs about humility. When we, for the first time in our life, look at it with an open mind we see that humility is a measure of self-worth, and a matter of "social intelligence" because people are drawn to us because we do not try to bring them down and elevate ourselves; we offer unconditional positive regard (we will discuss this concept shortly).

Humility is key to our efforts to rid ourselves of our character defects and replace them with character strengths. It leads to many other qualities that we need to keep sober, and it helps us lead a life of integrity and respect. This includes open-mindedness, which is a result of our humility, as it leads us to realize and admit that our way of thinking and living, which we were previously too stubborn to abandon, led us to addiction and failure, and that we must be open to new ways of thinking, new beliefs, and new ways of living to succeed. It also helps us to abandon our lack of gratitude for the positive things that we do have, and our resentment for the things we don't have. It leads us to stop blaming the world for our woes.

Importantly, humility leads us to leave behind our sense of inadequacy, our sense of unworthiness. This, in turn, is how we stop exaggerating our accomplishments, being envious of others, and generally making fools of ourselves. As such, humility does much more than win us the respect of those around us – it allows us to gain our own unconditional self-respect. What a wonderful way to be, especially in contrast to the mangled heap of ugly

[83]

emotions and motives that led us around by the nose for so long. As one alcoholic explains: "…one of the primary differences between alcoholics and non-alcoholics is that non-alcoholics change their behavior to meet their goals and alcoholics change their goals to meet their behavior" (Big Book, page 423).

*

Humility provides us with yet another mainstay of virtue: realistic self-awareness. Our minds have an instinctual need for affirmation from others. We crave approval from others, a deep psychological hang-up on being liked, respected, and admired. We become dependent on others to affirm us, even to validate us as people. We become preoccupied with what others think of us, and even start judging ourselves through their eyes. When we think we lack everyone's approval and high regard, we experience anxiety and psychological pain (that pesky cognitive dissonance again). This can lower our opinion of ourselves and it can make us do strange and counter-productive things to try to gain others' approval – such as lying about our accomplishments, buying a car we can't afford, getting cosmetic medical procedures, and so on. This self-defeating psychological need is inherent in all people, not just those with our disease. However, as usual when it comes to dysfunctional psychological processes, alcoholism-addiction multiplies the effects of this need for affirmation. Our beat-up self-esteem demands it.

When we slog along under our substance's cruel whip, we have an abnormally inflated pride, as we have already discussed. Our repulsive exertions and appearance, combined with the social stigma of what we have become, eventually result in us being held in very poor regard by others. We try to lie about our situation, and we aren't in a position to buy a new impressive car, so these efforts just make us look even more pathetic, and our longing for affirmation goes woefully unrealized. Our instinct is then to react with spite, and even violence, especially if someone dares verbalize or otherwise demonstrate their disapproval. This is a major impediment to our ability to accept anyone confronting us with the truth about our situation, even if it's done as an act of love and caring. Any help that is proffered is ferociously refused. No wonder the Twelve Steps see admission of who we really are as the first step to recovery.

This psychological need for affirmation plagues everyone, alcoholic-addict or not, to varying degrees... abstaining from substances of abuse does not shield us from its adverse effects. Given how battered our affirmation had been while drinking or using, we are exquisitely needy for it once in recovery, and likely to look for relief in drink or drug if that need isn't met. Our mind used our substance as a dysfunctional coping mechanism in the past, so we need to be sure it doesn't happen again. We must avoid obsessing over other people's assessment of us, and reacting to the psychological pain we feel by their perceived lack of approval. There is far too much mental effort involved and we end up lying or making bad decisions to try to win their approval. Let's look at an example.

Imagine you are happily sober and at work talking to a co-worker. Let's say you are pretty much average at your job but you, being you, see yourself as above average. Now, a co-worker makes a comment that you think suggests that you are average, and you immediately take offense. It leaves you smoldering with anger all day, probably longer. This can be a rock in your shoe that makes a bigger and bigger sore on your foot until you stop for a Band-Aid at the pub on the way home from work. Oops! Now let's say that the co-worker's comment made you angry, but not really so angry that you must have a drink to put out that fire. However, your alcoholic-addict mind is now carrying some anger and resentment that makes you irritable and sensitive to minor stressors: traffic, a slow copy machine, spilled coffee. This anger and resentment can build until your alcoholic-addict mind uses it to open the door to a drink or a drug a crack... and convinces you that you now have a reasonable excuse to stop for a drink or a pick-up on the way home, to de-stress. Just one drink or hit, that's all. Famous last words. I hope that doesn't sound preposterous to you, because this exact process occurs all the time. If only there was a way to stop it....

Luckily psychology – that subject that was such a pain in the ass when you took it in high school – has identified an antidote that defuses this powder keg of pride, denial, self-unawareness, and emotional reaction to the truth. This antidote is a concept known as *unconditional positive regard*, which means being seen by others with acceptance and respect, regardless of our

[85]

actions and words. This is not excusing the bad behavior, it is accepting someone simply based on their inestimable worth as a human being. This is seen very rarely in the world around us – even our loved ones come to view us with disgust for the things we say and do as active alcoholic-addicts (and rightfully so!). Basing our regard for others in a way commensurate with their words and actions is normal human behavior, and it's known in psychology as *conditional positive regard.* It takes a special person to give unconditional positive regard in any setting, especially to someone who is a pernicious drunk-addict. In fact, very few people in our world give unconditional positive regard to anyone at all, including to themselves.

Therapists try to establish an environment of unconditional positive regard in the therapeutic relationship, but it might be an act, as the therapist may well inwardly view the alcoholic-addict as a moral flunky. And it isn't difficult for us to see right through that. It is said that "only an alcoholic understands an alcoholic", but I would like to add to that: "only an alcoholic will not judge an alcoholic." Same for addicts. Does anyone other than an alcoholic-addict in sobriety truly believe, one hundred per cent and with no reservations, that alcoholism-addiction is not an issue of morality? That the alcoholic-addict is a victim and not a perpetrator? To be fair, there are always some exceptions to varying degrees, but what really matters is our perception of whether or not the person sitting in front of us has some kind of inward feeling of moral superiority or judgement. Regardless of what that person's true feelings are, if we perceive them as being judgemental because they are not "one of us", an impossible barrier exists. Nothing wipes out this heavily suppressive barrier completely except for shared experiences, shared "guilt", as it were. Oddly enough, while we look for unconditional positive regard from others, we don't get it from the person who matters most.

This is yet another paradox of human nature which is, like so many others, greatly magnified by our disease. We do not give our own selves unconditional positive regard. Quite the contrary, we are ruthlessly judgemental of ourselves… we tend to focus on what we have done badly rather than what we have done well. At least inwardly. On the outside we pump up our accomplishments to seek other people's affirmation, but in our own minds we know we are exaggerating or lying, which drops ourselves even lower in our own eyes. This happens to everybody (including and especially narcissistic personalities), but it happens especially harshly in alcoholic-addicts, and, until we find guided sobriety we ourselves will see our own disease as a failing of morality. No wonder we hide what we really are in our quest for affirmation from others. Fortunately, this perception of alcoholism-addiction as a failing of morality usually falls away after the first Twelve Step meeting we ever attend, where obviously good people freely introduce themselves as alcoholics, or addicts, or gamblers, etc.

Just an aside here about the morality question of alcoholism and addiction. Most people will concede that once hooked the alcoholic-addict cannot help but to continue in their addiction, that it is no longer a daily choice. However, many argue that at some point there was a very first drink or drug and that was a conscious choice and therefore everything started as an immoral act. I have even heard alcoholic-addicts say that. However, almost all people drink at some point in their life, and many will get "smashed" after a really stressful event, or to celebrate. Many people sleep off their drunk and move on with life with no further thought of alcohol. Many of us, though, – through the combination of genetics, brain chemistry, psychology, life situation, and upbringing (everything that is the subject of this book) – can't move off after our drinking episode without doing it again. We start slowly (or quickly) increasing the frequency and intensity of our drinking, and we circle down the drain of alcoholism. Everyone who has ever tasted alcohol has taken a first drink. It is not a morality issue any more than it is a morality issue to eat non-nutritious foods. The same logic applies to drug use. Many people try drugs, usually starting out with the "socially acceptable and socially encouraged" "soft" drugs (alcohol, ecstasy, marijuana… cocaine?) and progress from there. Some do not go on to become addicted, others do. The National Institute of Health's National Institute on Drug Abuse (NIDA) statistics tell us that by age 26 over 87% of Americans have used alcohol, and just over 50% have used illicit drugs.[3] These statistics are notoriously underestimated because many people falsely deny alcohol and drug use when surveyed. Either way, if making a decision to take the first drink or drug makes a person immoral, that's a lot of immoral people. Exposure to alcohol and drugs is increasingly becoming a normal part of life in our world. Now let's get back to the human need for affirmation.

[87]

This relentless, insatiable need for affirmation, for positive regard, is what drives people into dysfunctional relationships and sex addiction. If our self-esteem is low we will be driven to tremendous mental and physical exertions to find affirmation from others. This need is so strong – the lower the self-esteem the stronger the drive for affirmation – that our minds will compel us to lie about or exaggerate our accomplishments, and it drives us to find a romantic (or sexual) partner to affirm us. The affirmation we get from someone intimate is far more gratifying to our psyche. This is why some people are neurotically incapable being alone: as soon as one relationship ends they are frantically searching for the next. Ultimately it can lead to sex addiction, as sex may seem to us to be the ultimate affirmation: someone gives themselves over to us bodily, which we feel means that they must hold us in very high regard indeed. In some, this degenerates to the use of prostitutes, or other highly unhealthy sexual practices. And it makes us highly susceptible to co-dependency. These are deeply important issues in our recovery, and we will discuss these further in the chapter on psychotherapy.

As a scientist, I have been impressed by the Twelve Step fellowships as a rare true example of unconditional positive regard. From the first time we attend a gathering we are greeted by people who are truly pleased that we are there, regardless of how we look, what we have, and what we have done. They see our value as persons, looking beyond our alcoholic-addict behaviors. And this unconditional positive regard is genuine and freely given, in abundance. Why is this rarity of human nature present in these fellowships? For the simple reason that everyone there has been through what we have, some much worse, and they know that there is a good person who is sick under all that social gore, not an immoral charlatan. They know from personal experience that with the help of the Twelve Steps and the fellowship we can pull the inner good person out for the world to see. So they accept us and keep accepting us no matter what, even when we relapse, or are in jail, or whatever may befall us. It is this that keeps us coming back for more of what they have.

Our ingrained deep dysfunctional psychological need for affirmation can lead us into major life decisions, and cause some ugly emotions and actions. The problem is that we *lack insight* into this need. This is a term in psychology that means that a behavior or thought process occurs without us being aware of them… they occur automatically, subconsciously. We require self-awareness to recognize and curb this process, and we can only find this when we learn about these mental processes and learn to watch for them. The self-awareness that we need does not come naturally to us. The information we are discussing here can help us to be aware of these processes going on in our heads. So, we should endeavor to become aware when we are putting on a fake stage character or resorting to activities solely to gain affirmation from others. It may save us a lot of foolish and wasteful efforts. Better to earn their positive regard by behaving in a way consistent with our efforts to overcome our character defects and live with dignity and integrity.

*

It's hard to accomplish anything when we're drunk and high or sick all the time. However, there is more to why our lives come apart when we are captives of a substance. We have already discussed some substance-induced character defects and behaviors. Unfortunately, there is yet more to our psychology that alcohol and drugs use to bring about our ruination. In 1970 psychologist Abraham Maslow worked out a model of motivation that explains much about human behavior. Despite being almost 50 years old and simplistic, Maslow's model remains highly regarded and highly applicable, as it has stood up to scrutiny. If Maslow's name sounds familiar, it's because his ideas are taught in every basic high-school psychology and biology course. His model describes our *hierarchy of needs* and posits that our basic needs must be met before our attention is diverted to more elaborate, less biologically-necessary needs. Specifically, our most basic need is our physiological essentials. These are our basic survival needs and includes such things as food, water, shelter, sleep. Our attention will be laser-focussed on obtaining these things, and only when these physiological needs are met can our attention turn to satisfying our higher needs, which are, in order: safety needs (safe and secure environment), love and belongingness, self-esteem, and finally self-actualization (achieving self-fulfillment, becoming what we want to become).

Ordinarily, like anything that tries to generalize about the human body and mind, this hierarchy of needs is not set in stone, and can be somewhat flexible. For example, we might stay at work and miss supper and work late into the night, sacrificing our basic physiological needs of food and sleep so as to satisfy our higher needs of impressing our boss and achieving success in the workplace. However, when it comes to our human needs everything changes when we our substance takes over our mind. The substance becomes our number one physiological need. This is extremely odd, given that it is definitely not necessary to our biological survival – that's how powerful our addiction is. We are not willing to sacrifice our new artificial basic physiologic need in order to achieve any other needs... how many alcoholic-addicts skip a night of drinking or using to stay late at the office? If anything, the alcoholic-addict will leave work early to start imbibing. We will even ignore our real basic physiological needs in order to satisfy our obsession for our substance. Many of us eat little or nothing when we are drinking or using day after day. But, we do more than just ignore other needs.

Not only will we ignore our other needs in order to satisfy what has become our new supreme "physiological" need – alcohol or drugs – but we will actually throw away things that have already been achieved, to the detriment of our higher needs. Nothing is safe from getting "thrown under the bus" for our beloved substance. We've all done it; as we sink further into the distilled cesspool we lose our jobs, our homes, our loved ones, the fruits of our accomplishments, our safety and security, all we have worked for. In fact, we may even become glad to see some of these things go, as they were getting in the way of our drinking or using. A substance has become our new master. Robert Louis Stevenson put it well in Treasure Island: "I lived on rum, I tell you. It's been meat and drink, and man and wife, to me."

One friend in A.A. tells the story from his "pre-recovery" days about being at odds with his beautiful and supportive fiancée over his alcohol and drug use. She was not "one of us." She had been grinding along in their relationship despite his behavior, sticking with him and trying to get him to accept help. She was at the end of her rope and told him that if he didn't stop drinking and using she would finally leave him. He promised her right then and there that he was forever done with the drugs and alcohol... half an hour later she found him in the bathroom shooting up. Exasperated for the last time, she took off her engagement ring and threw it at him. He tells us that all he could think about was how much he could get for the ring so he could buy some cocaine and vodka. He sacrificed the loving person who satisfied many of his higher needs in order to gratify this one artificial physiological pariah that had hijacked his life. This is how we spiral downwards toward our bottom. Alcoholism and addiction truly are assassins of life.

*

Are there more ways our substances use our psychology to trip us up? Sadly, yes. You don't have to be a psychologist to know that it is human nature to ignore future consequences in order to find immediate gratification. Anyone who has tried dieting knows this first-hand! It's so easy to bite into that cake and worry about the consequences later. This aspect of our behavior is especially strong when the immediate gratification involves getting drunk or high. For us, pushing aside any thoughts of repercussions became learned behavior (remember: "operant conditioning"), and it became reinforced every day during our time "out there." Our recovery depends on us bettering it, but the learned behavior is always still there, and can manifest itself in other harmful ways – particularly in times of stress.

Under the pain of stress the human mind will seek immediate gratification by reaching for those dysfunctional coping mechanisms – eating when we're not hungry, sex outside of our relationship, pornography, gambling, compulsive shopping, smoking, anything that gives us that dopamine burst. This includes drinking and drugging. We need to be mindful of this mental drive to distract us from our problems by immediate gratification. Twelve Steppers will be familiar with the slogan "play the tape through to the end," which is an excellent way to address this aspect of our psychology. This excellent technique works for anyone, not just those who use the Twelve Step program. The idea is that whenever we feel an urge to reach for that drink or drug – or to walk into that casino, or whatever our poison – that we reflexively stop for a moment and think past the immediate gratification before us all the way to where it will lead… right back to that miserable way we once existed. This sounds easy enough, but it's not. The desire for that immediate gratification is very strong, and our mind will be fixated on it. The stronger the stress we're under the stronger that fixation will be. The ability to break that overpowering fixation long enough to "play the tape through to the end" takes some work to achieve. By far the very best way to do this is by the same meditation that we have already discussed. This meditation does two things to help us with this problem: 1) it helps us learn to focus our mind, so we can break the fixation during an urge, and 2) it helps us to imprint the "remember when" onto our mind so that we can play the tape through to the miserable end. And don't fool yourself: millions of alcoholics and addicts over decades have all found the same thing: that one drink or hit will put us right back to where we were. To believe otherwise is what we refer to as "the insanity of alcoholism-addiction," the subject of our next chapter.

There is another woeful dysfunctional coping mechanism our addiction-prone minds can compel us to seek: co-dependency.

*

Most of us are enormously mentally and emotionally vulnerable in early sobriety. After all, we have just been thrashed by "the lonely disease." We are fittingly said to be left with a void deep inside of us. I think of it as a cavern: deep, dark, damp, and shivery. Many will experience an unconscious urge to fill this cavernous void with a rushed romantic relationship based on immediate neediness. The Twelve Step program recognizes how dangerous this is and is very focussed on filling the emptiness inside us with some kind of a higher power and with good fellowship. To this end, another slogan is "never alone." We must be wary of the tendency of our addict-alcoholic mind to want to fill the void in other ways. Pursuing a relationship because we cannot stand being alone and need someone to prop us up is a recipe for disaster. Besides, we owe it to ourselves and the person we are with to be emotionally stable and comfortable in our own skin before we pursue anything like a romantic relationship. Besides our emotional neediness there is another aspect that can make relationships particularly perilous.

When we are newly in recovery we tend to not have a lot going for us in terms of a romantic relationship. Our dating profile would read: "alcoholic-addict newly sober, no remaining assets, emotionally broken, needy, physically sick seeks rescue-minded companion for unstable relationship." Well, that's how it should read, but our alcoholic-addict pride would have us being much less truthful in order use our "stage character" to draw someone to us. The people we will attract at that point in our lives are probably also struggling in life. If we find someone who needs us just as badly, we run the risk of co-dependency, which is when we have an excessive emotional or psychological reliance on a partner, particularly a partner who requires our support in return due to an illness or addiction; a very unhealthy situation that is likely to train-wreck. We risk mistaking loneliness and neediness for love: the mouse pulling the thorn from the lion's paw in the fairy tale. We should look for someone when we are strong and standing on our own, with our house in order, as well as our lives, so that we are attracted to someone for the right reasons and have something to offer in return. A little patience is prudent... it will come.

For those who are already in a relationship, patience is also required. Take heart... no matter how much the cats fight, there always seem to be plenty of kittens (so said Abraham Lincoln). We must recognize our partners' needs after all we have put them through. We are so excited and pumped up and confident about our recovery, we can hardly contain ourselves! We know that this time we truly do have something different, but our partners will still have those lingering doubts and memories, and may be outright distrustful and skeptical of our new-found sobriety. How many times have they heard empty promises and outright lies from us? We want only to forget the past and move on, but they are not yet ready or willing to forget. Our battered self-esteem desperately needs validation, and we are disappointed, perhaps even angry and resentful, when that isn't forthcoming. So, it can lead to bitter fights. For those who are using the Twelve Steps to achieve sobriety this is the time to try out our new-found empathy and selflessness skills. If we find it difficult to generate some empathy for our partners we should try asking ourselves: If my partner would have put me through what I put her through, would I have stayed by her? If my partner had lost all those things that were important to us like I did, would I be angry? Would I still be in this relationship? Would I trust her at this point? Now the empathy starts welling up... but, what should we do with that empathy?

For those who are involved in a complete program of recovery there is change and optimism in the air. We are finally seeing and ridding ourselves of those defects of character that made us drink and behave as we did – we are "cleaning house." However, our loved ones are not learning to "clean house" like we are. They have no Twelve Step program, or whatever program we are using, no fellowship helping them through the anger and resentments and emotional pain like we do. That is why I encourage involvement in al-anon, which is a Twelve Step program of fellowship for the loved ones affected by our behavior. In the meantime, we need to express our empathy by understanding our partners' pain and not responding in kind when they lash out at us. We must use the skills we are learning in our program to diffuse confrontation, avoid arguments, and avoid retaliation when emotions are high. This is an early and meaningful test of our ability to shed our character defects. It is the Twelve Steps, or whatever program we are using, being applied to our relationship. What about when our partner is also an alcoholic-addict?

It is a sad truth of psychology that "misery loves company." Once again, our disease amplifies this ugly aspect of our mental make-up. As we have discussed, when we are actively drinking or using we are consumed with guilt, shame, and regret. Our cognitive dissonance is profound, and our selfish alcoholic-addict mind can seek to reduce that dissonance by compelling us to surround ourselves with people who are doing the same as us, and also try to pull down those around us, including loved ones. After all, our behavior can't be that bad if everyone else is doing it too, right? This "misery loves company" syndrome typically occurs straightaway in relapse, and if someone at hand, such as our partner, is in recovery as well we see them as an easy target. In The Twelve Step fellowship the situation where one of a couple relapses and then strives to cause the other to fall is known as "hostage taking." An apt description.

A couple I know in recovery recently came back from a relapse. The husband, Matt, relapsed on his own, and then tried to get his wife Angela to relapse with him. She refused, and tried to help him but he kept pushing her, playing on her weaknesses until she finally did relapse. Now back in recovery, he feels awful about dragging her down with him, especially because she is having a tough time of it and had to return to a rehab facility. Matt loves Angela very much, but with his first drink his alcoholic-addict selfishness and cognitive dissonance returned with a vengeance, and "misery loves company" syndrome won out over his love. It compelled him to shove Angela under the bus. We must use our knowledge of "misery loves company" syndrome to avoid becoming that company when a friend or loved one relapses or is still "out there." So, how do we do that?

Barriers. People in general are gutless at establishing and enforcing barriers, and we alcoholic-addicts are no exception. In this context I refer to a barrier as a limit we place on other people's access to us in order to protect our own needs when they are inappropriately demanding of us. When someone's behavior around us or toward us may be a trigger to relapse it's time for a barrier, and we must withdraw. Establishing a barrier means we make sure the people in our lives know exactly what kind of behavior we will tolerate, and what kind we won't – but barriers are meaningless unless we enforce them. People have a way of wriggling around our barriers, especially fellow alcoholic-addicts, as we are masters of manipulation. But barriers are there to protect us from triggers, so we need to establish them for more than just people trying to entice us to drink or use with them. Anyone who brings out anger or undue stress – a family member who pushes our buttons, for example – needs to be barred from dragging us down. At least until such time that we are ready to handle that, if ever. It's about not allowing people to ruin our day... or our sobriety.

Fellow drunks and addicts are particularly skilled at dragging us down. They understand first-hand the insanity of our disease, and they will play on that. Misery loves company, so we must anticipate their efforts. A good example would be a drinking buddy who is still tethered to the bottle. Being around that person at all will without doubt be a trigger for us. We have discussed the need to find new places and new faces, and this is why. This is much more tricky with someone close to us, especially if it's our partner and we co-habitate. We can let our fuddled friends know that we will be there to help when they want to find sobriety, but until then we must withdraw. We are no good to them relapsed. Trying to help them is fine, but if they cross that barrier, we must withdraw. We need to follow the advice in the Big

[95]

Book… if they are drunk, leave them to their drink, as long as they are safe (not driving, etc.). When we do interact with them, we must be sure to walk away when they cross that barrier and try to play on our weaknesses: offering us alcohol or drug, pushing our buttons. Walking away might mean we have to go stay with someone else for a while. So be it. At least we are still in recovery.

Enforcing a barrier, no matter how appropriate the barrier, can be extremely difficult to do. We will feel heartless, cruel, uncaring, and the recipient of our enforcement will want to play on that. But this is tough love and it's needed because we are dealing with a deadly disease. It is very important to remember that we lack objectivity when we are dealing with someone we are emotionally tied to, so calling our sponsor or another "one of us" in recovery to communicate our situation and ask for objective guidance is important – lest those barriers be smashed down and us with them.

The keys here are 1) expecting the behavior, 2) establishing barriers, 3) walking away when those barriers are crossed, and 4) calling someone we trust for support. It is tough love, but we are no good to our friend or loved one if we relapse as well. First things first, right?

*

A veritable showcase of the contorted brain function and twisted psychology provoked by our disease is the so-called "pink cloud effect." The pink cloud effect is a psychological phenomenon seen in alcoholism-addiction recovery, first described by Alcoholics Anonymous. It can be defined as the "state of mind, usually experienced in early sobriety, characterized by unusual happiness and grandiosity in spite of rather difficult life circumstances."[5] Most of the psychology literature views it as being undesirable and a negative influence on recovery, despite the positive emotions it entails. It is described as the dubious elation of early recovery, an inability to accept and meet present life circumstances, and a coping mechanism. It is felt to be dangerous to our recovery because we can lose sight of problems in our life, including mental health issues, and we can easily become complacent and over-confident in our recovery. This may lead us to stray from our plan of action for recovery, and bring on the feeling that we're good now – that it's OK to drink or use again. As well, the pink cloud effect doesn't last forever – it seldom lasts longer than three to six months – and when we fall off the cloud, we can fall hard.

It's very important to distinguish between the pink cloud and the normal elation we will feel from life in the wake of our new-found freedom from addiction. We finally have this toxic tonic, this noxious narcotic, this vile vinofile villain of vitality off our back… and our brain. For the first time our mind is clear. Our time, energy, and thought are ours again, no longer sacrificed to fulfilling our obsession with obtaining and using our poison potion. Every one of our senses is alert and alive – we feel re-born. Long forgotten emotions awaken. We can live now, connect with people, we have time to do things. Yes, we have many problems, but we are learning how to feel good about ourselves, for once. We may belong to a fellowship of people who accept us, see the good in us, understand us, and show by their example that long-term recovery is realistic and wonderful. We are also learning to stop allowing our problems to "own" us. We are feeling good physically and mentally, things we lost are coming back to us, and we are slowly regaining the trust of ourselves and others. We may be exploring spirituality for the first time. So naturally we're going to feel pretty good about ourselves and our situation. However, some who are new to the ways of sobriety can feel so good that it interferes with their ability to function properly. That is when we have the pink cloud.

So how do we know if we or another is riding this dangerous pink cloud? There is a fine line between the normal elation of early sobriety, and this pink cloud. There is no blood test, no set way to determine if someone is too high on life, but it's usually clear after even a little time with the affected individual. The line is crossed when people have lost touch with reality, their emotions are not adjusting to reflect their real-life situation, and they are in denial about their problems and challenges. Over-confidence in their recovery is noticeable and concerning.

It's brain function and psychology rebounding from our substance that causes the rise and fall of the pink cloud. First of all, our emotions have been anesthetized by drugs and alcohol for so long, the sudden awakening of normal feelings can be intense. We alcoholics and addicts tend to operate in extremes, and our new-found return of emotions is no exception. As we discussed in the first chapter, our substance use causes our dopamine-soaked brain to down-regulate natural production of dopamine and dopamine-stimulated receptors in an effort to compensate for the abnormally elevated levels. When we stop using the offending substance our dopamine levels drop precipitously, but it can take a long time before the brain starts producing normal levels of dopamine and its receptors again. Dopamine levels are therefore bottomed-out and the effect is, as we discussed in the first chapter, a feeling of lifelessness, being down, lacking energy. It can take months before our brain has recovered its old dopamine system, and if the pink cloud effect wears off before this happens, we go from an extremely elevated mood to an extremely low mood, in a matter of hours. This sudden drop can knock us off our feet and cause a depression that will keep us off our feet. Obviously, this is not only a terrible outcome in itself, but it's also a major risk for relapse.

Even people whose dopamine system has normalized by the time the pink cloud wears off can run into problems. They may feel boredom after the high emotions give way to more modest feelings and stop doing the things they need to do to stay sober. They may feel despondent, fearing that something is wrong, and they may question if recovery is worthwhile... or even necessary.

It's proper to be happy in sobriety and to be proud of our accomplishment, but when it gets to the point of distraction from real-life and our necessary efforts for recovery, then it becomes dysfunctional and should be addressed. There is no magic way to directly address this, other than an awareness of the problem so that we can watch for it in ourselves and in those around us. Often people don't recognize they are "clouding," and might not be amenable to the suggestion. Gentle persistence and nurturing are the key. This is something that we must be aware of if we are serving as sponsor for a newcomer in recovery. Once people accept that they are on a pink cloud, they can't be talked off it, but they can be talked through it. Discussing their immediate life issues and a plan for addressing them helps them face reality. As well, it is key to explain what the pink cloud is and how it works. They must understand that the high emotions are temporary and will end, so that they can be mentally prepared. Close contact with friends in the know or a sponsor is crucial, so that help is there for the fall from the cloud. Isolation is characteristic of a low mood, so this should be watched for. Missing meetings and losing contact with friends and sponsor are concerning symptoms. It's good to encourage a visit with their doctor to see if any treatment for any depression would help. Trying to tough out depression results in needless suffering and a sharp risk of relapse. Working the Twelve Steps is tailor-made for helping someone through the experience safely.

The pink cloud effect is only one example of why a comprehensive program of recovery and an extensive support system are crucial when attempting to break free from alcohol or drugs. The program and fellowship of the Twelve Steps is one such comprehensive program, but I encourage everyone to seek and find one that works for them. The bottom line is this: we need you with us in sobriety – clean and sober, healthy and happy. We can't allow a rose-colored cloud prevent that.

\*

Another characteristic of the human mind that can trip up the alcoholic-addict is the need for control. This plays a major role in preventing us from seeking and accepting help and committing ourselves fully when we do seek it out. We are afraid that help will take away our control. I refer to this as our need to "keep the door open a crack." We have a psychological drive for that little piece of control to keep open a way back to our substance, just in case we "need it." This is done partly subconsciously and partly consciously. Despite thirsting for sobriety and finally doing something about it, a corner of our mind keeps that door to our substance open a crack. We want to keep that door open just in case recovery is too hard, or we have a really bad day and need something to "help us through it." This involves seemingly harmless trivialities that our mind will find excuses for: not deleting our dealer's number from our phone, going back to our old environment, holding back from what is suggested to us. The Twelve Step program refers to this as wanting to find an "easier, softer way" to our sobriety. Fortunately, there is an anti-venom for this psychological pitfall: surrender.

If we decide to attend a rehab facility we can be dominated by thoughts like: the food here sucks, I hate my roommate, that counselor is an idiot, I hate this activity, why can't I have my cell phone. Or, we can surrender ourselves, accept and be grateful for the opportunity to get healthy, and focus entirely on what we can get out of the program. It's about presenting ourselves as a clean slate: my way of doing things failed miserably, so I'm here to learn. We have to simply let go. It's all about our frame of mind. The same applies to attending a Twelve Step meeting, or anything else designed to help us: surrender, accept, and open the mind. It's about turning our focus to how we can benefit from what we have in front of us, rather than fixating on what we don't like about it.

Perspective is truly a remarkable thing. We can go through life angry and resentful over all the things we don't have, or over all the things about our life we don't like, and many among us live exactly like that. That is a recipe for misery and black emotions that will seep into our actions and relationships. Or, we can learn to be grateful for the things we do have, and the things about our life that we do like, and be generally happy and well-adjusted people. Same life, different perspective. Perspective is especially important in recovering from addiction-alcoholism, as it determines whether or not we accept help and allow good information to enter our mind and fight the addiction. Surrender is about allowing ourselves to have a positive perspective for the help we are offered. Our mind-set as active alcoholics or addicts is filled with anger and resentments, a need for control, and false pride, all of which fight against our ability to surrender ourselves to help.

*

It is immeasurably easier to crush a temptation right away – when it's still a puppy – than it is to allow it to balloon and fester and then have to face a wolf. For example, if we are having some friends over, and one of them calls to offer bringing some Vodka, it is easier for us to pipe up and say: "actually, I'm not drinking anymore and at this point I would prefer not having any alcohol in the house" than it is to say nothing and then allow the night to evolve to where our guests have come and gone and we are face-to-face with a half-full bottle of left-behind Vodka at two o'clock in the morning. Standing there tired, alone, within arms-reach of that bottle, it will take infinitely more resolve to do the right thing. Now, instead of simply saying no on the phone we must reach for and pick up that bottle, uncap it, pour it down the drain with the smell and taste of Vodka arousing our senses, recap it and have to look at it in our recycling bin the next day.

Psychological study of relapse tells us that many of us make a decision to relapse well before we touch that first drink or drug. If we don't halt a potential temptation in its tracks when it first appears – saying no on the phone in our example – perhaps it is because we had already decided that we would like to have an opportunity to access a drink or drug. We may even allow the insanity of our disease talk us into believing that we did so in order to test ourselves and prove how good our sobriety is by having alcohol or drugs in the house. As well, even if we do believe that it is safe to allow such a situation to develop, once the substance is in our house and in reach, our disease will work on our mind the whole evening, re-awakening the obsession. We may end up unable to think about anything else, and will certainly fall.

Defeating that temptation when it first appeared could be the difference between continued deliverance from our disease and a relapse lasting days, months, or years that takes us back to where we were and beyond – perhaps to the gates of death. Seizing victory over our disease – the one that's doing push-ups outside in the parking lot – by saying no on the phone in the beginning of our example would have felt intoxicating. Filching reprieve at the end of the night by pouring out the Vodka – if we can do it – won't. This is because despite winning out in the end, we know that we were defeated by allowing that situation to unravel in the first place. We just handed our old enemies – guilt and cognitive dissonance – a way to creep back in.

No matter how sound our recovery, our disease will persevere in its vile efforts to seduce us for the rest of our lives. When we don't nip temptation in the bud as soon as it appears, we are acting on that piece of our alcoholic-addict mind that wants to keep the door to our substance open a crack. Once that door is open a crack our mind will go through it and our body will follow our mind into bondage. In our example, while our friends are there our mind will start obsessing about that bottle of Vodka in our kitchen, scheming how to make sure it gets left behind with some left over, and building anxiety over it. When our friends finally leave we have already decided what we are going to do. Relapses are usually planned in advance, and it is this "leave the door open a crack" vulnerability that initiates the plan.

The way to overcome this mental process is to accept that surrendering isn't just about that first day we seek help – it has to be an ongoing process. We must surrender daily so that we slam that door shut every time our alcoholic-addict mind tries to push it open a crack. Part of that is making it a reflex to call our sponsor or a friend in the know the minute that wicked door creaks open. Very few of us relapse when we do that. It's surrender or die.

*

Everything we've discussed so far is about how our minds work when we are awake and thinking, but what about when we are asleep? Are we safe when we are sleeping? Many people in recovery are bedeviled with dreams of relapse. These dreams are among the most vivid and intense of any, to the point where people wake up feeling like they really did relapse. Nightmares tend to be vivid and affect us physically, but they pale in comparison to relapse dreams. People will actually taste their substance when they awaken. Some report waking up feeling drunk or hung over. Some are left with a powerful desire to drink or use. Even the emotions of relapse are there: guilt and shame over the event, and fear of relapse. These are powerful dreams. And scary. Are they a threat to our recovery?

Relapse dreams occur most frequently during detoxification and in early sobriety, and they tend to sharply decrease in frequency as we progress in sobriety, especially after the first six weeks. However, they can persist for a lifetime, albeit usually only occurring occasionally. One unfortunate peculiarity, however, is that although they decrease in frequency they do not decrease in intensity and believability. We can experience them just as vividly decades after our last drink or drug as we did when we were detoxifying. Theories abound about dreams, as we have no way of proving certain aspects of dreaming. I quite disagree with some ideas about them, such as that they are a reflection of our anxieties, or that they are brought on by some subconscious desire to relapse. It is becoming clear that relapse

[102]

dreams are not indicative of anything we have been doing wrong in our recovery.

Research has shown that the more relapse dreams we have the more likely we are to relapse.[4] However, the earlier a person is in recovery the more frequent the dreams, so obviously people early in recovery are at higher risk of relapse either way. Having said that, it certainly makes sense that they can trigger a relapse because people sometimes wake up from them with an urge to relapse. We must temper this concern with the fact that people usually report a deep sense of relief at realizing that the dream was not real, and thankfulness to be still in sobriety. Even then, however, the dreamer is quite shaken by the experience. Regardless, these dreams are not a sign of impending relapse and reading too much into them can be harmful.

Looking at some dream theories can help prove my point. The most famous dream theory is that of Sigmund Freud, the notorious Neurologist (contrary to popular belief, he was not a Psychiatrist) who brought us "penis envy" and "anal-retention." Freud theorized that dreams are expressions of subconscious desires that we wish to see fulfilled, and that our dreams are packed with symbolism that can be interpreted by a process similar to reading Taro cards. Today, his dream theories are widely discredited, and rightfully so. If dreams were expressions of our deepest desires all my dreams would be of cruising the Caribbean on a beautiful private yacht. Sleep experts widely discredit the idea that our dreams are packed with disguised meanings. Certainly the pseudo-science of "dream interpretation" has no basis in reality. Another theory that I don't believe deserves any credit is the "dreams-for-survival" theory, which posits that dreams are our brain's way of telling us information that is vital for our day-to-day survival. It just doesn't pass the common-sense test for me. I do, however, feel that dream researchers are spot-on with the *activation-synthesis* theory. This suggests that our brains produce random electrical discharges while we sleep, perhaps brought on by particular neurotransmitter changes (when it comes to relapse dreams, could this be our dopamine again, or our desire for dopamine?), and these impulses stimulate memory pathways and thought pathways in our brain. Our brains then weave these thoughts and memories together into some kind of coherent story (our dream). Any brain pathway can be stimulated, which is why our

[103]

dreams can be bizarre combinations of random memories, abstract thoughts, and imagination.

Our drinking and using memories are of events on which we were intensely focussed – our drinking or using had become our main focus in life – and that have been repeated multiple times, so the memory pathways involved are deeply ingrained. When one of these random electrical discharges hits that memory pathway it plays the whole memory rather than skipping around to a number of different memories and patching them together, as in a normal dream. Think of the memory pathways related to our drinking and using as being deep grooves in our memory banks, like a deep scratch on a record. When the needle hits that groove it gets stuck in it and follows it all the way to the end. Thus, the relapse dream is deep and vivid and complete – tastes, smells, emotions, hang-over, everything is there. Of course, the more prominent pathways are affected most, which is why our relapse dreams decrease as our memories of drinking decrease as we progress in our sobriety. Thus, using our "remember-when" meditation to engage the "creative-imagination" and "interference" processes of our memory (see previous chapter) to make that groove less and less deeply cut will actively reduce our vulnerability for relapse dreams. Although there is no direct research that I know of that confirms that last statement, it makes perfect physiologic sense to me. Yet another reason that meditation is so important for our recovery.

So, you can see that relapse dreams are the result of random electrical discharges that happen to hit a deeply ingrained memory, so I will repeat myself: do not read too much into a relapse dream; they are not felt to be an expression of any desire to relapse, even if they do result in thoughts of relapsing. Believing that they do reflect a desire to relapse leads a lot of us to avoid bringing it up at a meeting or with our sponsor, and can cause us undue anxiety over fears of impending relapse. Our secrets put us at risk of relapse, especially the ones related to our substance, and we must not allow these dreams to become a secret. If we fear that our dream is an expression of a hidden desire to drink or that it precedes a relapse, our fear can become a self-fulfilling prophesy. So, we need to get it out in the open and off our chest.

It is important that we call our sponsor, or another trusted friend in recovery, when we wake up from a relapse dream. It helps put things back in perspective and allows us to get the experience off our chest. Most likely, our sponsor has had them too. We must use these dreams, when they occur, to reaffirm that we are powerless over substances of abuse (Step One). We can take the relapse dream as a powerful reminder that no matter how far we are into our recovery, we remain powerless over our addiction. Certainly we wake up feeling very powerless after such a dream. Reaffirming our powerlessness also helps us to engage our recovery tools to address the after-effects of the dream. I would also suggest going to meetings and sharing about the dream, and engaging the support system – especially if there is any lingering fantasy of drinking or using or a "weird" feeling (as I have heard it described), or even shame or guilt left over from the dream. No use being powerless over a dream.

*

The central theme woven through this chapter is that alcoholism and addiction corrupt our psychology and push our mental processes far outside their normal limits of function. These processes are turned against us to compel us to continue satisfying our obsession for drink or drug, and to bring us back when we are trying to break free.

We can see, then, that we must fight our natural human psychology in order to achieve and maintain sobriety. These behaviors are hard-wired into our nature and we have a life-time of practice in them, despite the misery they bring on us. Fighting and changing them is an up-hill battle to say the least, and we really do lack the skills to do this on our own. It requires specific therapy… psychotherapy. Soon we will discuss how the Twelve Step program amounts to a superior form of psychotherapy for getting back control of these very processes. The knowledge we gained in this chapter will certainly help that process along. In the next chapter, we will discuss the "insanity of alcoholism-addiction", a truly perplexing specimen of normal psychology gone berserk.

[105]

# Five

## The "Insanity" of Alcoholism and Addiction

The "insanity" of alcoholism and addiction is mentioned many times at Twelve Step meetings, and in the Twelve Step literature. "The idea that somehow, someday he will control and his drinking is the great obsession of every abnormal drinker" (Big Book, page 30). This refers to our stubborn belief that if we take that first drink or drug, this time it will turn out differently... **this** time we will be able to control our drinking or using This is "insane" because we allow ourselves to believe it despite multiple previous failings. The name comes from Albert Einstein's famous line: "Insanity is doing the same thing over and over again and expecting different results." (By the way, it turns out that Einstein never said this. It has been misattributed to him). This surprisingly pervasive insanity has brought down addicts and alcoholics with many years of sobriety, so we must try to understand it and look at how we can deal with it, for our own safety and success in sobriety. In the chapters on the brain and memory, we learned about the permanent changes that occur to cause this pervasive vulnerability to relapse after even one ill-advised taste, and in this chapter we will discuss the psychology that leads us to believe that we can take a drink or use a drug and this time will be different.

We say that insanity is doing the same thing over and over again and expecting a different result. This is truer than we might realize. If we look at how our mind works, it is well-documented in the science of thinking and reasoning that our mind naturally go through a process called *means-ends analysis*. This process involves our minds repeatedly testing different solutions to get a desired outcome. So, for example, if we want to get from New York to Los Angeles by the weekend, our mind's process of figuring out how to achieve that goal is by this means-ends analysis: we will rapidly and almost unconsciously run through different ways of getting there. We will quickly consider walking, cycling, driving, taking a train, taking a flight. Our mind will throw out walking and cycling, will conclude that driving is do-able but not fast enough, and that taking the train is feasible, but taking a flight is faster and easier. So, we will likely decide on the flight, and away we go. Now, imagine if we were a bit naïve and decided to try walking first. We set out to walk to L.A., but by the time we get out of New York and a few miles down the highway we see how tired we are and how much time it took, so we realize that there is no way we could get to L.A. by the weekend. So, we abandon the notion of walking as a way of achieving our goal, and move on to considering a different solution. Now, let's say that we get back home, and the next day decide to try walking again. This time we are better prepared, and get a better result, this time getting ten miles further than yesterday, but again we realize it didn't work. Then, rather than abandon walking as a failed solution, we again work up our resolve and try walking to L.A. again the next morning. Again, we fail, but we end up trying twenty more times; sometimes we do quite well and make a good distance, other times we only make it a mile or two. Even then, we refuse to accept advice from people telling us that walking won't work, we refuse to acknowledge that there is help out there to get us to L.A. (an airline) and we suppress our mind's natural problem solving process (means-end analysis) and we stubbornly keep trying to walk to L.A.. Our original goal of getting to L.A. by the weekend has long been missed, so we adjust our goal to walking to Phoenix by the end of the month, and when that fails, rather than adjust our plan and give up on walking we instead again adjust our plan, saying we will walk to Chicago, and so on. I think we can agree that this behavior is insane; we are ignoring all the facts, all advice from others, and our own normal mental processes in order to satisfy our obsession with walking. Insanity is defined as: madness, extreme foolishness, irrationality. Our obsession with walking and our repeated tries at it is all of that.

Anyone who is one of "us" will immediately see how this example of insanity applies to the insanity of alcoholism-addiction. We keep trying time after time to quit drinking by sheer will-power. We ignore the advice of our friends, family, and doctor. We stubbornly refuse the hands of help that are extended to us. I got this! we say. We ignore constant failure and we suppress our brain's natural reasoning process. We expect a different result each time. Then, when we are in sobriety, we can easily fall victim to this same insane thinking that we can now take a drink or drug and handle it: we can drink or use responsibly **this** time. Even when we know that is not true, we can easily fall victim to it. And many do. This is the insanity of alcoholism-addiction.

Yes, thinking this way and then acting on it is insanity, and it's also very unhealthy. In psychology, we distinguish between two terms that are nearly identical in appearance, but very different in meaning: *perseverance* and *perseveration* (they really should pass a law limiting doctors to using three letter words). Note that just the endings are different in those two words. Persever*ance* is when we stick with a plan that leads us to a goal. That plan may require repetitive actions, but they are constructive actions and realistically lead to the goal. The actions are broken down into "bite-sized" chunks that we can take one bite at a time. For example, I required perseverance to become a medical doctor. I required ten years of university training and internship. I had to get up every morning and go to school or the hospital, day after day, for ten years. I was repeating a behavior over and over again, but it was a behavior realistically leading to my goal. I persevered, and became a doctor. Perseverance is hard, but it brings satisfaction, motivation, and other rewards. Even if we don't make it all the way to the goal, we can take pride in our efforts. Persever*ation*, on the other hand, is an illogical but persistent repetition of a behavior that continues despite increasing realization that it won't lead to the goal. It involves a "hail Mary" action that we want to lead us to our goal. Perseveration leads to frustration, depression, hopelessness, and despair. The insanity of alcoholism-addiction is persever*ation*, and it brings us down even lower than we were before. The Twelve Step program recognizes this and helps us to break this cycle of perseveration and learn to persevere with our recovery. The deceptively simple slogan "One Day at a Time" is about perseverance, and lets us know that we can realistically get to our goal by persevering in small one-day chunks of sobriety that will add up and lead to our goal of permanent sobriety. Research into thinking and reasoning in the human brain has shown that we improve our ability to achieve a difficult task if we divide the actions we need to take into intermediate steps, or sub-goals (the bite-sized chunks I refer to above). This science is used to our advantage when we break down our recovery to "one day at a time."

Another prominent feature of how our mind works in problem-solving – in this case the problem is our drinking or using – is that we have a natural tendency to ignore information that contradicts our initial plan for the solution and favor information that props it up. This is known as *confirmation bias*: we are biased to ignore information that goes against our plan of using will-power to break our addiction or trying to control our drinking or using, and favor anything that supports it... even if that information is skewed. It's a glaring example of our nature to be stubborn, and we alcoholic-addicts invented stubborn. Again, the Twelve Step program of recovery seems to understand this function of our brain by reminding us that to succeed in the program we need to keep an open mind. We are encouraged to do this so that our mind will stop ignoring information that tells us it is time to drop our tired, failed plan of quitting drinking/using by sheer will-power or believing we can control our drinking/using despite multiple failed tries at it, and be accepting of a different plan of action. Knowledge of our mind's natural process of confirmation bias will help us to do that, not only in our recovery but in life in general. How many arguments have we been in or how many times have we thrown good money after bad because our mind's confirmation bias wouldn't let us let go of a stupid idea?

In addition to the "insanity" we have just discussed, I would also like to add my own observations of certain strange behaviors that seem to be unique to addicts and alcoholics that also could be considered as insanity. One of these is the pride that we see in alcoholics, as we have discussed in the previous chapter. I consider ours to be a disease of paradoxes, and the pride of alcoholic-addicts is one such paradox. This pride exists even in people who have lost all their worldly possessions and loved ones, and who have no feelings of self-worth or self-esteem left. They have debased themselves to the point of being pathetic. Yet this false pride beams so strongly that it will prevent us from "lowering ourselves" to accept help and will prevent us from having the open-mindedness to new ideas and ways of doing things that may help us out of our squalid hole. Sounds kind of insane, doesn't it?

Another kind of insanity is the obsession-compulsion that drives our addiction. Obsession and compulsion is the cudgel our substance uses to keep us in its head-lock. Little or nothing we lose in life is enough for our brain to over-power this obsession and its best buddy compulsion. Even the brain's own destruction and the looming end of our life is not enough to spur it to action. Certainly, this mental dysfunction that drives us forward to the next drink or drug against all logic amounts to insanity. We discuss this obsession further in up-coming chapters.

I must point out that the word "insane" is not a medical term. It has no meaning in psychiatry. It once was used professionally, but is now a semi-derogatory slang term. I use it here because the expression "insanity of alcoholism-addiction" was coined a long time ago and is in common use, and I don't think it is at all demeaning to anyone in this context.

The A.A. publication The Little Red Book talks of the insanity of alcoholism-addiction at length in the chapter on Step Two. It asks: "How is the alcoholic to account for the insane impulse that prompts him or her to reach for that first drink that starts another binge?" (Page 26). We will answer that question by looking at the psychology behind the "insanity" of alcoholism-addiction, and we will also see why the Twelve Step program is perfect for correcting this abnormal psychology.

\*

All people, by adulthood, have psychological issues of some sort that cause them discomfort, unwanted thoughts, and color their actions in some detrimental way. Some more than others, to be sure. I use the term "psychological issue" to mean bothersome memories or thoughts that are pervasive and cause us problems in our daily lives. It is remarkable how much we can be haunted by psychological issues, and how much they can affect our decisions and actions, our interactions with other people, and even our physical health.

Given the power of the mind and its ability to dominate us, it is not at all surprising that alcoholism-addiction is deeply affected by the state of the mind. Conversely, given that addictive substances are mind-altering chemicals, it is hardly surprising that the reverse is also true. An alcoholic housewife telling her story illustrates this perfectly: "I never knew which came first, the thinking or the drinking. If I could only stop thinking, I wouldn't drink. If I could only stop drinking, maybe I wouldn't think. But they were all mixed up together, and I was all mixed up inside" (Big Book, page 297).

We recovering addicts and alcoholics love telling stories that highlight the disordered, warped thinking that dominated us during our time "out there." The fact that we can look back and laugh at ourselves is an indication of our wellness. Some of the things we did are so bizarre that they are funny... in hindsight. Some are not so funny. What's scary is that despite how ridiculous these stories are to us now, at the time we actually believed what we were saying and doing. One A.A. member I know tells the story of being a passenger in a car that was pulled over by the police back in his drinking days. When the policeman checked his ID and phoned in for a background check he found that this man had a number of DUI arrests. The policeman said to him: "I see you have a real problem with drinking and driving. Have you done anything about it?" He replied: "Yes, I have. I don't drive anymore." That story sounds like a professionally written joke, but at the time, in his alcoholic mind, this man was entirely serious. He wasn't kidding. Problem solved: I just don't drive anymore. Cheers!

I was not immune to this insanity. One day I was having dinner at my mother's house with some family. She happens to live across the street from a women's drug and alcohol detox facility, as well as across from a city park. There was a woman sitting on a park bench directly in front of my mother's window. Suddenly, she fell off the bench and lay still on the ground. I rushed over to see what was wrong. She was unconscious. I could see she was wearing a patient bracelet from the detox center, and that she had just signed herself out from there, as her suitcase was nearby. On her chest were a couple of Fentanyl patches, and on the bench were empty beer cans. I couldn't wake her, so I ripped off the Fentanyl patches, but she soon stopped breathing. I started CPR and called for an ambulance. The paramedics administered the narcotic antidote Narcan, and took her away to the hospital. Within an hour of that incident, where I resuscitated someone who momentarily died from combining drug and alcohol, I went home and washed down drugs with alcohol. At the time, the bitter irony of the situation escaped me. Now, I can see the insanity of it.

Another example of insane alcoholic behavior is found in the story of one alcoholic in the Big Book. This man, deep in the throes of alcoholism, was invited (out of pity) to have Thanksgiving dinner with a friend and his family: "There at the dinner table, I stood up and attempted suicide in front of everyone. The memory of that has always stuck in my mind as the definition of 'pitiful, incomprehensible demoralization' that the Big Book talks about. What is sadder is that my actions had made sense to me at the time" (page 488).

Simply the absence of drinking – being "dry" – does not cure this disordered thinking, as is pointed out in the A.A. publication Living Sober: "The ideas that got so deeply embedded in our lives during drinking do not all disappear quickly, as if by magic, the moment we start keeping the plug in the jug. Our days of wine and "Sweet Adeline" may be gone, but the malady lingers on" (page 69). The "stinking thinking", the residual disordered thinking that creeps into the mind of the alcoholic or addict in recovery, is an attempt by our disease to talk us into believing that it's OK to have a drink or drug: **this** time it'll be different. It's our subconscious cravings trying to manipulate our thought processes in order to satisfy these cravings. So, if we want to keep our sobriety, these obsessions and irrational thoughts that have ruled us for so long must be overcome. Psychological therapy – psychotherapy – of some sort is urgently needed. However, professional psychotherapy is very expensive, and many of us had already tried it and have continued on in our insanity. Luckily, there is a superior form of psychotherapy that is free of charge and widely accessible which has proven effective in millions of alcoholic-addicts over the last 80+ years. That psychotherapy is known as the Twelve Step program of recovery.

We will discuss psychological therapy and why the Twelve Steps is a superior form of it for our disease in an upcoming chapter. Even if you are not a Twelve Stepper you will find the information useful. For now, I'll quickly mention the things that psychotherapy must do for us to break the cycle of this insanity. First of all, we must firmly and truthfully accept that we have no power over our substance. Otherwise, our mind will keep on trying to convince us that we can learn to control our substance use Then, we need some sort of a moral compass to guide us back into living among "normal" people. Years of selfishness and willingness to do anything for our next drink or drug has robbed us of this. A crucial part of the whole process must be finding some kind of understanding that we are not as individuals the biggest most powerful thing in the universe. We must accept that there are some kind of powers in the universe greater than ourselves. This lets us know that although we were not powerful enough to beat our addiction, there is power to do that. This gives us our first glimmer of hope. We must also figure out what character defects we had that kept us locked in the denial of life that is addiction, and we must figure out how to rid ourselves of these defects, lest they bring us down again. We must also look for the things in our lives – past trauma, terrible events, being wronged – behind these character defects. Then we must accept responsibility for our own role in our demise, which is not something that comes naturally to us. Importantly, we must make amends to those who have suffered from our wrong-doings, lifting a huge burden from our conscience. You can see how this is going to bring our thoughts and behaviors back in line with our ingrained concept of how a good person should be, and this relieves the psychological pain, so that the mind no longer has to warp facts and logic in order to do so. In other words, we are ending our cognitive dissonance. As I pointed out in the last chapter, "peace of mind" is simply the absence of cognitive dissonance. We need peace of mind to achieve long-lasting recovery and to succeed and be happy in life.

Through this process we become a changed persons. As a professional I can assure you that we who accomplish these things are very psychologically different from the lump of psychological goo we were after our last drink or drug. We must stay with the process and its supports to continue to grow and not back-slide. We can thereby commit few new wrong-doings, and take quick corrective action when they do occur. No new dissonance is allowed to build. Taking a further ultimate step of growth by putting others before ourselves and doing service work is a death-blow to dissonance, because this makes our behavior even better than our concept of how a good person should behave. This is an end to the psychological pain that we had tried to smother with drink and drug for so long.

In the chapter on psychotherapy we will compare traditional clinical therapy methods with the psychotherapy that is the Twelve Steps for dealing with alcoholism-addiction. We will look at the science behind these interventions to see what it tells us about how or why they work... and if they work. I will also inject into the discussion my experience as a psychotherapy provider as well as my experience as a recipient of psychotherapy, and my experience in helping others through the Twelve Steps and a recipient of help going through the Twelve Steps. I will lay these things bare for all to see, but the chapter is also a discussion about what any reader can pull from either program to help them with their recovery, whether they are involved in the Twelve Steps, or seek out psychological therapy, or not.

Before we move on to talk about psychological therapy for our disease, let's first figure out when we are ready for that therapy, so that our 'efforts aren't just a fart in the wind (you have my permission to use that on a Valentine's Day card). If you or someone you know is not ready yet, we'll discuss how to get there. That is the subject of our next chapter.

# Six

## When is Someone Ready for Recovery?

At risk of sounding clinical or like I'm trying to shoe-horn all of us into one mold, I break down the mental readiness for accepting help for addiction-alcoholism into four "phases." In medical terminology we call this projection of how a disease plays out its *natural history*. To be sure, everyone is an individual and has their own story. However, I think my concept of the natural history of readiness for recovery from alcoholism-addiction holds up quite well for most of us. See what you think, I'd appreciate an email with any comments you may care to share. Most people who find themselves drinking or using drugs, or gambling, or stuck on some addictive behavior too much are able to shake themselves off, walk away from it, and never look back. However, those of us who can't – true alcoholic-addicts – follow a remarkably similar path, which I have broken into four phases. These are:

Phase 1: This begins when we realize that our substance use has become abnormally frequent, and we are seeing the beginnings of it being detrimental to our health, family, job, and well-being. We are having arguments at home over our drinking or using and our behaviors around it. We are noticing that we are covering up for things we messed up or neglected to do. We are not willing to stop our drinking or using; even if we could stop at this point we would not. We become annoyed when people talk about our drinking or using. We try to get them off our back by hiding our substance use and telling them that we'll stop, even though we have no intention of doing so. We are starting to choose our substance over people and things, as we are willing to endure frayed relationships, sagging job performance, loss of hobbies and activities, and material loss for our substance. We are developing tolerance to our substance. We begin to be attracted to other people and places that support our substance use. We are getting physically sick from our substance use. Cognitive dissonance is getting noticeably uncomfortable. We sense that we are somehow becoming a different person, doing things we previously would have considered selfish and stupid.

Phase 2. This begins when we reach the point where we do want to stop, but we think we can do it on our own. "I got this," "I can stop: I've done it before," "as of Monday I'll stop" becomes our mantra to concerned family and friends. We really mean it when we say these things. We believe that will-power and determination will do it. Everything becomes "tomorrow." Tomorrow is when we'll deal with the bank problem, fix the broken garage door, have that talk with our boss, take the kids to the movies. And we believe it every time we say it. Even though we are going to great lengths to hide our alcohol or drug use, it is well known to everyone around us. Family and friends are repeatedly trying to get us to talk to the doctor, go to rehab, go to A.A., but we come up with every reason, every excuse not to. We still don't believe we need any help. Our alcoholic-addict pride, and our insane thinking are in full swing. We still believe we have power over our substance. Even if we did follow their requests and seek help we wouldn't accept what was offered, because we still need to keep that door to our substance open, and we still think we can do it our way, on our own. We would only pretend to seek help to get our family off our back.

At this point we are trying – over and over and over again – to control or stop our drinking or using. But it has to be our way: on our own with us in control. We are still looking for the easier, softer way. "I'll just drink on weekends," "I'll switch to beer, or weed," "I'll cut back my using," "I won't drink or use until after work," are our new plan. Each new low makes us swear off the drugs or alcohol, and we mean it. Sometimes we do stop. It will last a day or two, sometimes a week or more, but we always end right back where we started. Despite all our failures, we still cling to the belief that we can do this on our own. We are under the spell of the insanity of our disease.

We are losing things from our life, and we will continue losing them as long as we remain in this phase of our disease. Marriage, job, money, house, drivers' licence, access to our children, all progressively fall away. If we don't get out of this phase we will end up finding ourselves homeless, edging toward "jails, institutions, and death." We are having serious health problems. We are sick all the time. If we don't get out of this phase we will die.

Phase 3. Those lucky enough will enter this phase of our disease before they have lost too much. We are in this phase when we are finally desperate enough to seek and accept help. This is what is referred to in the Twelve Steps as "hitting our bottom." The crucial ingredient to entering this phase is described in the Big Book: "We learned that we had to fully concede to our innermost selves that we were alcoholics [or addicts]. This is the first step in recovery. The delusion that we are like other people, or presently may be, has to be smashed" (page 30).

At this point we will find ourselves being funneled toward detox, an in- or out-patient rehab program, or a program of recovery like a Twelve Step program. Our doctor, friends, family, whomever we go to for help will want us to do this. There is still one barrier between us and recovery at this point: surrender.

Once we surrender, we find sobriety. Surrender or die.

Phase 4. This phase is not part of our disease unless we fail to find sobriety in Phase 3 and give up trying. We have tried rehab, Twelve Step or other programs numerous times but have always found ourselves back drowning in our substance. This phase begins when we finally give up, and accept that we will ride our disease to the end. This is where we find the Wernicke-Korsakoff syndrome, advanced liver cirrhosis, alcoholic cardiomyopathy, and other advanced physical consequences of our disease. This is where we find those living on the fringes of society, who look and act like outcasts. This phase of our disease is uniformly fatal. However, there are still those who escape the grave and find sobriety if they finally become willing to surrender themselves to the solution.

*

[117]

It's helpful to understand the mindset of those who are ready to accept help. Our mindset usually involves feeling utterly overwhelmed. It's incredible how overwhelmed we are when we are actively addicted to alcohol or drugs, and how much it keeps us from getting sober. We feel a crushing weight on our back, and it occurs on three levels:

1. we are overwhelmed by the thought of living without our substance,
2. we are overwhelmed by all of life's problems that have piled up and worsened, and
3. we are overwhelmed by the guilt, shame, fear, self-loathing, and anger we feel.

Because this sense of being overwhelmed is such a deterrent to accepting help, let's look at each of the three aspects in turn. First of all, we are overwhelmed by the thought of living without our drug or alcohol. By the time we reach phase three of our addiction, most of us have tried multiple times to stop on our own, but we have failed. Life is so hard and we fear withdrawal so much that we can't imagine life without our drink or drug. We have failed all our previous attempts to control or stop our substance use, and we have concluded that it's not possible for us. Our guilt and shame and self-loathing are so huge that we don't even believe we deserve to be sober and living a good life.

Our multiple failed attempts at controlling or stopping our drug use or drinking have convinced us that we are too addicted to be able to recover. Our guilt, remorse, shame, and self-loathing from all the things we have done in our addiction has us believing that we have messed up too many things in life to be able to get sober, that even in sobriety our life would be too messed up to bear. Also, all the weird thought processes, moods, and feelings that have dominated our mind make us believe that we are too messed up in the head to be able to get sober. We are overwhelmed.

Part of the abnormal psychology of alcoholism/addiction is a terrible tendency to blow things up in our mind and thereby terrify ourselves - the "making a mountain out of a molehill" thing. We lay awake at night mulling things over in our mind, thinking up worst-case scenarios, making things look

[118]

ten times worse than they are. When we think of living without drugs or alcohol to cope, we project it as being too much for us.

When we talk to someone who is in recovery, go to a recovery meeting, spend a week in a detox facility, or check into a rehab facility we meet people talking who have variable amounts of time in recovery. Even hearing someone say: *I have 30 days clean and sober* can overwhelm us. We think: *30 days?!? I don't even know if I can make it through today, let alone 30 days!* We are overwhelmed.

The best way to crush this feeling of being overwhelmed by the thought of life without our substance is to borrow a principle from the Twelve Step program: "one day at a time." We need to learn to just concern ourselves with today: we need to do the things we need to do to stay sober today, and then let tomorrow look after itself. Focussing on today is easy enough, focussing on 30 days or a lifetime is not when we are in an overwhelmed frame of mind.

**We are overwhelmed by life problems.** For most of us, the stress of life's problems had a lot to do with bringing us to our alcohol or drug addiction. We used our substance as a dysfunctional coping mechanism because the stress of life was too hard. Then, as we became more and more withdrawn from life our problems worsened and accumulated. The stress got worse, and we drank or used more. It is the common experience of millions of addict-alcoholics that once they got sober, things started to get better. It almost always turns out that we have blown our problems way out of proportion in our mind, as alcoholics and addicts do. But we can't see that when we are sitting there contemplating getting sober. We are overwhelmed.

Once again, the best solution to this overwhelmed mind-set is to take life, like our recovery, "one day at a time." There is no point to projecting our problems into the future and laying awake all night worrying about them. Here, we need to approach life one day at a time by not worrying about what happened yesterday, or last year, and not worrying about what might happen tomorrow. Rather, we concern ourselves with doing today what we can to help the problems that we can help, and accepting the problems that we can't do anything about. Then, we let tomorrow take care of itself. It sounds simple, but this remarkable approach to life gives many people – alcoholic-addict or not – a piece of mind that they have never before known.

[119]

Things have a way of working themselves out, as long as we take care of ONE thing: remaining sober. Things we thought were gone forever come back to us. Bridges that we had burned open up to us again. And we are able to live with our problems and do what we can to help them along. We can expect things to come back to us in sobriety, but we mustn't try to get sober just to get those things back. If we try to get sober for anything but ourselves we will fail. That has been the experience of the millions of people who did this before us. We have to do it for ourselves only. While that sounds selfish, it's not. The grip of our disease is strong, and we will never break it unless we are focussed on ourselves. If we were capable of getting sober for our kids, or for our job, or for our marriage we would have done so long ago. All those we love and all those things that are important to us will remain lost unless we focus on ourselves while we break these chains.

One of the reasons behind the effectiveness of recovery programs that involve frequent contact with other alcoholics or addicts is because we can see that we are not alone in our experience. We meet people and hear their stories and see how they overcame all the destruction from their drinking or using days. It greatly deflates our feelings of being overwhelmed when we see that we are no more messed up and no different from the millions of people who came before us and managed to find life-long sobriety. The Big Book and other Twelve Step literature are filled with stories from such people who came before us. By reading about people we can identify with we can see that our own situation is typical, not extraordinary and certainly not insurmountable.

Once we are sober, it is crucial to deal with the black emotions and feelings, all the dysfunctional thought processes, all the harmful brain changes... all the stuff we are discussing in this book. Simply not drinking or using is not enough. Years of experience have taught us that we must correct the pathological changes that our disease brought on and get those burdensome emotions off our back... or we will ultimately go back. That is why it is wise to get involved with a recovery program that addresses our disease as part of our recovery. That is also why there is no "pill" that makes us sober... we must address the thoughts, feelings, emotions, and pain behind our addiction. Even Naltrexone - recently being touted as the new cure for drinking - has barely an 11% success rate, and even that is short-term. No pill

[120]

gets us out from under all our mental baggage. If you do use a medication, I suggest doing it along with a recovery program.

One more piece of information that helps make recovery less overwhelming is this: **alcoholism and addiction is a disease of biology, and not a failure of morality!** All those awful behaviors fall under the umbrella of symptoms that are the hallmark of the disease of addiction, and are not at all indicative of a "bad person."

We should not allow feeling "overwhelmed" to keep us from a sober life.

\*

We learn in this book many of the barriers to getting sober, which need to be addressed as part of the initial process of finding sobriety. Some we have already discussed, such as the "insanity" of alcoholism-addiction, and some we will discuss in the coming chapters, such as concurrent mental health disorders. I believe that the solutions to all these barriers lie within the Twelve Step program, although this should sometimes be coupled with some outside help. We discuss all these solutions in this book, especially in the next chapter.

In the next section we will discuss how we should go about helping a loved one or a friend who is caught in addiction-alcoholism. Before that, I would like to point out that it is my opinion that anyone who is attempting to break free of substance addiction should strongly consider doing so by checking into a seven day medically supervised detox facility. This allows addict-alcoholics to detoxify safely, which is especially important in those who were using alcohol regularly, as withdrawal from alcohol use can be dangerous, even deadly. While discussing the medical aspects of detoxification from alcohol is not a part of this book, there is detailed information on my website about the subject (www.alcoholism-addiction-psychology.com, click on "Alcohol withdrawal and seizures").

In addition to allowing for safe detoxification, a detox facility makes the process easier by allowing addict-alcoholics to interact with other alcoholic-addicts who are also detoxing, and allowing access to medical assistance to help ease the withdrawal symptoms. As well, the councillors provide recommendations and information pertaining to options for further help, such as community supports, rehab facilities, outpatient rehab programs, and sober-living housing. Usually, Twelve Step members come into detox facilities to provide support and Twelve Step meetings, and offer sponsorship and support for after discharge.

A detox facility is a great way to commit to getting better. It's a safe place to ride out the withdrawal symptoms, escape from all the worries of the world for the week and focus on recovery, and come up with a viable plan of action for ongoing recovery.

*

If a friend or loved one is caught in addiction or alcoholism we must be aware of the phases of readiness for accepting help, because if we push for sobriety and treatment in phase 1 or 2 we will have little chance of success and will only alienate our loved one. The Twelve Step program goes into great detail about how to recognize and deal with people who are still "in their cups." The program also details how to approach and feel out an alcoholic-addict and establish that connection that will lead to sobriety. This appears on pages 89-103 of the Big Book. However, one of the requirements of this process – and we will see in the next chapter why this is a crucial requirement – is that this approach be done by a fellow alcoholic-addict who is familiar with the program.

There is a major impediment that is characteristic of alcoholic-addicts to accepting advice or help from family or friends, especially if they are not alcoholic-addicts themselves. If we are too close, we are not in a good position to help them break free. Our advice tends to be offered repeatedly and quickly becomes viewed as "nagging," pushing our sick loved one away. Besides that, one of the hallmark symptoms of alcoholism and addiction is the ability to masterfully manipulate family and friends, so that when these people think they are helping their sick loved ones, they are actually enabling their drinking or using. This is especially the case when it comes to giving material support. When we are too close to the person, we lose perspective and objectivity. Besides, unless we are an alcoholic or addict in recovery we really don't know what we are dealing with. So, it is best to let an outsider who is an alcoholic-addict in recovery become involved.

A friend with more than twenty years in recovery from drug and alcohol addiction found himself with a teenaged daughter who had followed his earlier path of addiction. She came to him for help. Even though he had more than twenty years of recovery experience and had helped many other alcoholics and addicts into sobriety during his time in A.A., he knew he wasn't the one to help her. He brought her to a Twelve Step meeting, introduced her to the first female he saw, and then left. He knew that if he tried to help her himself that he would try to be her father and her sponsor, and tell her what to do. He knew this wouldn't work, and he was correct. His daughter is now five years into her own recovery, by the way.

The best thing we can do for people in the throes of their disease is to recognize what phase of their illness they are in, and resist our overwhelming desire to push them to "just stop." We need to understand their frame of mind even though it may be foreign to us. I hope that reading this book will enable us all to do that famously. Then we need to involve an outsider who knows what he or she is doing. I suggest calling the local A.A. number and asking for help. They will send someone over who will extend the hand of help in a way that addict-alcoholics can identify with. If they are not ready to accept help, the A.A. caller will back off, but will make sure that sick loved ones know that help is there when they are ready.

Once loved ones have accepted help, now is the time for family and friends to throw their support openly behind them. Allow them to set the tone, and the pace. Get in touch with their sponsor or councillor with any questions. It means a lot to an addict-alcoholic in early recovery to know that family and friends are there for them. Keep the conversation light, they often are far from ready to discuss their situation, allow them to set the pace and drive the subject of conversation. Easy does it.

When we back away from the situation, our addict-alcoholic loved ones are surprised by our understanding, and relieved by our restraint from pushing them toward something they are not ready for. We can't will these people into recovery, but we can understand them and gain their trust. Once they are ready, it is time to get them better, the subject of our next chapter.

# Seven

---

## The Twelve Steps as Psychotherapy

Freud himself said the aim of psychoanalysis is to relieve people of their neurotic unhappiness so that they can be normally unhappy. Hmmm, verrrry interesting. Luckily, Freud's methods are no longer in use. Every one of us – alcoholic-addict or not – has psychological issues of some sort that cause us discomfort, unwanted thoughts, and color our actions in some detrimental way. Some more than others, to be sure. What I call a psychological issue is simply something affecting or arising in the mind, relating to the mental and emotional state of a person. It's remarkable how much we can be haunted by these troubles… how much they can affect our decisions and actions, our interactions with other people, and even our physical health. For many, they rob us of our happiness.

Even in the absence of mental health disorders or alcoholism-addiction the things that trouble a person's mind can cause quite a bit of turmoil. Most people go through life schlepping these psychological issues, functioning as best they can. We get so used to carrying our issues around that it becomes "normal" for us. We become resigned that there is nothing that can be done about them: I have always been this way and I always will. They pollute our views of ourselves and others, and molest our best intentions. These distasteful memories and emotions are the slag heap of our less-than-glorious past: abuses, failings, embarrassments, conflicts. They bring uncapped angers, frustrations, prejudices, biases, fears, and insecurities that pitch their tents on top of our values. These things never get properly dealt with, so they seep out through every outlet: complaining, gossip, road rage, anger, hatefulness, trepidations, dysfunctional coping mechanisms. Yet we all can be freed from these burdens by proper psychological therapy, also known as psychotherapy. We learned in the chapter on psychology that these issues – particularly fear, anger, and resentments – are the biggest causes of our obsessive drinking or using... so, then, we alcoholic-addicts would especially benefit from such therapy.

It may surprise you to hear that, in my professional opinion, by far the most effective psychotherapy technique that exists is the 80+ year-old Twelve Step program. I know it surprised me. I am trained in the various techniques of psychotherapy, which certainly have their merits and uses, but I have seen nothing produce the remarkable transformations that we see with the Twelve Steps. And these occur in alcoholic-addicts, who tend to have some pretty dreadful issues, to say the least. What is perplexing to academics like me is that this psychotherapy is delivered by laypeople – fellow Twelve Steppers – with no training as therapists, who probably don't even realize that what they are doing is providing psychotherapy. If this secret gets out people like me will be out of work. Shhh!

Moreover, the Twelve Step program (of psychotherapy) is free, and... well, the rest of this chapter is going to finish that sentence. We will walk through how this gem of a program specifically addresses the psychological issues that underlie our intemperance, and find out what it is about it that makes it so effective. There is an opportunity for mutual benefit here – anyone doing the Steps or sponsoring others through the Steps will benefit from increasing their knowledge of the psychology of the Twelve Steps as therapy, and professional psychotherapists will benefit from adding some principles from the Twelve Step program into their practice. People who do not use the Twelve Steps will gain valuable knowledge for their own use. So let's get to it.

*

The healing power of the mind is well-documented. Consistently across all diseases the placebo effect, the physical healing from a fake medication (a sugar pill), is about 33%. The patient thinks themselves better. I have personally witnessed many real-life examples of people mentally giving up and quickly succumbing to their illness, as well as examples of people who were determined and mentally strong beating the odds and getting better. It doesn't happen every time – there is only so much the mind can do – but it sure happens a lot. The mind has healing power over our bodies... but it can also be harmful.

Given the power of the mind and its capacity over our behavior, it is not surprising that mind-altering drugs, including alcohol, deeply affect our behavior. As we have seen in our reading so far, what makes our alcoholism-addiction a disease is that it afflicts our mind so as to manipulate our mind's processes to change our behavior. The behaviors it elicits perpetuate our substance use and so catches us in a vicious cycle that defies all logic. We are sucked deeper and deeper into sickness and will ultimately die. Our sickness harms us in order to sustain itself – that is what a disease does.

Thus, we alcoholic-addicts are famous for our twisted, illogical, "insane" thinking patterns – it is a symptom of our disease. At this point in your reading you have become an expert on how our brain biology, our genes, memory, and our psychology are turned against us by this disease. Let's now recall a concept we discussed earlier on: cognitive dissonance. To quickly review, alcoholism-addiction forces our mind to an extreme form of "rationalization", which is the strongly ingrained human nature to substantiate our behavior with logical, plausible reasons, even if they are outright lies. Cognitive dissonance is the psychological discomfort we feel from the conflict produced when our inebriated miscreant actions clash with our set beliefs about how we should behave. This inconsistency between our ideas, beliefs, and values and our actions creates dissonance, a great psychological discomfort, which we feel as guilt, remorse, shame, and self-loathing. These emotions are painful to us, and the bigger the gulf between our beliefs and our actions the greater the pain. Interestingly, the mind doesn't try to reform our beliefs to match our actions, or change our behaviors to match our beliefs, it just lies to itself about what our actions are. Part of those lies is that we start blaming others for everything that's wrong in our lives, creating tremendous anger and resentments. As with other mental functions alcoholism-addiction pushes the mental process of cognitive dissonance to extremes.

Simply the absence of substance use does not cure this psychological pain and the associated disordered thinking. Our dissonance-burdened mind still seeks relief – however dysfunctional – from some kind of coping mechanism. Our dopamine-hungry mind tries to convince us that this time we can drink or use responsibly, and we allow ourselves to believe it. So, this dysfunctional psychology that has ruled us must be purged. Psychological therapy of some sort is urgently needed. However, psychotherapy costs a fortune, and many of us had already tried it and failed (as I had). Luckily, there is a superior form of psychotherapy that has proven effective in millions of drunks and addicts over the last 80 years. As you know, I am talking about the Twelve Step program of recovery.

Counselling and psychotherapy was a big part of my medical practice, something I enjoyed. I can therefore say this in a qualified way: the Twelve Steps is a five-star system of psychotherapy. In order to get the same level of therapy elsewhere, we would spend tens of thousands of dollars and a very long period of time, probably years, with a psychotherapist. If we could even find a psychotherapist capable of that level of intervention. Even then, it is unlikely that we would achieve the same level of deep introspection, resolution of conflict within and with others, self-improvement, and life-changes that we achieve from properly working the Twelve Steps. Not to mention stopping our substance use.

I am not demeaning the field of psychotherapy, nor the skill of its practitioners. What we are going to demonstrate in this chapter is that it is lacking as a choice for sole treatment for the disease of alcoholism-addiction. Its usefulness lies in helping some of us through some troubling factors that led to our alcoholism or addiction, as part of a broader plan of recovery. We suffer from a disease so tough to beat that we need more than what traditional psychotherapy provides on its own.

Strictly speaking, psychotherapy is the use of psychological methods to help a person to: 1) overcome problems, 2) resolve troublesome thoughts, behaviors, compulsions, or emotions, and 3) improve social and relationship skills in a healthy way. This field of therapy includes a range of procedures and techniques that can be considered psychotherapy. (Note that the "psycho" part of the word is short for psychological, not psychotic). Psychotherapy has a role in the treatment of many mental issues and some mental health disorders. It works well in some situations, not so well in others. Its track-record in alcoholism-addiction is not very good, but it can be useful in helping alcoholic-addicts deal with some related issues such, as a history of abuse.

Psychological therapy is available from many types of practitioners, some qualified, some not so much. In general, PhD psychologists, social workers, and some MDs will be best qualified to provide this kind of care. I took extra training during my medical schooling in order to be able to do this kind of work. I gained a lot of experience in it by working at a pediatric mental health unit, and by doing it as part of my medical practice regularly over a period of more than 13 years. I worked with people with mental health disorders, marital problems, obsessions, post-traumatic problems (including from experiences dating back to childhood), social problems, and alcoholism-addictions. So, naturally, I would have to tendency to seek out psychotherapy myself when I found myself unable to stop my drinking and drug use.

After finding out the hard way time and again that I couldn't quit using drugs and alcohol on my own (the insanity of alcoholism), I thought I would try psychotherapy. I attended sessions faithfully for over a year, spending almost $5,000, and was just as schnockered during and after as before. Then, after a few more "bottoms", my family funded my return to therapy, again to no avail despite my best efforts. But I fiercely wanted to be free of alcohol and drugs. My family had been pushing me toward A.A. from the beginning, and my therapist recommended it, but I was too head-strong. I couldn't – or wouldn't – see how a room full of drunks could get me to cork the bottle. If I had listened to my therapist and committed to A.A. I would have found what I needed. But I didn't… I was still in "phase 2" of my disease.

I lived in utter despair, by this time convinced that death was my only way out. During one particularly pernicious binge some friends and family took me to a detox facility. I went willingly, definitely being in "phase 3" of my illness by then, but I didn't hold out much hope for a good outcome. There I was introduced to A.A., two meetings a day. I couldn't fathom why people who were sober for years would take time out of their day and come put on meetings at the detox center for a bunch of sickly, tremulous, opinionated sots. Someone gave me a Big Book. I gave the book a chance, hungrily drawn into it once I saw that it was all about my secrets and behaviors, that I was not alone. I bought into the program and committed with everything I had. From that moment I have not used drugs or alcohol, and I am justifiably confident to never again fall under their spell. As I got to know the program and worked the Steps I realized: Schmeesh! This is actually psychotherapy! Swag!

For a psychotherapist to take on active drinking/using patients and expect to get them drug and alcohol-free with a cardinal shift in character would be a lofty goal indeed, unlikely to be achieved. Even if it were, the results would not likely survive beyond the end of the therapy. Yet we see exactly that endpoint regularly in those who commit to the Twelve Step program and make it a part of their life. Fortunately, most therapists recognize that and strongly recommend attending a Twelve Step program.

So, here I was professionally and personally dazzled by the unexpected gem I uncovered in the Twelve Steps. As a scientist I had to find out how and why this antique and unpretentious system works so well. I was planning some time off, so I proceeded to dissect the Twelve Step program and hold it up to the established psychotherapy methods to unearth its magical ingredients. I ransacked the scientific and medical research literature, and the Twelve Step and recovery literature, commingling them in my search. Most importantly, I soaked up the stories and wisdom of Twelve Step fellowship members, "long-timers" and newcomers alike. I was looking for answers and I succeeded. This chapter is about what I discovered.

The unique characteristics of the Twelve Step program that make it a superior form of psychotherapy for our disease are:

•The ability to extract complete honesty and openness
•The up-front promise of recovery
•Involvement of a higher power
•A.A. is not "talk-therapy", but a program of action
•The presence of a massive, always available, altruistic support system
•Accountability to the program
•The use of fellowship meetings
•Sponsorship
•The experience of a "spiritual awakening"
•Focus on internal locus of control
•The absence of professional detachment

[129]

•Universal availability: at no cost
•Not delivered an hour at a session, once or twice a week
•The availability of extensive supporting literature
•The use of service work, emphasis on selflessness
•Life-long duration of the program.

\*

Honesty. It's a key ingredient to success... if you can fake honesty, you've got it made. At least that's how we alcoholics and addicts see it. We take our bullshit and sugar-coat it and call it the truth. We are skilled liars, our acumen sharpened by years of practice. We lie to prop up our alcoholic-addict false pride, we lie to hide our behaviors, we lie to get our substance, we lie to cover our lies. When we attend therapy, we must tell our story if we are to realize any benefits... but we must tell the TRUE story. If there isn't complete disclosure to the therapist, everything that transpires is worthless. How can you deal with a problem you won't even acknowledge? That's a problem in the therapist's office, and scientific research has proven that we lie to our therapists. The Twelve Step program has brilliantly cracked this problem.

As we discussed in the chapter on psychology, human nature drives us to cover our defects, to exaggerate our good, to put ourselves in the best possible light, and our disease inflates this tendency titanically. In fact, dishonesty is a defining characteristic of alcoholism and addiction: "more than most people, the alcoholic [and addict] leads a double life. He is very much the actor. To the outer world he presents his stage character. This is the one he likes his fellows to see. He wants to enjoy a certain reputation, but knows in his heart he doesn't deserve it." (Big Book, page 73). This is a problem: we aren't going to get anywhere unless we lay it all on the table... but science has shown that in a therapist's office, we ain't tellin' the truth.

There has been some entertaining research into how much we lie to our therapist. One article from Psychology Today[1] starts out: "People lie while lying on the couch. It happens all the time. You've done it. I've done it. Nearly everyone has some sofa subterfuge on their therapy resume." Sofa subterfuge! I love it! This very clever and illuminating article features an interview with Matt Blanchard, a psychology researcher on lying in therapy. The interviewer askes: "we know that lying is common in therapy, but how common is it?" Blanchard responds: "our results suggest it is very common. Our first study of 547 therapy clients found 93 percent could recall specific topics about which they have lied to their therapist in the past. This might involve denying suicidal thoughts, hiding drug use, concealing criminal acts, or downplaying the extent of their emotional suffering. We found it particularly interesting that 72.6 percent reported lying about therapy itself: pretending to like their therapist's comments, or pretending to find therapy more helpful than they really do." These results were upheld by further experiments.

Interesting. Those things that 93% of people lie about in therapy are exactly the things that characterize our lives while drinking or using. While no one has similar data on how much people lie when working the Twelve Steps, I will posit that it is very low indeed. According Blanchard's research one piece of information that patients lie about and deny more about than any others is whether they are contemplating or have contemplated or attempted suicide. My experience in the Twelve Step fellowship has consistently been that people are very up front about this, even when they share in front of others at meetings or speak at the podium, situations which we would expect to cower them into concealing this information. Many even share this information about themselves in print. The same applies to criminal behaviors, extra-marital affairs, and many other deep dark secrets of our sordid past. There are few secrets kept in this fellowship, unlike in the clinical therapy setting. It is, after all, famously a program of rigorous honesty.

Eighty-plus years of experience of A.A. has shown that one of the hallmarks of beginning a successful, permanent sobriety is being 100% open and honest. "Time after time newcomers have tried to keep to themselves certain facts about their lives. Trying to avoid this humbling experience, they have turned to easier methods. Almost invariably they got drunk... the reason is they never completed their housecleaning. They took inventory all right, but hung on to the worst items in stock... until they told someone else all their life story" (Big Book, pages 72-3).

[131]

The Twelve Step program is up front about demanding rigorous honesty and about the fact that without it there will be no sobriety. A therapist will be up front about the need for honesty if anything is to be gained as well. But, unlike therapists, the fellowship obtains it. Even newcomers seem to be eager to share this intensely personal information, as if to "fit in" with their new friends of similar experiences. Even more than that, these people were dying (pardon the pun) to get this information off their chest, and are relieved to find someone who has paddled the same canoe.

A crucial lubricant for honesty lies within the program: only an alcoholic can understand an alcoholic; only an addict can understand an addict. This value of this is underscored on page 18 of the Big Book:

> "Highly competent psychiatrists who have dealt with us have found it sometimes impossible to persuade an alcoholic to discuss his situation without reserve. Strangely enough, wives, parents and intimate friends usually find us even more unapproachable than do the psychiatrist and the doctor.
>
> "But the ex-problem drinker who has found this solution, who is properly armed with facts about himself, can generally win the entire confidence of another alcoholic in a few hours. Until such an understanding is reached, little or nothing can be accomplished."

I repeat that last part: "...little or nothing can be accomplished." If people don't get us, how, then, can they give us meaningful advice? How will they convince us to follow this advice that is not based in understanding? The mind of an alcoholic-addict is a strange place, and it takes an alcoholic-addict to truly understand it, and to call us out on our bullshit. How many times have we been asked "why don't you just stop?" I was there, I was the therapist with all the education and book smarts, but my personal journey in alcoholism-addiction and recovery taught me how little I knew. It does take an alcoholic-addict to get another to let down walls and start being honest. And it takes an alcoholic-addict to recognize honesty. But it's more than that... we need to know we are going to be understood before we give honesty; we need to identify before we let go. The result: "We know but few instances where we have given these doctors a fair break. We have seldom told them the whole truth nor have we followed their advice" (Big Book, page 73).

In the book *Experience, Strength, and Hope*, a collection of stories of recovery, one woman speaks of how she had run the gamut of treatments for alcoholism, as her wealthy family tried in vain to help her overcome her alcohol addiction. Being the early days of A.A., fate brought her to the A.A. Foundation office in New York, where she met Bill W., co-founder of A.A.: "He did not take out a folder and say, 'What is the nature of your problem?' He said to me, gently and simply, 'Do you think that you are one of us?' Never in my entire life had anyone asked me 'Are you one of us?' Never had I felt a sense of belonging. I found myself nodding my head." (Stars Don't Fall, page 347). She found sobriety from that moment. The sense of belonging that she had been unable to find in the offices of therapists was what finally saved her.

Examples abound. Says one "hopeless" alcoholic: "…a sober member of Alcoholics Anonymous sat me down in her office and told me her story – how she drank, what happened, and how she got sober. No one had ever done this before. I had been preached to, analyzed, cursed, and counseled, but no one had ever said, 'I identify with what's going on with you. It happened to me, and this is what I did about it.' She got me to my first A.A. meeting that same evening." (Big Book, page 449). This hopeless drunk never tasted alcohol again.

What if the therapist happens to be a recovering addict or alcoholic? Self-disclosure is forbidden among doctors and therapists, so we may be completely unaware that they are "one of us." Even if the patient is aware of this, the counselor or doctor will not share their personal story or experiences; they will remain aloof to maintain the therapist-patient boundary. Certainly, they will not commiserate with the patient. Therefore, little or nothing can be accomplished.

Another "hopeless" drunk who was rescued by another alcoholic: "Of far more importance was the fact that he was the first living human being with whom I had ever talked, who knew what he was talking about in regards to alcoholism from actual experience. In other words, he talked my language. He knew all the answers, and certainly not because he had picked them up

[133]

from a book" (Big Book, page 180). This was someone who got nowhere with counselors who had learned about alcoholism from reading about it. By the way, it was a doctor who said this (Dr. Bob, the co-founder of AA).

Further, whether the counselor or doctor is an addict in recovery or not, and whether the patient is aware of it or not, there remains that separation, that lack of a personal bond, as required to maintain the "therapeutic relationship" (which I've always seen as a pompous concept). This is required of therapists by their professional licencing boards because it is felt to threaten the professional detachment that must be kept between the therapist and the patient. For example, my father died of pancreatic cancer, but whenever I had a patient with pancreatic cancer I would never share my own experience with the patient or family... it would have been considered professional misconduct. This is a fundamental rule. Therapists are taught to show empathy, also never to put themselves on the same level as the patient. So much more so if the therapist is an alcoholic or addict. This cripples the effectiveness of professional therapy for alcoholics. Says one alcoholic after meeting Dr. Bob and Bill W.: "If I had thought they didn't know what they are talking about, I wouldn't have been willing to talk to them at all." (Big Book, page 185).

As if to further deepen the chasm created by professional detachment, the therapist will keep detailed clinical notes of the session, doing so right in front of the patient during the conversation. This further formalizes the relationship, widening the inter-personal divide. These notes are in fact a legal document that can be subpoenaed and become a matter of public record. Few people will share the sordid details of their life on record, especially incriminating details. All this serves to form a large barrier to effective therapy, one that is innate to and required of professional therapists. The very principles that govern clinical therapy lower the cone of silence over the alcoholic. None of this is present between an alcoholic-addict and the sponsor.

*

We alcoholic-addicts are constantly wary of the social stigma of our disease. As well, as formerly "normally-functioning" people, we are overly conscious that we are broke, broken, and otherwise not at our best. Certainly, awareness of this stigma may be particularly acute when we are sitting in the office of a counselor who is well-dressed, well-paid, and has (apparently) life in order. This fear of being judged will cause our alcoholic-addict pride to kick in. As we have discussed in a previous chapter, the alcoholic-addict's pride is a defence mechanism. It makes us very indignant and defensive when our shortcomings are exposed, and it makes us lie about our situation. This is not a good way to start a therapeutic relationship that requires honesty and forwardness.

So, how is it that the Twelve Step program is able to overcome this dishonesty? Certainly, sitting in a clinical setting in front of a therapist engaged in "professional detachment," who is taking notes and is there to talk to you because she is paid to, we are not inspired to self-disclose, to drop our "stage character." The fear of being judged – or others finding out our secrets – would be overwhelming for anybody, alcoholic-addict or not. The research I mentioned above identified that the weaker the bond between the patient and the therapist the more strangled the honesty will be. The disheveled, sick, guilt-ridden, defensive alcoholic-addict is unlikely to feel much of a bond with the sharply dressed, professional, slick therapist with the stuffy office. We need someone we identify with in a comfortable, neutral environment. Nothing puts us at ease quite like a fellowship of people just like us, with complete anonymity. Stigma and the barriers to honesty that come with it are left outside the door.

The people in Twelve Step fellowships who reach out to us are from all walks of life: "All sections of this country and many of its occupations are represented, as well as many political, economic, social, and religious backgrounds. We are people who normally would not mix. But there exists among us a fellowship, a friendliness, and an understanding which is indescribably wonderful" (Big Book, page 17). A favorite story of mine in the Big Book is "Physician Heal Thyself!" (pages 301-308). In this story, a highly credentialed surgeon (and psychiatrist) found irony in the fact that it was in his butcher, baker, and carpenter (who were A.A. members) that he finally found the help that got him sober. This fellowship is uniquely

[135]

compelling at breaking down barriers of social standing, religion, and culture... it's the United Nations of alcoholics and addicts.

The Twelve Step program has "...no attitude of Holier Than Thou,... no fees to pay, no axes to grind, no people to please, no lectures to be endured..." (Big Book, page 18). The alcoholic-addict will hear none of the aggravating interrogations that scandalize us: "Why don't you just stop?", "Can't you stop for your kids?", "Don't you have any will-power?" The members who reach out to us – initiating the process of psychotherapy – start by telling their story with full disclosure and all honesty, with all the humiliating sordid details, thus allowing us to see that we are not alone. This disarms our alcoholic pride, as we no longer need to compensate for a feeling of inferiority, and it makes us want to reciprocate with our own story... all of it. Human nature is to identify, to emphasize commonalities. It draws us together. We want to be a part of the group. This is the start of a highly effective therapeutic relationship, with pride out of the way, a bond of fellowship in place, and a desire to be honest and forthright. This is a prerequisite to getting anywhere at all in any kind of therapy, and the Twelve Step fellowship achieves this. This is a key ingredient in its recipe for success.

*

Oddly, one of the foremost reasons for the success of the Twelve Step program is also one of its seemingly thorniest issues... for some.

Dr. W. Silkworth, an early friend and supporter of A.A., was Medical Director of a hospital for the treatment of addictions in the first part of the 20th century. It was under his care that the "hopeless" drunk Bill W., co-founder of A.A., finally achieved sobriety... and began divining his ideas on recovery. Dr. Silkworth wrote an opinion about his impressions of the concepts of A.A., which is printed in the Big Book (The Doctor's Opinion). In this passage he says that for alcoholics [and addicts]: "frothy emotional appeal seldom suffices. The message that can interest and hold these alcoholic people must have depth and weight. In nearly all cases, their ideals must be grounded in a power greater than themselves, if they are to recreate their lives" (page xxviii). He affirms that: "unless this person can experience an entire psychic change there is little hope of his recovery" and that "something more than human power is needed to produce the essential psychic change" (same page). He was correct – and prophetically so, because his observation remains just as valid today as it was over 80 years ago. Let's look at the psychology behind that.

The acceptance of the existence of a power greater than ourselves has deep psychological implications that help explain why this crucial part of the Twelve Step program is so important. The cover story of the December 2010 issue of Monitor on Psychology is an article that examines the subject. In the article, the author demonstrates that belief in a higher power satisfies our need to seek order from chaos, helps us to form and hold together social groups, and helps us to make some kind of sense of the world around us.[2]

Belief in a power greater than ourselves reduces our anxiety over things that are beyond our control and gives us a moral compass – a set of rules – to strive for and to guide our life. Otherwise, our morals, our beliefs in what is right or wrong, are left to be based on the law, which would be scary. Abraham Maslow (whom we met in chapter four), in his 1954 book *Motivation and Personality*,[3] pointed out that faith in a higher power provides strong motivation for personal growth. The need for giving ourselves to something bigger than ourselves, to find spiritual enlightenment, the desire to positively transform ourselves and society, is at the apex of our needs (he refers to this as "self-transcendence"). This self-actualization is also known as self-discovery, self-reflection, self-realisation, self-exploration. Those who are "self-actualized are described by Maslow as living creatively and fully using their potentials. He described the characteristics of the self-actualized as being able to: correctly and honestly judge situations, accept their own human nature and flaws, form their own opinions, and remain true to themselves rather than to others' expectations. They are also: comfortable being alone, task-centered, autonomous, appreciative of life's goods, capable of profound interpersonal relationships, and compassionate. This belief opens them to "peak experiences," which is the same as what is referred to as a "spiritual awakening" in the Twelve Step program. These are all things we need to break free from the character defects and pain that kept us addicted, and to maintain sobriety These are also things that empower us to a life of integrity and peace of mind. Belief in a higher power, according to this eminent and accomplished psychologist, can do a lot for us. Not tapping into this power would be amiss.

This higher power involvement is missing from traditional clinical psychotherapy, sometimes emphatically so. These things are absent from traditional therapies in order to not offend sensitivities, or because of a lack of background in the concept of a higher power on the part of the therapist. There has been a recent urgency in the professional psychotherapy literature to train therapists in incorporating spirituality and a higher power into their treatment models, in acknowledgement of the proven healing power of these previously untapped assets. Acceptance that we cannot defeat the obsession of alcoholism-addiction alone, that there is something or someone somewhere or somehow in the universe that is more powerful than the individual is fundamental to the Twelve Step program. Acceptance of this enables the first three Steps, which are absolutely essential before proceeding further with the process of therapy offered by the Twelve Steps.

Unfortunately this can be a sticking point for some of us, because of doubts about the existence of a higher power, and a reluctance to seek help in that power. In my upcoming book *Science and Spirituality: a User's Guide* I provide a scientific and mathematical argument for the existence of a higher power, creator, superior intelligence, intelligent designer, God or whatever you want to call it. That argument is beyond the scope of this book, but some may find *Science and Spirituality* an interesting read. The great thing about the Twelve Step approach to this is that it is all-inclusive. We are all free to choose whatever a higher power means to us. It's worth a brief diversion here to point out how that can fit with anybody's beliefs and comfort level.

A common misconception is that the Twelve Steps is a religious program. It is a spiritual program, not a religious one. I define spirituality as our connections outside ourselves. These connections outside ourselves occur on three levels: 1) connections with other people, 2) connections with the world around us, and, for some, 3) connections with a power greater than ourselves. Most alcoholic-addicts in the dregs of their disease have ruined relationships with family and friends. They isolate themselves and don't connect with the outside world. For those who have a higher power, that connection is usually suffering as well. We are spiritually sick.

There are three ways we can be ill, not functioning properly, or suffering. One is physically, another is mentally, and the other is spiritually. Some sicknesses or diseases are more of one than others, some are a mixture. For example, if you break your finger, you are physically ill. It does little to impact your mental or spiritual health. Depression affects us mentally as well as physically. People with depression not only suffer from a depressed mental mood, but they also suffer physical symptoms: fatigue, body pain, headaches, nausea, for example. They have abnormal sleep and eating patterns that affect them physically. Alcoholism-addiction makes us physically sick (it causes multiple organ damage and dysfunction), it makes us mentally sick (addiction-alcoholism is, in fact, classified as a mental illness known as "substance use disorder"), and it makes us spiritually sick.

I will illustrate how alcoholism-addiction makes us spiritually sick by using my own example. As I mentioned above, spirituality is defined as connections outside ourselves, which can occur on three levels: 1) connections with others, 2) connections with the world around us, and 3) connections with a power greater than ourselves. When I was out of control drinking and using I destroyed my connections with others. I used and abused those I cared about. I pushed them away with my intolerable behavior. And, I was glad to see them go. I was tired of them interfering with my alcohol and drug use, and I was tired of their nagging. They call alcoholism-addiction the lonely disease, and we are happy to be alone. Any "friendships" we do maintain tend to be people we drink or use with, a flimsy sodality between people overwhelmed by selfishness. Many people who have over-dosed and survived say that when they lay there dying their using friends didn't call for help but instead robbed them of their money and drugs and left them to die. None of my drinking or using friends ever came to see me when I was languishing in the hospital, nor are they happy for me now that I am well and in sobriety. I had no meaningful connections with other people, so I was spiritually sick on that level.

On the second level of spirituality, I was also empty. I had no connections with the outside world. I only left the house when I absolutely had to. I stayed home, blinds drawn, passing out and coming to on no schedule. I would look at the clock and see that it was 7 o'clock but have no idea if it was morning or night. Nor did I care. I didn't answer my phone. I had no connection with the outside world.

I was also spiritually barren on the third level: connection with a higher power. I always believed in and had a fairly close relationship with God, who was my higher power. However, I was angry at God for making my life so miserable. Why me? What did I do to God that I would be so cursed in life? I was angry and resentful to my higher power. I hated God.

After working through the Twelve Steps, I found myself to be in better spiritual health than I had ever been, because the program takes care to guide us to spiritual growth. First of all, I had to give up my repeated failed attempts to get off the drink and drug on my own, and instead I had to let fellow alcoholic-addicts in recovery into my closed world. I began connecting with them at meetings, by phone or text, and by getting together in friendship and fellowship. I now have a very robust and healthy spiritual connection with many wonderful people outside myself. With my character defects being tamed, my relationships with loved ones is strong. I have become an early riser, and I now start my days with a walk outside, and I drink in the beauty of the sights, sounds, and smells of the world around me. I take time to gaze at the stars. I am interested in world events. I have many things going on in my connections with the world around me. I also have a healthy and intensely satisfying relationship with a higher power, as I understand it, that has enriched my life. I am spiritually healthy on all three levels.

So, our disease is one that affects us physically, mentally, and spiritually. However, there is no physical cure: we will never go see our doctor and walk out no longer an addict-alcoholic. There is no mental cure: no psychiatrist or counselor with fix us. A spiritual cure has to be our approach to our disease. When we take a spiritual approach to treating our disease and we stop drinking or using, our physical and mental health soon follow.

This addiction sickness must be addressed as part of the whole package: mental, physical, and spiritual. We must come at this disease from every direction. To leave out the spiritual aspect is a grave mistake. It is unfortunate that the view of the Twelve Step program as being religious pervades, because it keeps many people from benefitting from a highly effective, life-saving resource.

Those who already have a belief in a higher power are fortunate; they have a ready-made answer. For those who doubt the existence of a higher intelligence, they can use their fellowship group as their higher power: after all, the group is a collective intelligence that has beat alcoholism-addiction… so they must be more powerful than me, the individual who couldn't beat it. Their collective intelligence and support is higher than my individual intelligence and solitary self.

I am always dismayed to see people detoxing, physically sick and with clouded minds, refusing to accept the Twelve Step program because they don't get the higher power thing. How could they instantly figure out the higher power thing in their present physical and mental state?. Besides, it's the nature of the alcoholic-addict pride that we resist the idea that **I** am not the greatest power in the universe. They have never before in their life spent any time reflecting on what a higher power might be, and in their present ailing condition they certainly won't be able to. I advise people to go with the program to get sober, and the higher power thing will work itself out. Let's focus on what's important right now. After all, we will be much clearer in thought once we are no longer snowed by our substance, and have had some time to consider it. If it means that we use the telephone pole outside our window as our higher power for now, then that is fine – the important thing is that we get and stay sober, not that we figure out the universe.

The Twelve Step program has had, from the start, a highly inclusive view of the concept of a higher power. Bill W., co-founder of A.A. said: "Our concepts of a Higher Power and God – as we understand Him – afford everyone a nearly unlimited choice of spiritual belief and action." (A.A. Grapevine, 1961). It is not religion, although those who practice a religious faith are fortunate in that their higher power is already defined for them. Although the Big Book of Alcoholics Anonymous uses the word "God" often, it also emphasizes that the higher power can be anything to anyone. The Big Book addresses this specifically in the chapter "We Agnostics." One of the key requirements in the program is open-mindedness; being *open to the possibility* of a higher power is all that is asked. Some kind of inadvertent personal clarity always follows later in the program, there is no point in forcing it by trying to figure it out all up front.

Some examples of a higher power that are used by A.A. members are: music, nature, the universe, science, the A.A. group, energy... or even something unknown, undefined. One friend in recovery tells me that he has never figured out what a higher power is to him, and maybe never will. When he prays he just says the words and "throws them out there." He doesn't know where the prayer goes, he just knows that it makes him feel better and it helps him. It works for him because he was a hard-core drunk and junkie who has found long-term sobriety in the Twelve Step program using that understanding of a higher power. He did not allow his inability to figure out what a higher power is to him prevent him from getting sober in the program.

There is a story in the Big Book that highlights the fact that there is no call for a preconceived idea of or belief in a higher power to participate in the program, and it also illustrates the value of the higher power concept in bringing us to sobriety. The alcoholic in this story had been brought to an A.A. meeting by a friend. He didn't think A.A. was for him, but he reluctantly went along. He tells his story: "It was the second meeting that clinched my sobriety... the chairperson called upon me to share.... As I spoke, I looked around the room. More importantly, I looked at the faces of the people in the room and I saw it. I saw the understanding, the empathy, the love. Today I believe I saw my Higher Power for the first time in those faces. While still up at the podium, it hit me – this is what I had been looking for all of my life. This was the answer, right here in front of me. Indescribable relief came over me; I knew the fight was over" (Big Book, page 326). This man experienced a "spiritual awakening", the vitalizing experience that launches most A.A. members into recovery. This is the same thing as Maslow's "peak experience" that we discussed above.

The world-renowned Psychiatrist Carl Jung recognized the value of a spiritual awakening, which he referred to as a "vital spiritual experience." When discussing alcoholics – he spoke of alcoholics but what he said applies to all of us – for whom all medical treatment has failed, he referred to them as utterly hopeless, and doomed. He did, however, admit that exceptions do exist to the prognosis if one thing takes place in the hopeless drunk: "here and there, once in a while, alcoholics have had what are called vital spiritual experiences. To me these occurrences are phenomena. They appear to be in the nature of huge emotional displacements and rearrangements. Ideas,

[142]

emotions, and attitudes which were once the guiding forces of the lives of these men are suddenly cast to one side, and a completely new set of conceptions and motives begin to dominate them" (Big Book, page 27).

The Big Book quotes an unnamed doctor (I think it was certainly the noted addictions specialist Dr. Silkworth): "...the general hopelessness of the average alcoholic's plight is, in my opinion, correct.... Though not a religious person, I have profound respect for the spiritual approach in such cases as yours. For most cases, there is virtually no other solution" (Big Book, page 43). So, we can see that this spiritual awakening is a potent force in bringing even the most forlorn of alcoholic-addicts to sobriety. Leaving the spiritual aspect out of our recovery is a fatal flaw.

These medical specialists and alcoholic-addicts all point to this vital spiritual experience as being of paramount importance for the "hopeless" alcoholic-addict. The strong presence of this experience in the Twelve Step program is a key aspect of its effectiveness, which is unfortunately absent in traditional psychotherapy. Such a powerful resource, unused, is squandered.

*

Let's look at another unique aspect of the Twelve Step program that has much to do with its success: sponsorship. For you non-Twelve Steppers a sponsor is "an [alcoholic-addict] who has made some progress in the recovery program [and] shares that experience on a continuous, individual basis with another [alcoholic-addict] who is attempting to attain or maintain sobriety..." (A.A. pamphlet "Questions and Answers on Sponsorship"). Our sponsor is not our boss, not our instructor, but an equal, as are all people in the fellowship. A clinical psychotherapist is a mentor of sorts, but doesn't amount to what a sponsor provides. A mentor is a wise and trusted counselor, which is hopefully what we get when we spend the time and money on a therapist. However, a sponsor is not only a mentor, but also a teacher, a big brother/sister, a best friend, someone who feels a responsibility toward us. While a therapist may feel responsible, that feeling soon peters out as soon as we can no longer pay for our sessions. A sponsor will drive us to meetings, is available to talk any time of day or night, and will be there when we are in

[143]

need. As well, the sponsor's family is a valuable resource made available to our traumatized families. The beauty of sponsorship is that no matter how much a sponsor helps us, we are helping our sponsor even more, for helping others is the secret ingredient of staying sober.

Sponsorship is a mentor-disciple relationship, but a very special one. In his excellent paper on mentorship, Dr. Alex Lickerman makes some observations:

> "...in a true mentor-disciple relationship, the mentor, contrary to what many believe, is not intrinsically superior to the disciple. Human beings have a tendency to conceive of all relationships in terms of power and authority: all of us tend to think of other people as either superior, equal, or inferior to us. A mentor-disciple relationship, on the other hand, functions optimally only when both mentor and disciple consider themselves fundamentally equal. If they don't, the greatest hope they share—that the disciple will surpass the mentor in accomplishment—will almost certainly never come to pass. For a disciple to learn most effectively from a mentor, he must resist the impulse to place the mentor on a pedestal and himself at the mentor's feet, because if he refuses to believe that he can become as great as the mentor, he never will. Though almost by definition a disciple is inferior in knowledge and experience in comparison to the mentor, in their degree of commitment to achieving mastery and creating the most value possible with their skills, and most importantly, in their commitment to accomplishing their shared mission—whatever it may be—a disciple must be, in every way, the mentor's equal. They must fight side by side, never one behind the other, or one for the other. That way lies subservience, ego, and failure. A true disciple shares the dream of the mentor as his or her own." [4]

The therapist-patient professional detachment expressly creates a power differential, which would necessarily fall short of what Dr. Lickerman describes as a true and effective mentorship. The sponsor-sponsee relationship, on the other hand, follows precisely what Dr. Lickerman advises.

As a fellow alcoholic-addict the sponsor draws out our elusive honesty, and therefore knows the secrets deep inside our black pit of garbled emotions. He or she has been where we are. The sponsor is the antidote to our lack of objectivity when it comes to ourselves... in other words, the sponsor calls out our bullshit. Dr. Lickerman continues:

> "Choosing a mentor with whom we establish an active and enduring connection... brings a benefit not seen in momentary mentor-disciple relationships: trust. In feeling trust in a mentor, we open our hearts in a particularly important way: we become willing to listen to him or her in a way we aren't willing to listen to others. When our mentor speaks, we automatically prepare ourselves to receive value. We therefore open ourselves to change. We relax our biases, our attachment to our ego, and tend to absorb even negative feedback in a constructive way, thereby opening the door to the possibility of genuine self-improvement. Thus the greatest benefit, in the end, to choosing a mentor is the way it opens our minds to hearing difficult truths and makes possible our growth in a way no other relationship can."[4]

There is much to gain from this level of mentorship, but the operative word here is trust. Someone who just gives us advice, but to whom we lie, is not going to generate the situation Dr. Lickerman speaks of. We have already spoken of the value of the shared experiences, the anonymity, and the comfortable informality present in Twelve Step fellowships that draws the honesty and trust from us. This is what leads to that special relationship that Dr. Lickerman speaks of, and the same does not derive from the professional therapist as a mentor.

If the therapist is willing and able to stand in as a mentor to the alcoholic-addict, that relationship will be one-sided, one-way, formal (within the boundaries of the therapeutic relationship), and will be very unlikely to include unlimited access. And it will terminate as soon as we can no longer pay the fees.

The sponsor-sponsee relationship, always equal right from the start, blossoms as it progresses. Just tonight at a meeting I heard one woman say of her sponsee: "sometimes I wonder who's the sponsor and who's the sponsee!" She had been helped through many of her own life trials and tribulations by her sponsee over the years. The connection extends beyond the sponsor-sponsee link, as spouses and families often get involved, introducing a multi-layered support system for all affected. We all find out that we are never alone. What a great feeling!

*

Alcoholism-addiction is a disease of loneliness. "[We] remember feeling isolated even when we were among a lot of happy, celebrating people. We often felt a deep sense of not belonging, even when we cheerfully acted sociable" (Living Sober, page 33). Our drinking "... momentarily helped us to behave socially, or temporarily assuaged our inner lonesomeness. But when that effect of alcohol wore off, we were left feeling more set apart, more left out, more 'different' than ever, and sadder. If we felt guilty or ashamed of either our drunkenness itself or anything we did while drinking, that compounded our feeling of being an outcast" (ibid, pages 33-34). We alcoholic-addicts often say that our initial attraction to drinking or using was to overcome shyness and fit in socially. Such bitter irony that it led to our profound loneliness! While social acceptance was our initial experience, when the alcohol or drugs took over our lives "the lonely road ahead looked bleak, dark, and unending. It was too painful to talk about; and to avoid thinking about it, we soon drank again" (ibid, page 34).

Alcohol and drugs sentence their hostages to a deep, painful social isolation. Our friends tried to help us, but we always disappointed them. And we trashed them. Even if they are still with us we can't reach out to them because how can they understand what we have done? "No wonder, then, that when we first listen to recovered alcoholics [and addicts] in A.A. talking freely and honestly about themselves, we are stunned.... We discover – but can hardly dare to believe right at first – that we are not alone. We are not totally unlike everybody, after all" (ibid, page 34). These are the budding

[146]

seeds of fellowship being planted from our first visit to a Twelve Step meeting.

Even when we had friends during our drinking or using days loneliness became our lot. They became tired of our antics, and we became tired of their interference with our love affair with our substance. Loneliness is a depressing place to be, it makes us want to drink or use drugs. Suddenly, when we accept the helping hand of the Twelve Step fellowship we step into the light of warm and welcoming friendships, people who fathom and accept us, and it feels good to reciprocate. We begin to inhabit each other's lives, and that connection grows gratifyingly as our sobriety grows.

Even if we manage to recover our previous friendships, we still need this fellowship of friends in recovery because it keeps us sober. This is important because many of our former associates are the people we used to drink or use with. Our new friends have none of our drinking/using triggers associated with them. If anything, they are triggers for our sobriety.

In his Psychology Today discussion "The Importance of Friendship"[5] Dr. Saul Levine describes the kind of friendship that breeds a better life. He researched physical, mental, and emotional health as well as other measures of happiness. "Good friends are open, genuine and honest with each other. They tolerate each other's frailties, appreciate their differences, and honestly criticize when necessary. Over many years, they participate in each other's celebrations and marriages, and in their children's and grandchildren's milestones. They are there for each other during illnesses and setbacks, and some are left to mourn the losses of their dear old friends, almost as a loss of a part of themselves." Because the nettlesome complexities of our disease, it takes a special person to be that friend that Dr. Levine describes. Few "normal" friends will "honestly criticize when necessary" because they don't see through our manipulative lies when we decide to drink or use... it takes a fellow alcoholic-addict to do this. Few "normal" friends will tolerate our frailties and appreciate our differences, especially when these involve our "immorality" as alcoholic-addicts. Few friends will be there as recovering alcoholic-addicts need someone to be there: happy to receive a call at 3 a.m. because we feel an urge to relapse or can't settle our mind down. Few "normal" friends would know what to say if we did call them.

[147]

These are the kinds of friendships that are found among Twelve Step members. Our "normal" friends are not to be faulted... it takes an alcoholic-addict to fathom this unusual type of friendship that we need. Attending psychotherapy does not give us any such friends. Even group counselling lacks the fellowship unique to the Twelve Step program. The Twelve Step program has a set culture of fellowship that is ingrained into the program and that cradles us from the first time we gingerly walk through the door.

Friendship expert Karen Karbo points out that friendship is established through self-disclosure and reciprocity, and that satisfying friendships are more likely when we know what to say in response to another person's self-disclosure.[6] Emotional expressiveness and unconditional support, as well as acceptance, loyalty, and trust are essential for truly deep bonds. Our Twelve Step friends singularly satisfy all of the above characteristics. Our non-alcoholic-addict friends may no longer satisfy our new deepest friendship needs to the same degree because we are unable to self-disclose and expect reciprocity. I recently attended an A.A. meeting where a fellow alcoholic-addict had recently come back from a relapse, and tearfully shared that he ended up broke, and resorted to drinking mouthwash during his sojourn back to the bottle. He said that he needed to get this off his chest and he could only do so at A.A. He said that hearing other people share honestly gives him the strength to be honest. His admission and tears were met with reciprocity: an empathy and understanding and acceptance that was unconditional. His Twelve Step friends were fulfilling a need that no other friend could do. That was the only place he could get that off his chest.

Karbo quotes psychological research by Carolyn Weisz and Lisa F. Wood involving our deep need for friendships that satisfy our need for social identity. This psychological need takes precedence even over the need for intimacy. That is why support groups thrive: people who have survived similar tragedies identify with each other and like to stick together. When our social identity includes something socially stigmatized, such as alcoholism and addiction, we have a particularly strong need for social identity in our friendships – being around other people with the same background, whom we can identify with. Humans are social animals and we have a strong psychological drive for acceptance, and our sense of self in the group is satisfied only when others in that group share our background. Nowhere else will we find people who completely understand us, are unreservedly non-judgemental about our past, and supportive... providing us with social identity support. This factor alone has been identified as the best predictor of whether a friend becomes a "best" friend.

Our drive for social identity support is powerful: "We stick with people who support our social identity and withdraw from those who don't. We may even switch friends when the original ones don't support our current view of ourselves."[6] This includes after a major life change that involves a new or changed social identity. Going from "normal" to alcoholism-addiction and then to sobriety is one such change, and we now seek out those we can identify with as recovering alcoholic-addicts.

Further research by Carolyn Weisz demonstrated that people with substance abuse problems, like us, are more likely to find sobriety when we feel more socially in sync with sobriety than we do with substance use. Being a part of the Twelve Step fellowship group provides precisely this social framework, where we can align our views of our social roles and our sense of self with other people focussed on recovery, thus and away from those who are focussed on getting high or drunk. This same effect is huge in preventing our relapse. Continued friendship and participation with this group (people in sobriety) helps us to maintain this sense of our role in society and our sense of self that supports our sobriety. Our strong drive for social identity support does that for us when we are with a group who focusses on maintaining sobriety.

So, we see that having friends with the same problem is critical when we suffer from a disease... even more so when that disease is socially unacceptable and our drive for social identity support is otherwise unattainable. Says one alcoholic: "I have a wealth of friends and, with my A.A. friends, an unusual quality of fellowship. For, to these people, I am truly related. First, through mutual pain and despair, and later through mutual objectives and new-found faith and hope. And, as the years go by, working together, sharing our experiences with one another, and also sharing a mutual trust, understanding, and love – without strings, without obligation – we acquire relationships that are unique and priceless." (Big Book, page 276). The Twelve Step fellowship embosoms all who have a desire to stop drinking or using... and those who would fall again, or have fallen. The Responsibility

Pledge renders the matter academic: "I am responsible. When anyone, anywhere reaches out for help, I want the hand of A.A. always to be there. And for that, I am responsible!" One recovering alcoholic expresses it well: "When I'm afraid, I reach for the hand of another alcoholic to steady me" (Big Book, page 318).

Importantly, the company of other people who are admitted problem drinkers or drug users and who are committed to sobriety helps us to feel "normal" as we move forward in our recovery. This is a counter-weight to the odd behavior of unknowing people who egg us on to have a drink at social occasions. "But we know now that we do not have to proceed all on our own. It is far more sensible, safer, and surer to do it in the company of the whole happy fleet going in the same direction. And none of us need feel any shame at all at using help, since we all help each other" (Big Book, page. 35).

The program realizes the danger of loneliness in our sobriety, as it is a risk factor for relapse. We must avoid slipping into our well-learned habits of social isolation. If we suffer from depression or other mental health problems that manifest isolation as a symptom, this is particularly important. We will discuss this further in the chapter on mental health and alcoholism-addiction. "Thoughts of a drink seem to sneak into our minds much more smoothly and slyly when we are alone. And when we feel lonesome, and an urge for a drink strikes, it seems to have a special speed and strength. Such ideas and desires are much less likely to occur when we are with other people, especially other non-drinkers. If they do occur, they seem less potent and more easily put aside while we are in touch with fellow A.A. members" (Living Sober, page 36). The program addresses this by the widespread practice of members exchanging phone numbers and using them. As well, many social activities outside of meetings are organized. Part of my program of recovery involves talking to another alcoholic-addict in recovery every day, of which I avail myself in the greatest amounts when I'm not having such a great day.

As someone fascinated by human psychology, I have always found the dynamic of returning from relapse particularly interesting. In a group full of success stories of recovery and emphasis on life-long abstinence, it is easy to understand how someone returning to a Twelve Step meeting following a relapse would be filled with more than the usual amount of shame and regret. I often wonder if I would be able to show my face again if I relapsed.

However, all who do come back are welcomed with acceptance and delight at their return. There is no judgement, contempt, or discouragement, only warm support. And hard advice and tough love from people who know exactly what we have been through... many of whom have relapsed themselves once or twice.

The fellowship isn't all roses and lollipops. It's also about tough-love and accountability. I have been amazed by the ability of members to suss out the bullshit of others when they hear it and to confront them on it. Abraham Lincoln described tact as the ability to describe others as they see themselves. If this is so, then our friends in the Twelve Steps have no tact whatsoever, and that's why we need them. I can say from my own experience that any time in my recovery that I experienced thoughts of drinking or picking up drugs, that a powerful influence in not allowing these thoughts to take root in me was the overwhelming thought that I can't let down my fellow Twelve Steppers. I don't want to disappoint them, I don't want to make them think that all the time and effort they put into me was for nothing, and I don't want my own fall to cause others to waver. The fellowship is at once confederate and guardian.

There is one tough pill to swallow in the fellowship that does have a silver lining in favor of our sobriety, and that is that we see friends relapse and die. While it is morbid to think that would somehow help us, the dead often speak the loudest, and to close our ears to them would be to squander an opportunity. Death of a fellow lost to relapse serves to curtly remind us that we are dealing with a deadly illness, not to be taken lightly.

Continuing participation in this fellowship must be a part of our plan for long-term sobriety. Sadly, a commonly heard confession is of relapse years into recovery after ceasing attending meetings. Daily affirmation of our powerlessness over alcohol, whether we are sober 30 days or 30 years, will remind us that we need to continue in the program for life. This keeps us from succumbing to the "insanity of alcoholism" by deciding that enough time has gone by that we can now drink "responsibly". When we share our recovery with others like us, this powerful "insanity" has a much tougher time of taking ahold of our mind.

As we can see, the fellowship of the Twelve Step program, on an ongoing basis, has deep-reaching implications for our recovery from our disease. The fellowship alone makes the program invaluable. It is a rewarding and effective aspect, but it is only one of many. One reason that continuing in the fellowship is vital to our perpetual sobriety is because it allows us to partake in a powerful asset in our recovery toolbox: service work.

*

Peculiar to the Twelve Step program is a concept that defies logic, yet its role in long-term sobriety is rightfully given great reverence: service work – taking the message to the drunk or addict who still suffers. This is definitely not a part of any traditional psychotherapy program. However, the Twelve Step program holds service work sacred… in fact it is part of the final of the Twelve Steps. Service work can be as simple as helping set up chairs for a meeting, making coffee, or even helping a neighbor carry her trash to the curb. In its purest form, it means reaching out to alcoholics and addicts who still suffer. We are told that we must seek sobriety for ourselves, so insisting on service work seems a contradiction. Worse, we are instructed to give without seeking anything in return. This definitely isn't consistent with seeking recovery for ourselves.

Or is it?

*Drop the Rock* sheds light on who really benefits from service work: "We no longer ask only what everyone can do for us; we also ask what we can do for them. We no longer only seek out situations that comfort only us; we also discover ways to comfort. We find that we feel better about ourselves when we help others. We learn from our Program that what we may have been searching for our whole lives is wrapped up in service to others" (page 42).

Doctor Bob, co-founder of A.A., explained: "I spend a great deal of time passing on what I have learned to others who want it and need it badly. I do it for four reasons:

1. Sense of duty.
2. It is a pleasure.
3. Because in so doing I am paying my debt to the man who took time to pass it on to me.

[152]

4. Because every time I do it I take out a little more insurance for myself against a possible slip" (Big Book, pages 180-1).

So powerful was this effect that he made it part of the Twelve Steps to sobriety.

Once we are at a point in our recovery where we are ready for service work, the level of commitment demanded by the Twelfth Step is deep:

> "Never avoid these responsibilities, but be sure you are doing the right thing if you assume them. Helping others is the foundation stone of your recovery. A kindly act once in a while isn't enough. You have to act the Good Samaritan every day, if need be. It may mean the loss of many nights' sleep, great interference with your pleasures, interruptions to your business. It may mean sharing your money and your home, counseling frantic wives and relatives, innumerable trips to police courts, sanitariums, hospitals, jails, and asylums. Your telephone may jangle at any time of the day or night. Your wife may sometimes say she is neglected. A drunk may smash your furniture or burn your mattress. You may have to fight with him if he is violent. Sometimes you will have to call a doctor and administer sedatives under his direction. Another time you may have to send for the police or an ambulance. Occasionally you will have to meet such conditions." (Big Book, page 97).

Fortunately, it is seldom or never that we will be called to this level of service, but that level of commitment radiates through the fellowship.

The Big Book is clear about the importance of service work: "Practical experience shows us that nothing will so much ensure immunity from drinking as intensive work with alcoholics. It works when other activities fail" (page 89). It further elaborates: "Carry this message to other alcoholics! You can help when no one else can. You can secure their confidence when others fail.... Life will take on new meaning. To watch people recover, to see them help others, to watch loneliness vanish, to see a fellowship grow up about you, to have a host of friends – this is an experience you must not miss…. Frequent contact with newcomers and with each other is the bright spot of our lives" (page 89).

Service work is win-win. "Even the newest of newcomers finds undreamed of rewards as he tries to help his brother alcoholic, the one who is even blinder than he. This is indeed the kind of giving that actually demands nothing. He does not expect his brother sufferer to pay him, or even to love him. And then he discovers that by the divine paradox of this kind of giving he has found his own reward, whether his brother has yet received anything or not….Practically every A.A. member declares that no satisfaction has been deeper and no joy greater than in a Twelfth Step job well done" (Twelve Steps and Twelve Traditions, pages 109-10).

It's counter-intuitive, but somehow this giving to strangers and asking nothing in return in fact benefits us greatly. Another A.A. member describes his experience of service work: "In telling newcomers how to change their lives and attitudes, all of a sudden I found I was doing a little changing myself…. I discovered in pointing out to the new man his wrong attitudes and actions that I was really taking my own inventory, and that if I expected him to change, I would have to work on myself too… [and] the dividends have been tremendous" (Big Book, page 230). Although we ask for nothing in return, we receive much.

Service work is how we grow in our sobriety – if we stagnate we fall. Other less obvious dividends abound. We are never fully able to make amends to those we have harmed: someone can't be located… someone would be harmed by our amends… someone is offended by our efforts… a certain amend would land us in jail to no one's benefit… or there is nothing we could do that would equal the harm we have brought on someone. Some alcoholic-addicts working the Steps are deeply bothered by this. Service work provides us a way of making amends indirectly, by doing good now to counter past evils, to our immense psychological relief. Further, as we help others, so others will help us in our times of need. It makes the Twelve Step community much more than the fellowship it claims to be… it makes it a kinship, a brotherhood/sisterhood. And there is more. No matter how well we hide our good deeds, they become known to others, inside and outside of the program. We earn respect and trust from people without even being aware of it. We reap benefits from this that far outweigh the efforts we put forth. Trust

[154]

and respect of others is a deep psychological need whose satisfaction cannot be bought. As you may have predicted, I can't resist the opportunity to explain the psychology of service work's benefit to our recovery.

We discussed in earlier chapters the psychological dysfunctions that fuel our alcoholism and addiction. You will recall that it has much to do with cognitive dissonance, the psychological discomfort we feel when how we act doesn't line up with how we believe a good person should act. Working through the Twelve Steps alleviates this dissonance, this pain, by bringing our actions back in line with our set beliefs and values. However, service work nails it for us, because by putting others before ourselves and by giving with no expectations of anything in return we make our actions even better than our set beliefs about how we should behave. Service work is a stake through the heart of cognitive dissonance. Instead of pain, our actions now bring us joy. No wonder they help us maintain our sobriety. We don't need drugs or alcohol to feel joy in our lives.

In his excellent article in the British Psychological Society journal Psychologist Tom Farsides examines altruism, the selfless giving of ourselves to others – what we call service work.[7] He describes empathy as being a key factor in altruistic behavior. We are more likely to be sincerely altruistic toward people we empathize with, and less likely to do so based solely on moral principles. When we have a shared hardship with the people we are helping, we are naturally and effortlessly empathetic and much more likely to be truly altruistic with them. So, we are naturally geared to being altruistic with our fellow alcoholic-addicts.

Although altruism is about giving to others and expecting nothing in return, Dr. Farsides points out that we are motivated to altruism not only over concern for others, but also when we feel there is some benefit to us. To deny that we are partly motivated by the good we reap from our service work would be to lie to ourselves. We are, after all, human. The Twelve Steps acknowledges this by letting us know that we must give in order to get back. We are guided toward service work with the promise that this is what will keep us sober. And it turns out to be absolutely true!

We need more than just empathy to rise to this challenge. Dr. Farsides points out that we are more likely to be altruistic if we see others doing the same. I know that my experience is shared by many Twelve Steppers when I

[155]

say that watching my sponsor engaged in service work certainly inspires me to do the same. As do all those who have extended a helping hand to me in my recovery. This is how the fellowship sets the example for all newcomers to emulate, and the altruism keeps going.

As we will discuss in the next section, actions have a weightier impact on our minds than do words. By carrying out the action of service work our minds become much more committed to our program of recovery. Our minds strive to justify our efforts, especially if we are not receiving material compensation in return, by increasing our belief in the value of what we are doing. We become much more psychologically committed to our own recovery by helping others with theirs.

When we talked about memory in an earlier chapter, we discussed a powerful form of learning called operant conditioning, where an action is rewarded and we learn to repeat that action in order to repeat the reward. Alcohol and drugs cunningly hijack this process by rewarding our drinking or using behavior with increased dopamine release in the brain, which teaches us to repeat the behavior. In doing service work, we feel good about ourselves, we enjoy the fellowship of those we help, and we receive thanks (sometimes) for what we do. This pleasurable feeling teaches the brain to do more service work to receive more of this reward. It is reasonable to believe that with repeated altruistic behavior this new learned behavior pathway in the brain will start to become more entrenched and therefore more likely to be accessed than the older, slowly fading learned pathways of our alcohol-drug-dopamine behaviors! Helping others gives us the ease and relief that we used to get with that first drink or drug, and that becomes our go-to feel-good coping mechanism as we practice it more and more.

Service work roots out other old tendencies. Alcoholism and addiction drag us into deep selfishness, and service work is the authoritative antidote for selfishness. Our minds follow our actions, and by acting selfless our minds accept ourselves as selfless, and this stamps out the last flames of selfishness and keeps it from smouldering back to life. Service work also helps us in our humility, a virtue that is central to our purging of character defects. Both of these virtuous character strengths are key to our recovery and are strengthened by our service work.

The dividends are tremendous, as it is through this service work that Twelve Step members stay sober for life. A commonly held sentiment is: "I could not expect to keep what I had unless I gave it away" (Big Book, page 253). So, this is a major part of the success of the Twelve Step program of psychotherapy. Yet this is definitely not a part of traditional clinical psychotherapy. No psychotherapist will ever advise a patient to go out and start recruiting and counseling other patients and then leading them through a program of psychotherapy. Yet this is the basis of the service work of the Twelve Step program, which has kept millions of people sober over the last four-score years.

*

Psychotherapy is called "talk-therapy" because, well, that's what it is. However, it's a fact that when we talk about something, we deal with thoughts and abstract ideas that we may not internalize, especially when it is the therapist doing the talking. Remember: we lie to therapists. We do not necessarily feel engaged by these words, or committed to the concept they represent. However, when we do something – when we take physical action – we feel a psychological commitment to that action, and to the ideas behind it. It is well-known that we believe what we do, that our minds follow our actions. This is well recognized in the Twelve Step program, as one recovering alcoholic illustrates: "If asked what the two most important things in recovery are, I would have to say willingness and *action* [italics are mine]" (Big Book, page 317).

Let's look at a few of the psychological effects of action. First of all, we can't control our feelings... we can't will ourselves happy. We can think about how a certain emotion came about, and try to convince ourselves that we shouldn't feel that way, but it won't help us. This is a cobweb for us because in the past we have tried to suppress our emotions with alcohol or drugs. Ignoring our feelings won't help, we must acknowledge them... then we can influence them by action. A good example is that if we are feeling fear about doing our taxes, we may end up sleepless over it, procrastinating on the couch, even becoming depressed over it. We can tell ourselves that all will be well, but it probably won't help. If choose action and do some work toward getting our taxes done, then we start to feel better. When we move to act, negative emotions fade.

A few tips for using action to deal with fear and worry: begin action with the ends in mind. In other words, don't just start doing something, first figure out what the end result is, plan the steps that you will take to get there, and then start acting. This is being proactive, which calms our mind by giving us an ability to see that there is a viable solution to our worries. It also helps make sure that the actions we take are leading logically toward a solution. We should also commit ourselves mentally to the action. Rather than stew in self-pity or fear while we are acting, we must focus on what we are doing, so that we are detracting from the fear rather than building it. As well, we must remember that all action does not necessarily have to be focussed on solving a problem that is causing the fear and worry. Pulling out some healthy coping mechanisms are helpful. A hike on a beautiful day with a loved one is therapeutic for many unwanted feelings. I am heavily into meditation, which I use as a great tool to help my peace and serenity. It, too, is an action, a healthy coping mechanism.

It is important to note that it is not only negative emotions that should prompt us to take action. Many alcoholic-addicts find any extremes of emotion to be a trigger... even times of great joy. Many say that it is when things are good that the grasp of alcohol or drugs reaches for them the most.

The Steps that take us through the process of "cleaning house" are called the "action Steps." Cleaning house is about clearing out all the mental debris that contributed to making us addicted and further accumulated while we were drinking or using. This involves listing in full our wrong-doings, and identifying and removing the defects of character that led to these wrong-doings. It's the process of ridding ourselves of the anger, resentments, fears, self-pity, selfishness, and dishonesty that have "owned" us for so long. Then, we finish cleaning out our dissonant mind by making amends to those we have harmed, as best we can. Self-forgiveness begins to materialize. This process is how we put memories of traumatic events of the past in perspective. It is how we find the amazing gift of peace and serenity, and it is done by action, thus engaging our mind and making the experience memorable and real. It is not done by sitting in someone's office talking for

[158]

an hour twice a week. Even after cleaning house, we are led to repeat this process on a daily basis to keep the house clean, and to reach out and help others who suffer. Few people could disagree that results require direct and specific actions.

The "action" involved in living the Twelve Step program involves more than the action required in completing the Steps. It also requires that our day-to-day actions reflect our new way of living... we live the program's principles. We live with humility, respect, and dignity. We are challenged to consider: if I couldn't speak, would people know by my actions what I stand for? We gain much more than we give by living principled lives. A good example of this is trust.

As active alcoholics and addicts, we seem to trust only our alcohol or drugs. We are not trusting of any person, and we run in circles that demand that we not trust anyone lest we be ripped off, robbed, or assaulted. The years of denial, broken promises made with good intentions, obsession-driven selfishness, and the continually growing list of lies and rationalizations leave us with zero credibility with anyone... we even stop trusting ourselves (what a horrible thing that is). Our words are meaningless, no one believes a word we say anymore. Only action will rebuild trust: "Trust comes through action. By acting worthy of trust, we gain the trust of others and ourselves" (Drop the Rock, pages 86-7). This is just one example of the necessity of action to settle our dissonance and start gaining back our lives; talk is not enough. Being trusted by others is psychologically important to us – all people worry and obsess about it. I remember that as I inched along day by day in my early recovery, people in my life began to see for themselves that I meant business, only because I showed them that I meant business, through my actions. I had long ago used up the credibility of my words, only my actions had any voice. I had to earn back my credibility. Trust began to fall back in place and it felt wonderful! However, that trust comes from our actions, not from our words.

*

"Rarely have we seen a person fail who has thoroughly followed our path" touts the Big Book (page 58). As a psychological therapist I have never said to a patient: "Have a seat and we will start therapy and I can promise you that if you do what I say you will no longer use drugs or alcohol and will experience a fundamental change in character and a spiritual awakening that will change your life." For a therapist, making promises about the outcome of therapy is taboo (imagine the lawsuits!). Yet that promise is made expressly to anyone who comes through the door at a Twelve Step meeting. The psychotherapist couldn't back up such a claim, but the Twelve Step program can and does. The evidence, like the promise, is up front: the alcoholic-addict at a meeting will meet many recovering alcoholic-addicts who are eager to tell their story: stories that are repeated in the literature, stories representative of the millions of people who have realized the promises of this time-tested program of recovery. This solidly backed-up promise has a therapeutic effect: it immediately instills hope and generates a willingness to commit to sobriety. We are much more likely to commit to something when we know it will work. Crucially, it engages us with a call to action, an end to passivity. This is not talk therapy, it is a program of action. The promise is not un-qualified… recovery will follow if the alcoholic-addict will do "a few simple things." (In fact, studies funded by the U.S. National Institute of Health since 2005 have demonstrated the Twelve Step program to be the most successful approach to treating addictions.)

One A.A. member describes perfectly the effect that this promise of recovery has on the newcomer. Before she had ever been to any A.A. gathering she was given a copy of the Big Book: "I stayed up all night reading this book. For me it was a wonderful experience. It explained so much I had not understood about myself, and, best of all, it promised recovery if I would do a few simple things and be willing to have the desire to drink removed. Here was hope. Maybe I could find my way out of this agonizing existence. Perhaps I could find freedom and peace, and be able once again to call my soul my own" (Big Book, page 273).

Making an up-front promise is considered a weakness in therapy, but it is one of the strengths of the Twelve Step program.

*

We can see how the Twelve Step program embodies features that makes it a particularly suitable form of psychotherapy for alcoholism and addiction – features that are not part of traditional clinical methods. However, I once counted myself among clinical psychotherapists, and I am not trying to diminish the value of clinical psychological therapy. It is a useful and important adjunct to the overall effort of recovery, particularly in alcoholics and addicts with serious psychological issues, such as a history of abuse. But it must be an *adjunct* to our program; if we consult a psychotherapist as our sole effort for sobriety we stand little chance of success. Fortunately, many therapists recognize this and recommend attendance at Twelve Step meetings; some will even hand out a Big Book. I would be wary of any counselor or therapist who does not try to steer the alcoholic-addict toward a comprehensive program of recovery and support system, such as the Twelve Steps.

Certainly, the Twelve Step program recognizes the need for professional help in our lives when we need it, including a psychological counselor. Living Sober devotes a chapter to this ("Seeking Professional Help," Chapter 23). Here, it is acknowledged that: "probably every recovered alcoholic has needed and sought professional help of the sort A.A. does not provide" (page 58), and members are encouraged to seek out such help when needed. Members are reassured: "fortunately, we have found no conflict between A.A. ideas and the good advice of a professional with expert understanding of alcoholism" (page 58). Having made this point, let's have a closer look at clinical psychotherapy in alcoholism-addiction.

There are different types of psychotherapy, which are different styles or philosophies of how to manipulate the mind into a healthy way of operating. Humanistic therapy, Psychoanalysis, Cognitive therapies, Behavioral therapies, and, of course, Cognitive-behavioral therapy (CBT) are among the approaches currently in popular use. I have a problem with these "doctrinal" philosophies of therapy – meaning that the therapist sticks to a narrowly defined procedure – because the therapist should be open to many different ideas and be flexible and accommodating when working with patients. After all, we and our situations are all different, and one inflexible approach rarely works for everyone. While the specifics are beyond the scope of this book, suffice it to say that each of these methods has shortcomings in terms of the

[161]

psychology of alcoholism and addiction. For example, they may serve to enhance our self-pity, external locus of control, and resentments by encouraging us to search our past for things to blame our disease on. While that might massage our alcoholic-addict pride and be easier on our ego, it's not going to help us beat our disease.

We have learned that cognitive dissonance is a major psychological factor that keeps us drinking and brings on other character defects, such as pride, selfishness, anger, and resentments. Only by "cleaning house" can we remove our dissonance, by making good past wrongs and beginning to lead a principled life. As well, our external locus of control, another major cause of our disease, cannot be extinguished without accepting our own part in our downfall, and turning our focus away from the actions of others in our lives. We must learn to focus on the things we can change, and accept the things we cannot. That this is recognized by the Twelve Step program is highlighted by the Serenity Prayer, which is used to open every meeting: "God grant me the serenity to accept the things I cannot change; courage to change the things I can; and wisdom to know the difference." It's worth taking a short diversion here to dissect the psychology of this prayer. I am going to use the Serenity Prayer to demonstrate the shortcomings of various psychotherapy models for alcoholism-addiction. Let's use our knowledge of psychology to do this.

The Serenity Prayer was written by American minister Reinhold Niebuhr in 1934, and fatefully came to the attention to A.A. co-founder Bill W. in 1941. Bill recognized the value of this prayer and adopted its first verse into the A.A. program. Despite not knowing the psychology involved, Bill recognized the power of the message contained in this short supplication. First of all, it indicates that acceptance of things around us that we have no control over requires serenity, meaning that we must have some peace of mind before we can stop obsessing over things we can't control: other people's actions, the weather, bad luck, and our past misfortunes. To achieve this acceptance we must first extinguish the burning obsession over our anger and resentments, and thereby find serenity. It is only then that we are primed to move to an internal locus of control. It is only when we accept the things we cannot change that we can start focussing on the things we can. The prayer asks for the courage to do this. Courage is necessary, because we previously lacked that courage and instead hid behind alcohol or drugs. Even when sober, we can still resort to distraction and procrastination or denial when it is time to face up to our problems. The second line of the prayer reminds us to give attention to this, and reminds us that it takes courage to do so. Finally, we ask for the wisdom to know the difference. Why does this take wisdom? Because it is human nature to fly off the handle and complain and rail whenever something happens that deviates from our plan for life. This happens to everyone, including non-alcoholic-addicts. Wisdom to not allow this to happen requires insight into our psychology, so that we can recognize when our mind tries to run away on us, as well as the self-awareness to halt that process before it has us angry and resentful and blaming others when we could instead be doing something productive about the situation. Better to spend our time and exertions on things we can do something about than to burn energy railing about things we can do nothing about. This amounts to wisdom. This short prayer, in three lines, gives a fantastic overview of what the program does for us in dealing with life, and reminds us to "practice these principles in all our affairs.". Now, back to our discussion of psychotherapy.

Behavioral therapy, essentially using operant conditioning to teach us to "unlearn" our addicted behavior, falls far short of the thorough identification and elimination of root causes of our disease that must be undertaken to have any hope of recovery. We have long ago found out for ourselves that the mind finds no reward greater than the continued use of alcohol or drug. This makes the action-reward pairing of behavioral therapy of limited use for an alcoholic-addict. We are fighting against the far more powerful action-reward pairing that our substance provides. We can't teach ourselves to be sober.

Cognitive therapy attempts to teach us to think our way through our issues. Cognitive therapy has virtually no role in alcoholism-addiction because we are powerless to "talk ourselves out of" drinking or using. I am not over-simplifying here, it's as simple as that. We have all tried.

Cognitive-behavioral therapy, or CBT, is the merging of both types of therapy. It has enjoyed some success in conditions such as anxiety and depression, where it has been shown to be as effective as medications, in some cases. It is helpful for people who can control their drinking or using, and need a little push to stop. However, for the type of "hopeless" alcoholic-addict who needs the Twelve Step program it has had very little success as a stand-alone therapy. It is, however, of great use for helping with issues of

[163]

great psychological impact, such as a history of abuse. As a stand-alone approach to getting sober, it has limited value.

The Humanistic approach to therapy is, in my opinion, downright dangerous in treating alcoholism and addiction. This type of therapy emphasizes that we are able to make rational choices on our own as long as these choices and their benefits are pointed out to us. As well, this method of therapy searches out events and people from our past in order to affix blame for our shortcomings, purposely taking responsibility for our problems away from us and placing it on external causes. This directly flies in the face of the step crucial to finding sustainable recovery by establishing an internal locus of control. It also inflames our resentments and anger as it gives us new targets for blame. The search for such causes often amounts to a fishing expedition to draw out anything unhappy that's ever happened to us, in effect inventing problems out of things that may never have been a factor for us. While it is true that outside influences contributed to our drinking, it is wrong to focus on those things rather than their effects on our character. This approach fortifies an external locus of control, whose eradication must be a fundamental goal of psychological therapy. The therapist will take a hands-off approach, allowing the patient to explore solutions to problems. Guidance is provided mostly in the search for the external reasons for our woes and teaching us that we are not at fault. However, people with our disease require a comprehensive internal review, not a review of other people and events. It is a matter of focussing on the things we can change, rather than the things we cannot change.

There are other methods in use, but they are generally all derivations from techniques we just discussed. By far, the most common psychotherapy approach in use today is CBT, which has become so in vogue that it's even a house-hold term. There has not been a lot of research in support of psychotherapy as a treatment modality for alcohol and drug addiction. However, data published by the National Institute of Health showed the effect of CBT as "small."[8] This is unfortunate, given that CBT is usually the mainstay of psychotherapy in alcoholism and addictions.

Another approach to treating addiction that frightens me is the attempt to bring alcoholic-addicts to a point where we can drink or use moderately – "responsibly." Obviously, if we were in any way capable of that we would

[164]

have done so long ago on our own. I, myself, attended a group therapy program where the goal was responsible drinking and using. As any Twelve Stepper could have predicted, I failed miserably at my guided "responsible" drinking. I was looking for the easier, softer way.

The Big Book records a fateful conversation with the third ever member of A.A. – Bill D. – who was once again enfeebled in a hospital bed due to his relentless drinking. Not his first time confined to a hospital bed, he was shackled due to his hysterical agitation. The first two A.A. members – Dr. Bob and Bill W. – appeared at the bedside. Bill D. tells the story:

> "One of the fellows, I think it was Doc, said, 'Well, you want to quit?' I said, 'Yes, Doc, I would like to quit, at least for five, six, or eight months, until I get things straightened up, and begin to get the respect of my wife and some other people back, and get my finances fixed up and so on.' And they both laughed very heartily and said, 'That's better than you've been doing, isn't it?' Which of course was true. They said, 'We've got some bad news for you. It was bad news for us, and it will probably be bad news for you. Whether you quit six days, months, or years, if you go out and take a drink or two, you'll end up in this hospital tied down, just like you have been in these past six months. You are an alcoholic.' As far as I know, this was the first time I had ever paid any attention to that word. I figured I was just a drunk. And they said, 'No, you have a disease, and it doesn't make any difference how long you do without it, after a drink or two you'll end up just like you are now.' That certainly was real disheartening news, at the time" (Big Book, pages 187-8).

Eighty years of experience of countless alcoholic and addict members since this discussion took place has proven this to be absolutely true. Trying to teach an alcoholic-addict to become a "responsible" drinker or user is a losing proposition. If you can drink or use "responsibly" and control it, then you are probably not an alcoholic-addict.

By the way, you will be pleased to know that after speaking at length with Dr. Bob and Bill W., Bill D. was overwhelmed with inspiration – what

[165]

we might call a spiritual awakening – got dressed and left the hospital, never to drink again.

Among my attempts to find sobriety I sought help from a certified addictions counselor. He told me to not refer to myself as an alcoholic or addict, because these terms are demeaning, and it is not good to demean oneself. This is an example of the liberal "humanistic" approach to addiction treatment: "it's not your fault, don't blame yourself." This counselor was not at all supportive of me attending a Twelve Step program. In fact, his advice to not refer to myself as an alcoholic or addict contradicts Step One of that program. He wasn't able to help me get sober. I later saw him again, admittedly only 10 days into my recovery, this time after finding sobriety in the Twelve Step program. I had experienced a spiritual awakening, and I was bubbling over with enthusiasm as I extolled what I had found in the program. He was visibly unimpressed, and no congratulations or supportive comments were offered. I was stunned by the utter lack of knowledge that he, a trained addictions counselor, had about Twelve Step programs. He said that it was only ten days and that my aplomb was misplaced. That stunned me, because I was at a Twelve Step meeting that very morning, only one hour prior to seeing this counselor, and while sharing I mentioned that I was feeling good in my recovery today, but that I had "only" 10 days sober. After the meeting half a dozen members assailed me: "Don't ever say 'only 10 days' or 'just 10 days' man! Any amount of sobriety is something to be proud of and this is a program of 'one day at a time'. So don't ever say 'I have only 10 days'. Say 'I have 10 days!' and be proud of it." I felt very good after hearing that, and then downcast after hearing the counselor's words. I had been 10 days dry in the past, but was white-knuckling it and always broke and went back to my drugs and drink. This time, however, I knew I had something, and I knew I could do it. The Big Book says that "we are neither cocky nor are we afraid" (page 85), and that's exactly how I felt. I remain sober still. I never went back to see that counselor again.

Many therapists strongly advise their alcoholic and addict patients to seek out a Twelve Step program. Unfortunately, many patients do not heed this advice, as they are still not convinced of their powerlessness. If the therapist would guide the patient toward this conclusion, there would be a better response to this advice. When I was attending psychotherapy I was advised to consider attending A.A., but I never did. My acceptance of my powerlessness over drugs and alcohol came much later, unfortunately. In my years of working with alcoholics and addicts I always suggested participation in a Twelve Step program, but I knew almost nothing about it. Knowing what I know now, I wish I had been helping my alcoholic and addict patients move toward becoming mentally ready for accepting help (see Chapter Six), and I should have been giving out copies of the Big Book. Ten years of medical training left me woefully lacking in knowledge about this amazing resource. I am saddened by therapists who don't support Twelve Step programs, and I view with heavy heart inpatient "rehab" programs that are "Not Twelve Step Based". I have seen many graduates of these programs whose only support afterwards is a weekly "aftercare" meeting, which is often a considerable distance away. There is no sponsor, no close contacts, no fellowship, no other meetings, no literature. Many will not go to Twelve Step meetings as they have not had any exposure to the program. They miss out on the massive support system, the widely available meetings, the benefits of having a sponsor, the continuity of effort, and the excellent therapy of the Twelve Steps itself.

Psychotherapy, no matter how well delivered, lacks the deep self-searching and the brutal truth about ourselves that we require. We have already discussed the therapists' inability to extract the honesty necessary to accomplish this. Psychotherapy is well suited to addressing a specific stressor in life, such as a traumatic event, but is not empowered to effect the massive "house-cleaning" we need to do to resolve our disease. We need tough love and the wisdom gained of a well of personal experience by fellow alcoholic-addicts in recovery. They have accomplished what we want to do and they can help us do the same.

\*

People like me, of the medical community, have failed the alcoholic-addict from the beginning. My own experience in medical school and residency did little to foster good and understanding care of this disease. There was very little classroom instruction on the subject, and what there was did not match at all with my present understanding of this disease, as one who is recovering from it. In fact, there was a "we vs. they" mentality about it, especially those addicted to narcotics. They were viewed as creatures of scurrilous intent who were wilfully trying to manipulate us into prescribing them narcotics. Although they were in fact trying to get prescriptions from us under false pretenses, it was lost on us that their disease had driven them to depths of desperation that had nothing to do with the person within, hiding under the suffocating armor of addiction. I failed to see that it was their armor, not their skin. My attention was on exposing their intrigue and invoking the authorities, not on looking through the superficial and helping them take off that armor, which weighs them down so heavily. In hindsight, I am saddened that I could have done so much better by these unfortunates, had I known what I know now. It was A.A. that taught me everything I know about our disease, not medical school.

I hope that the medical education establishment and practitioners at large are doing better at this by now, and they are, but there is still a long way to go. The National Center on Addiction and Substance Abuse published a book correlating medical studies on the subject of various therapies.[9] Their findings identified a wide-spread problem of unqualified or poorly-qualified practitioners who treat people with our disease. The addiction treatment workforce (counselors) was given a particularly poor report in terms of qualifications, and were found to be lacking even in the knowledge of where to look for information about treatment of addictions. Medical doctors were found to be lacking in their screening for alcohol and drug addiction, as well as in implementation of treatment. I would advise any professional who works in addictions to consult this report (available as a free download) for a hard look at the current state of addictions treatment. We have a long way to go to measure up.

*

There is a demon within that glares down at us with glacial eyes: self-pity. It is our nature to feed this beast, which had much to do with our chemical misfortunes. Of course, "normal" people will wallow in self-pity, but – as usual – our disease takes our psychology to extremes, and self-pity becomes a beast as we travel further and further down our sordid path. With our fortified external locus of control, we feel like life's helpless victims. Abstaining from our drug doesn't cure it, in fact we can add our drinking or using mishaps to our "poor-me" list: "Why am I a slave to alcohol/drugs, when so many other people can take it or leave it?" We have discussed the critical process of changing our external to an internal locus of control as a major requirement of any kind of therapy if it is to equip us for success and some measure of fulfillment in life. This can't happen until we stamp out the self-pity.

As the alcoholic-addict stumbles down the path of tragedy and loss the sentiment deepens. "Why me? Why am I the one to lose my job, my family, my happiness?" We become bitter, resentful, and we begin to hate people, places, things, institutions, the world, even God. Placing blame on everyone else is the essence of an external locus of control... and of self-pity.

Self-pity is an odd entity, because we seem to like it. We actually enjoy adding to our list of poor-me's and then telling anyone who will listen all about it. "Self-pity is an enticing swamp. Sinking into it takes so much less effort than hope, or faith, or just plain moving" (Living Sober, pages 55-56). Mired up to our chest in the swamp of self-pity is a comfortable place for us to be – our mind finds relief in the belief that our woes are not a consequence of anything we did or didn't do. Our mind loves believing that we are not at fault for our misfortunes. Even if we *are* suffering from someone else's unprovoked actions, what good does it do to relentlessly allow it to "own" us by stoking our self-pity? It's the epitome of external locus of control. And it makes us feel hopeless and it makes us drink or use.

Self-pity loves to have other people confirm it, so it makes us seek out pity from others. This never works well, because people tire of our constant negative attitude and our obsessive talk about our problems. People recognize our self-pity for what it is. We may even seek out failure as a way of confirming our view of ourselves as victims and gaining other people's pity. People caught up in self-pity are focussed on the past, crave sympathy, and are unable to laugh at life and themselves. They act with the goal of attracting attention, empathy or help, instead of acting to solve their problems. They

[169]

look outside of themselves for the source of their problems (external locus of control), which only leads to a downward spiral of their life issues.

Self-pity, known as *self-victimization* to psychologists, is a horrible mental trap. It is an expression of learned helplessness, which we have previously discussed, and is a symptom and causative factor in depression. It appears in many dysfunctional situations, where we feel or pretend to feel that we are passive victims.

Manipulators often play the victim role by portraying themselves as victims of circumstances or someone else's behavior in order to obtain pity or benefits from others. The manipulator often finds it easy and rewarding to play on sympathy to get things from others. Even abusers will use it to gain forgiveness or absolution from their acts of abuse. "I was sexually abused as a child" is the mantra of the rapist.

More to the point, we alcoholic-addicts will use self-victimization to excuse our substance use and associated behaviors. "You'd drink/use too, if you had my life," we say. This does two things for us psychologically. First, it helps placate our cognitive dissonance by telling ourselves that our drinking or using is not our fault, and second, it helps us to manipulate others into excusing our behavior, and perhaps even enabling our continued drinking or using. It gives us justification – in our own mind – for our behavior, and gives our mind the green light to continue drinking and using.

Like many of the dysfunctional mental processes that are active in alcoholic-addicts, self-victimization does not just disappear with the last drink or drug. Even in sobriety it remains a reason for us to avoid our problems, wallowing in passive helplessness. We may still cling to the belief that our fate is controlled by external forces, so any efforts to improve our situation will be useless. This caused us to drink or use and excused our substance use in the past, so it must be dealt with ASAP lest we fall again. We must part company with this external locus of control, once and forevermore.

Obviously, self-pity must be a major target of any effort to achieve lasting sobriety. This effort must continue as long as we wish to remain sober, for sobriety alone does not defeat it. Self-pity is not the exclusive domain of the practicing alcoholic-addict. It is a widespread affliction of all people, to some degree. Sobriety provides no immunity to it.

Even in situations where we truly are victims of someone else's malice or some bad luck, self-victimization is destructive. We need to accept the things that are, and look into how we can change things for the better, just like the Serenity Prayer suggests we do. We must invoke the Twelve Step slogan and live "Life on Life's Terms." To break the hold of the passivity of victim-hood, requires taking responsibility for our own goals and actions. We must abandon the comfort of our own feelings of impotence (comforting because they excuse us from responsibility for our failings) and accept that we have power to change our lives. We ask for the courage to do so through the Serenity Prayer. Only then can we start planning out the actions we need to do to reach our goals.

Sitting with the therapist in her comfortable office, with her luxury car parked outside, good job, no problems in life (that are visible to us), we become even more aware of our losses, and this feeling of self-pity becomes magnified. This is not a good start to a process that needs to quash self-pity. However, being around other recovering alcoholic-addicts in the Twelve Step fellowship enables us to discover that it isn't "just me" after all. Our experiences, including our losses and illnesses and pain are shared, even exceeded, by many others. This somehow brings us immense comfort. Misery does love company, but that's not what comforts us here... it's the lifting of our self-pity that soothes us. We see that people in our fellowship don't obsess with blaming others for their problems, they own up to their part in it. They don't seek our pity and they don't complain. Then, hearing how sobriety meant recovery of life and happiness in these same people stirs us and replaces the self-pity with hope and motivation. And courage to change the things we can.

Shared hardship forges the strongest of bonds between people, as has been recognized for millennia. Commiserating with a fellow alcoholic-addict breaks down many walls and is largely responsible for the honesty and trust that is seen in the fellowship. However, it is also the antidote for this attitude of self-pity that causes us to not allow anyone in. People in the fellowship recognize self-pity from a mile away and don't let us get away with it. This virtue is inherent to the Twelve Step program and we feel it from the very first gathering we attend.

The Twelve Step program uniquely provides us with an opportunity to quash our poor-me mentality, and moves us toward the critical internal locus of control. We are made to realize that the joys of life are not a given... we must seize them. But, they are there for the taking.

*

One glaring shortcoming of clinical psychotherapy is its finite duration. As soon as the money runs out, or the health insurance has maxed out, the therapy ends. Hopefully the gains made in therapy persist for a while, but there is no further support... nothing. That may be fine for some with limited issues, but not for alcoholic-addicts. We are not "fixed" when we leave the therapist's office the last time. Our disease requires ongoing attention for life. Other diseases are like that too. I know numerous alcoholic-addicts who relapsed shortly after they stopped doing what they needed to do to stay sober. We've said that our disease is always right outside the door doing push-ups, waiting for us to weaken a bit. I would say that my addiction is bench-pressing, and doing chin-ups and sit-ups waiting for me!

Unlike clinical therapy, "A.A. is not a plan for recovery that can be finished and done with. It is a way of life, and the challenge contained in its principles is great enough to keep any human being striving for as long as he lives. We do not, cannot, outgrow this plan. As arrested alcoholics, we must have a program for living that allows for limitless expansion. Keeping one foot in front of the other is essential for maintaining our arrestment" (Big Book, page 275).

Let's look back at the science that we have learned. We know from the chapter on the brain that the brain pathways that were created in alcoholism-addiction remain in place for life, always waiting to once again jump into action. We know that our genetics pre-dispose us to our disease, and our genetics don't change: we remain pre-wired for substance abuse. We know that our psychology, left to its own devices, will slip back into the poor-me, helpless, angry, resentful, selfish, blame the world way of thinking that brought us to seek refuge in the bottle or needle in the past. We must maintain our defenses every day in order to maintain our higher level of thinking and functioning, lest we slip back to where our brain, genetics, and mind would take us.

I compare alcoholism-addiction to diabetes – they are very similar in some aspects. Both are caused by chemical changes in the body that occur due to things we ingest. Both are lethal if untreated. Both can be put into remission by daily treatment, but both will come right back as soon as we stop our daily attention to them. I will leave the diabetics to their own devices, but the Twelve Step program prescribes we alcoholic-addicts with a daily treatment regimen, and we just have to follow it.

A friend of mine in A.A. relapsed nine years into his sobriety, and experienced an eight-month binge that cost him his home, his business, his wife, and nearly his life. Upon his return to A.A. and renewed sobriety, he said that his relapse came after he became complacent and stopped attending meetings and stopped his 15 minute sessions of reading and meditation/prayer that he undertook every morning. He found a high price to giving up his daily therapy, even nine years into sobriety. Unfortunately, I have heard the same story as his many times. We must have a long-term program.

The fact that we are alcoholic-addicts for life is a central message of the Twelve Step program. It follows that to maintain sobriety the program must remain a part of our lives as long as we expect to remain in remission. To be sure, as time goes on many members require fewer meetings than they once did, but the principles and practices must remain in place. Experience has shown that many have fallen after slowly dropping the program from their life, always in the confidence that they longer needed it. It's the insanity of our disease at work, but it's also a natural sentiment once we have years of sobriety under our belt. The character defects that we strive to control easily worm themselves back in, and these are the demons that once led us to our substance use. We got sober by beginning a new life, informed by our old lives, but invented anew. This new life must continue to be fueled by what got us sober and keeps us there. Staying with the program is no hardship… we have chosen a path that has led to success and we happily embrace the journey.

*

One dazzling strength of the Twelve Steps over other forms of psychotherapy is the availability of an outstanding network of supporting literature. Literature can be taken home by the alcoholic and read anytime anywhere. Much of it is free, in the form of pamphlets on a variety of subjects, made available at meetings or as free downloads, and the books are offered at cost, or as free downloads. While many psychotherapists may recommend a certain book, or may have available some pamphlets about various topics, they lack the solid foundation of the variety of coherent literature available to the fellowship. This literature is time-tested; this is no "fad" self-help scam of the week featured on Dr. Phil.

As an academic, I have been singularly impressed by the effectiveness of the Twelve Step literature. I have seen many occasions where an addict-alcoholic first "got it" and found sobriety and commitment to the program from reading the Big Book. This was my experience. My copy of the Big Book is tattered and worn, because I have been through it many times. I study it. I find its message to be profound, and every time I read it I peel back a new layer only to find another layer underneath. I find new truths in it every time I read it. Other than new stories being added and old ones deleted in the back part, the basic text has had one single word change in the 80 years and four editions since it was first published. Like I said: time-tested. That book has saved many lives, including my own. Let's just have a quick look at exactly how amazing this book really is.

The Big Book is one of the best-selling books of all time, having sold 30 million copies, as of 2009. In 2011, Time magazine placed the book on its list of the 100 best and most influential books since 1923 (Time magazines first year in print). In 2012, the U.S. Library of Congress designated it as one of the 88 "Books that Shaped America". The Big Book got its nickname because the very first edition was printed on thick, heavy paper, making the book physically big. Earlier, I referred to the Big Book as the Swiss Army knife of recovery. Two of its tools are that it is a manual of psychotherapy and a medical textbook. It amazes me that this book addresses the science (the brain, genetics, and psychology) of alcoholism-addiction and recovery so completely, as we have shown in this book, despite being written years before the science was known to humankind. The program amounts to a superior form of psychotherapy, and the Big Book is a manual for training providers of this therapy, and for helping "patients." There is no other medical or psychology textbook that can claim being unchanged in 80 years. Consideration has been given to re-writing the text to remove the male pronouns that prevail, the 1930s terminology, and the references to God as a Higher Power, but the text has been left alone because of its immense success in its present form. Its words have proven true, so no changes are likely to occur, for better or for worse. This book is an amazing resource, there for the taking. No extended health insurance required.

Besides its unparalleled success, what grabs my attention most about the Big Book is how it came about. It was written by Bill W., a stock-broker with no literary or medical training, yet it is a transformative book of therapy that even today still holds up to medical scrutiny in its original form. Despite being dictated by Bill while leaning over his secretary's shoulder, without benefit of a word-processor for editing, it is superbly written literature. Its effect on people is profound, it has certainly saved millions of lives and restored loved ones to their place in their family and the world. It has transformed people's very personality and enabled the most dysfunctional among us to achieve a successful bearing in the world. It's an uncanny piece of composition produced by a failed stock-broker in 1939. Not bad for his first ever try at writing a book. I feel comfortable as a man of science when I say that I believe that the Big Book was inspired by someone or something greater than us all.

The Twelve Step literature is widely disseminated and available to all, including the illiterate. There are free apps and websites that make the Big Book available in audio form in many languages. Brail is also available. Twelve Step publications are in print in 43 languages, and can be found around the world.

*

"I can't get sober until I deal with my past."

What does it mean to "deal with" a traumatic experience from the past? People generally believe it means that the offending experience is forgotten and no longer bothersome. That's not a realistic expectation, but many will cling to this forlorn hope for a lifetime. Realistically, "dealing with" a traumatic event means arriving at a point where we can get through our days without the event dominating our thoughts and dictating our actions; in other words so that we can have peace and function normally, so that these events no longer "own" us. Medicine calls this disruption of normal functioning due to past events Post-Traumatic Stress Disorder (PTSD). PTSD is one of the few psychiatric disorders that medicine is not very good at treating. Medications do not help very much. Psychotherapy can help, somewhat.

Addressing past traumatic experiences is an exquisitely delicate issue. Offending the traumatized is easy and unsafe to do. Even experienced therapists find it a challenge to work with these unfortunates. I have worked with people who suffer ongoing effects of past events, and find it one of the most difficult of challenges. However, I have found the Twelve Step approach to therapy to be an appropriate and effective method for helping people grapple with past traumas. This method of therapy helps by allowing the sufferer to take a powerful external event – the trauma – and establish an internal locus of control around the event. As well, it also addresses any dysfunctional coping mechanisms in use, which are commonplace given that medical therapy usually fails these people. Let's look at that specifically.

People with PTSD carry a higher risk of alcoholism and addiction, as they understandably seek to "self-medicate" in their desperation to relieve their pain and suffering. It's an attractive but dysfunctional coping mechanism. Not surprisingly, this coping mechanism leads to a much worse situation, where we now have comorbidity, which is the presence of substance use as well as another psychiatric disorder. In the National Comorbidity Survey, PTSD was associated with alcoholism in 52% of males and 28% of females, and drug addiction was in 35% and 27%, respectively.[10] These surveys notoriously under-estimate true prevalence rates because of the reluctance of "us people" to disclose that we are alcoholics or addicts when asked in a survey... or by our doctor. We will discuss PTSD more in the next chapter.

It's important to remember that even in the absence of PTSD, many of us are yoked to past issues that burden us with pain. Just because we don't have full-blown PTSD doesn't mean we don't suffer from memories of horrible past events in our life. As I mentioned earlier, everybody has something from their past that somehow colors their thoughts, beliefs, and actions in a negative way. These things, too, have a role in our disease, and they should be confronted in our search for peace of mind.

The above statistics show that "dealing with" past trauma is crucial to helping us to find sobriety, and finding sobriety is likewise crucial to dealing with past trauma. Luckily, the Twelve Step program does both. Simultaneously. It is my professional opinion that the Twelve Step program provides excellent psychotherapy for dealing with past traumas. However, with deep emotional trauma I strongly advise also involving outside help, in the form of a therapist experienced in that particular type of trauma, as well as a medical professional. The Twelve Step program shares in that recommendation, as we have already seen.

I will discuss, briefly, the impact of past trauma, including sexual abuse, on us and our recovery. Please do not allow my brevity and my suggestion that there is a way to come to terms with these tragedies to imply that I am trying to minimize or trivialize the impact of these tragedies on our lives. The legacy of these events is the cruelest of prisons. However, this issue, so common among those who seek refuge in the bottle or narcotic, must necessarily be discussed. It is the elephant in the room that is blocking the door to our sobriety.

Past trauma may not be from one specific event. It may be from accumulated events, such as ongoing poor treatment in the workplace, bullying during the school years, or how a child is treated over years. As well, its effect is based on the person's perception of events and memories. Events that may be traumatic for one person may be easily shaken off by another. We must remember to give space and empathy to those affected, because unless one has been through it personally, it is impossible to fully appreciate the psychological effects of past trauma… especially if it was in childhood… especially if it was repeated and prolonged… especially if it was at the hands of those who should have been be providing care and protection… and especially if it involved sexual abuse. Little wonder that victims of abuse tend to be angry and defensive people. They understandably feel vulnerable and threatened by the world, and characteristically respond aggressively when

[177]

they feel challenged or threatened. They also feel chronically misunderstood, which also brews up anger and aggression.

While I believe the Twelve Steps to be an excellent path toward peace for these people, emotional and mental scars will never heal. While a complete discussion is beyond the scope of this book, there are many deeply seated psychological issues that can be at work, such as an impaired self-reference, dissociative behaviors, disturbed relatedness, and dysfunctional coping mechanisms (including avoidance behaviors, indiscriminate sexual behaviors, addiction and alcoholism, and self-harm - cutting, eating disorders, suicide). The scars will remain, but many among us have shed the dominance of these events from our lives. It can be done.

Past traumas can play a leading part in bringing us to our alcohol and drug use – understandably so. However, if we fixate on blaming our addiction problems on these events, it just further blows up our resentments over these events, which will be an insurmountable barrier to our recovery as well as our ability to find peace. But it is in our nature to resist letting go of these things – we want to continue to hate and punish. Somehow the hate and anger we lavish on past events and those responsible is satisfying to us psychologically. But this long-standing preoccupation has to end if we are to be happy and free.

There is a story from a member of A.A. who was well known in my area, until his recent passing. I am sure he would not mind me sharing his story, as he shared it many times as a speaker, and would certainly be pleased that the legacy of his story continues to help others. This man, Paul, got involved in the outlaw biker scene at a very early age. He fit the bill: big, ugly, arrogant, and ruthless. He lived the life just like you see in the movies, and ended up addicted to just about anything, and in prison for murder. While in prison he found sobriety through A.A., where he also found his higher power and a fundamental change in character. Grateful for his recovery he sought to give back in service work to try to right some of his many wrongs. Upon release from prison he remained active in A.A. and lived a life commensurate with the principles he learned in the program and with his new-found peace and serenity. Then, unspeakable disaster struck.

Late one night Paul was awakened by a soul-shocking phone call: his twenty-something daughter had been found dead. She had been savagely raped to death. A man was in custody. To attempt to describe the blinding mix of emotions that Paul felt at that moment would be futile. Under great strain, his old biker instincts seized every fiber of his being: he had to kill this beast who had savaged his girl… right after picking up a bottle of Vodka. He set out to do murder, fully capable of it. However, a little mental burr caught Paul in his trance, and caused him to call his A.A. sponsor. His sponsor talked him down, and Paul collected himself. Paul was able to use his "tools" from A.A. – prayer, meditation, talking with other alcoholic-addicts, going to meetings, working his Steps – to ride through the anguish that turned the minutes to hours. Paul's sponsor helped him to see that the rapist was himself an alcoholic and addict, and therefore sick, and needed help. Paul found his peace again.

Times passed, and the depraved rapist was sentenced to prison for his vile deeds. In prison, this man found sobriety in A.A., and, like Paul, experienced the healing power of his higher power. A fundamental change in his character paralleled that of Paul's. He worked with other alcoholics and addicts in prison. Grateful to his higher power, who was God, he studied and became an ordained minister. His behavior in prison was exemplary.

Paul was surprised one day by a call from a member of the parole board. His daughter's killer was applying for early parole. This was being seriously considered by the parole board, but they would allow a parole hearing only if Paul consented. Nobody in the world would condemn Paul for outright forbidding any consideration of early parole, but that's not what happened. Instead, Paul went and met his daughter's murderer in the flesh. He offered his forgiveness, a defining moment of courage and humility. He came away with the realization that remaining in prison wouldn't help this man or anybody else. Release from prison would allow this man to take his message of A.A. and God to others, so Paul consented to the hearing. The man was granted early parole, and went on to do exactly the service work that he said he would do.

Paul gives us an example we can only hope to emulate. He found peace after an extremely traumatic experience, to the point of forgiveness of someone who didn't deserve forgiveness, and showing that individual an act of mercy. Although deceased, Paul lives on as an inspiring example of the healing power of the Twelve Steps.

*Drop the Rock* relates a story from an A.A. member in recovery: "Without the knowledge from understanding and working the Sixth and Seventh Steps [the Steps whereby we endeavor to shed our character defects], I can go to any lengths in any direction imaginable to be compulsive. I've gotten over having a chip on my shoulder about this quirk of nature and don't blame my parents. Even if I had 'perfect parents' (which really don't exist), I would have been quite a challenge to them anyway. I tell many newcomers they may have to do some work about their parents, but there is a big trap in blaming them while working the Steps. It's too easy to get stuck blaming our parents, which continues to make the past a reliable source of unhappiness. Our parents don't work the Steps for us" (pages 87-8).

We must not try to trivialize what some have lived through in the past. Even after 15 years of practicing medicine I still hear in the rooms of A.A. stories of past traumas that leave me speechless. The point is that we can't change what has happened in the past, we can only change what we do with it now. It may seem stark and heartless to boil it down to that, but that is the hard truth. We can either lurk through life with a black cloud of resentment (or fear, or self-loathing) over our head and isolate ourselves and express our anger toward those around us and try to smother the emotions with drugs and alcohol, or we can choose to "deal with" that black cloud as best we can. It is the Serenity Prayer applied to life. The freedom we experience from the release from the black cloud over our head is immense, as can be seen by the testimonials from addicts and alcoholics who have done so. It's about whether we allow these things to own us. Talking it over with a Twelve Step member who shares a similar history of trauma is therapeutic. One doesn't have to look too far to find that in the fellowship. There is nothing so salubrious nor better medicine for our suffering than bonding with someone who understands our troubles first-hand. Support groups and friends in the Twelve Step fellowship can provide those opportunities.

Another alcoholic who found peace and serenity in A.A. was able to let go of her resentment toward her parents: "…I don't blame my parents for my alcoholism. Kids with a lot worse upbringing than mine did not turn out alcoholic, while some that had it a lot better did. In fact, I stopped wondering, 'Why me?' a long time ago. It's like a man standing on a bridge in the middle of a river with his pants on fire wondering why his pants are on fire. It doesn't matter. Just jump in! And that is exactly what I did with A.A. once I finally crossed the river of denial!" (Big Book, page 328).

This woman makes my point perfectly. When we have horrible events in our past, we will never be able to forget, and maybe never forgive. Nothing will take these terrible memories away. However, we can take action to stop these memories' power to own us, to control our thoughts and actions, to drag us down. To build on the above analogy, the man with the burning pants will always have scars on his body from his burning pants. However, by choosing to jump in the river he can stop the burning. However, if he chooses to remain on the bridge to obsess about why his pants are burning and who or what caused it, he will surely be consumed by the fire.

This freedom is worth the work. People who live in the past have often forgotten what it is like to feel "normal." Many consumed by this level of anger and resentment find it to be the last thing they think of when they go to bed at night, and the first thing they think of when they come to in the morning... if they can sleep. Their inner fury boils over into their daily lives, causing them to be quick to anger and impatience, lashing out at faultless people for the smallest of offences. What a wonderful thing to be released from this servitude of pain and to find true peace of mind and serenity! I recommend giving the Twelve Steps a try if that is your situation. The program gives so much more than sobriety. It is a widespread observation among members that they came to the program looking for sobriety and found so much more. But we must first be willing to let go of that strangely satisfying anger over the past, and face our demons head-on. One alcoholic woman, Karen, illustrates this well.

Karen was deeply affected by an essay by Martha Roth that she found in her daily meditation book. Karen paraphrases: "The essay talked about people who analyze themselves to death. They know exactly what makes them do the things they do: the tyrannical mothers, the abusive husbands, the poverty they were raised in, or the childhood of extreme indulgence and privilege. They have great insight, but instead of using that insight as a means to develop new and hopefully better behavior, they use it as a reason to continue with old, destructive behavior. They are not willing to go through the pain it takes to change, even though the pain of staying the same is killing them" (*Drop the Rock*, pages 6-7).

[181]

Psychology researcher Dr. Ervin Staub[11] has done some interesting work with survivors of traumatic abuse and has demonstrated a tendency among many to altruism, something he refers to as *altruism born of suffering*. His work has shown that helping others appears to be highly therapeutic for people suffering from past traumatic events. The Twelve Step program heavily emphasizes service work – helping others – which Dr. Staub's research shows will be of great help. The program provides an excellent framework for exploring this potentially therapeutic avenue.

A special case is those who live life with a deep sense of insecurity and mistrust because of past trauma. Getting close to anyone – including people in the Twelve Step fellowship – is unthinkable to some of these people. These unfortunates should work closely with a qualified therapist to get to a point where they can ease their way into trusting relationships. This is a slow process and a sponsor in the Twelve Steps with a similar background is helpful.

I hope that anyone living with horrible memories and emotional and physical scars from life's injustices will come to the Twelve Steps with the open-mindedness to allow peace back into their lives. It's an important step to finding life-long sobriety.

\*

So, we have made the case that the Twelve Steps are in fact a form of psychotherapy, and that they are a superior form of psychotherapy for our disease. But, is the program of the Twelve Steps simply suited to the problem of addiction and alcoholism? Absolutely not!

The Twelve Step program knows that sobriety is more than "just saying no" to drugs and alcohol and addictive behaviors. To achieve sobriety we need a whole new set of life-skills, a new design for living. Our very character has been changed by our experiences during our alcoholism-addiction, and we must "clean house" if we wish to stay sober. I see the Twelve Step program as a swag-bag of skills for living. These same skills for living, applied to anyone's life whether they are "one of us" or not, can only bring positive changes.

[182]

In the Twelve Steps we found a superior form of psychotherapy that helped us see and defeat things that have tied us down for most of our lives. We found a change in character that gives us strength, peace, and integrity. We found a new way of thinking and new habits that allow us to function well in the world. We didn't just learn to live without our substance, we learned how to live without needing it. We were enabled to live life on life's terms. And we live.

Many Twelve Step members describe themselves as "grateful alcoholics or addicts," a gigantic contradiction in terms. However, they are grateful because if it wasn't for their alcoholism-addiction they would never have experienced the miraculous life-changes that they found in the Twelve Steps. There they found new life skills that they had never known, even before their substance problem began. As for me, I wish I would have found my way to the Twelve Steps earlier on in my life, long before I was an alcoholic-addict, because I would surely have done so much better in life – socially, professionally, and in happiness. I can only dream of a life do-over with the life skills I have now.

I mentioned at the beginning of this chapter that every person in the world – alcoholic-addict or not – has psychological issues to some degree and would benefit from the psychological therapy of the Twelve Step program. You don't have to look hard to see that there are many people around us who have anger and resentments that controls their actions. My experience with counselling couples is that most of the strife that infects troubled marriages has a basis in anger and resentments that have nothing to do with the marriage or the spouse. People widely have unresolved issues. All would benefit from cleaning house. This is underscored by the fact that some 300 programs of personal improvement unrelated to addiction also use the Twelve Step program, under licence from Alcoholics Anonymous.

What a wonderful world this would be if we all bought into the principles of the Twelve Steps! Every one of us striving to root out our anger and resentments, to curb that part of our nature that breeds selfishness, greed, defensiveness, ego, and falsehood. All people committing to helping others and expecting nothing in return. An end to suffering under the dark rule of some species of chemical. No longer cowered on bended knee under the stinging glare of our past and our problems. We are all born filled with the capacity for this, we just need to learn to avail ourselves, something that may ever escape our attention.

Well, we can't change the world. But we can change ourselves.

# Eight

---

## Mental Health and Alcoholism-Addiction

Diagnosis and treatment of mental health disorders – the focus of psychiatry – has always been a big part of my medical practice. It's an inevitable part of general medical practice, and it's an area of medicine that has enticed me. How could it not? As a people-watcher the only thing I find more fascinating than normal psychology is abnormal psychology. It's also an area of medicine where a motivated doctor can tellingly impact people's lives. Most of my time in practice has been in a region where psychiatrists are in scarce supply, so I had no shortage of this kind of work. Unfortunately, some people with mental illness carry a label of being somewhat demanding and difficult to deal with, so many doctors don't relish seeing them. Many of my colleagues say they will see *some* people with mental illness because they feel they should "do their part." However, these patients deserve better than doctors who are seeing them just to "do their part."

Doctors seem to love coming up with complex words to describe simple things. True to form, they use the word *comorbidity* to describe a mental health disorder and alcoholism-addiction present at the same time in the same person. You may also hear them referred to as *concurrent disorders* or *dual diagnosis*.

Many people have mental issues that bother them, but what makes it a mental health *disorder* is when these issues cause problems to the point of interfering with the ability to function in life. We have names for these disorders of mental function: depression, anxiety disorders, schizophrenia, bipolar disorder, and anorexia are some among many. The definitions of the various mental health disorders are standardized in an internationally accepted book known as the DSM-5 (Diagnostic and Statistical Manual of Mental Disorders, the fifth version of which is currently in use).

What we know of as alcoholism and addiction are technically not proper medical terms, because they do not appear in the DSM-5. Instead, substance addictions are collectively referred to as *substance use disorders*, and a list of all the substances that fall into this category are given. This list includes alcohol and many other addictive substances. However, regardless of medical terminology, what we call alcoholism and addiction are considered to be a mental health disorder. I prefer just calling them "our disease."

The interaction of our disease with mental health disorders can have serious ramifications. When people with a mental health disorder add drugs or alcohol to the mix – in other words, when they suffer from comorbidity – they experience:

•more severe psychiatric symptoms,
•more dramatic effects from using substances, including more blackouts,
•lower likelihood of following treatment plans,
•more physical health problems,
•increased experiences of social stigma,
•increased financial problems and homelessness,
•poorer management of personal affairs,
•more serious relationship problems, including with family,
•more verbal hostility, tendency to argue, disruptive behaviour, aggression,
•greater likelihood of ending up in jail, and
•increased suicidal thoughts and action.

As put by the U.S. National Institute on Drug Abuse (NIDA): "[alcoholism-addiction] is a complex brain disease characterized by compulsive, at times uncontrollable drug craving, seeking, and use despite devastating consequences— behaviors that stem from drug-induced changes in brain structure and function."[1] We are already familiar with these brain changes, as we have discussed them in earlier chapters. These changes occur in some of the same brain areas and affect the same neurotransmitters that are responsible for other mental health disorders, such as depression, anxiety, or schizophrenia. It is therefore not surprising that there is such a high rate of comorbidity between alcoholism-addiction and other mental illnesses.

In Chapter Two we discussed how our genes can have a significant impact on our vulnerability to alcoholism-addiction. We saw that the genetics of our disease are complex, with many different genes interacting to produce the factors that come together and lead us to becoming addicted to a substance while other people can take it or leave it. Likewise, mental health disorders are instigated by numerous genetic factors that intermingle to make us more likely to develop these problems. Unsurprisingly, given the overlap in brain locations, neurotransmitters, and symptoms between alcoholism-addiction and mental health disorders, there are also overlapping genetic vulnerabilities. This means that the same genes that can make us more likely to become substance addicted can also make us more likely to develop a mental health disorder... and vice-versa.

While the influence of genetics is powerful, there are many other factors that contribute to our mental health. These are known as our "environment" – our life situation and experiences, how we grew up, the quality of our diet, our education, all of the many influences on our life as we live and breathe and interact in the world. Many of the things we are exposed to in life that can bring on alcoholism-addiction are also risk-factors for mental illness, such as: growing up in an unstable household, poor education, lack of life opportunities, poor nutrition, abuse and other trauma, to name a few.

Mental health disorders and alcoholism-addiction share more than causes. Because the same brain areas and neurotransmitters are affected, there are overlapping symptoms, making diagnosis and treatment challenging. Correct diagnosis is critical to ensuring appropriate and effective treatment, and failure to identify and treat a comorbid mental health disorder can jeopardize an alcoholic-addict's chance of recovery. There is, however, one area where the overlap is, sadly, missing.

Within healthcare systems different professionals and clinics address substance use disorders and other mental illnesses separately. Each is treated in assorted venues by a mix of health care professionals with different backgrounds. While each has an understanding of the other, neither system may have sufficiently broad expertise to address the full range of problems presented by comorbid patients. As well, there is almost always a physical separation between the two systems, and a resulting bias against close communication between treating professionals. Baffling to me is the bias that exists in some substance use treatment centers against using any medications, including those necessary to treat serious mental illness. This is counter-productive, as many do not stand a chance against their alcoholism-addiction unless their mental health problem is treated.

Many of those with undiagnosed or untreated alcoholism-addiction or mental health illness end up in the criminal justice system, brought there by their disease-induced behavior. It is undeniable that alcoholism-addiction and some mental health disorders make a person much more likely to end up on the wrong side of the law, especially when comorbidity exists. However, adequate treatment services for both substance use disorders and other mental illnesses are greatly lacking within the criminal justice system. These people end up being treated as disciplinary problems. Our jails and prisons are filled with people whose presence there is simply a symptom of a treatable disease.

Also heartbreaking is that people of unfortunate circumstances – such as the socio-economically disadvantaged – tend to have markedly reduced access to healthcare, rehab facilities, and medications. Meanwhile, this population is disproportionately represented in the ranks of those who suffer alcoholism-addiction and other mental health disorders. Those most affected are those with the least access to help.

Yet another barrier to effective diagnosis and treatment of these often comorbid problems is the social stigma carried by both. The stigma contributes to many people living in denial of their conditions, or with difficulty in finding the courage to come forward for help. They are understandably psychologically resistant to being diagnosed and taking on these new identities – labels – that are viewed as negative, even by friends, family, lovers, and employers.

Another challenge to diagnosing mental health problems is that we may not realize we are suffering from one. We may have lived with the condition for so long that we have long forgotten what it is like to feel "normal." As well, many mental health disorders are characterized by what is referred to as a "lack of insight." The medical profession, true to form, has chosen the simple name *anosognosia* for this symptom. (If you've somehow managed to make it this far through life without knowing that word, you're probably safe to continue on without it). This means that affected people are unaware of the symptoms they are experiencing, sometimes incapable of being aware. This is seen in bipolar disorder – where they are unaware of symptoms but able to accept the truth when confronted with enough evidence – and schizophrenia, where they remain completely oblivious to the symptoms, no matter how much they are told otherwise. This is a baffling thing to see in real-life, because their psychiatric symptoms are so obvious that it's hard to believe they are not aware they are ill. For the uninitiated, this impaired awareness of illness is difficult to comprehend. It may cause conflict because people will think those with anosognosia are faking or trying to pull one over on them, and the affected people are defensive about the suggestion there is something wrong with them. The main concern about people lacking insight into their illness is that they will not seek help, will resist help when offered, and be unlikely to cooperate with treatment. They don't believe there is anything wrong, so why would they want treatment? (Sounds a lot like another disease we know, doesn't it?)

Let's look at a few mental health illnesses that are particularly relevant to alcoholism and addiction.

*

Alcoholism-addiction, Obsession, and OCD

Alcoholism-addiction is a disease of obsession and compulsion. We've talked about that quite a bit in this book, but let's dig a little deeper for a page or two. I'm sure many people have heard of OCD – Obsessive-Compulsive Disorder. Like most mental health disorders, OCD occurs on a spectrum, meaning that some people have a very mild form while others have a form where they are so afflicted that it disrupts their ability to function in life, sometimes severely (like Howard Hughes, who was an extreme example). Our disease, despite being characterized by obsession and compulsion and definitely disruptive of our ability to function, is not considered to be OCD.

This is how it works. An obsession is a pervasive thought about something, a thought that we can't purge from our mind. It overrides all other thoughts, so that it's difficult or even impossible to think about or concentrate on anything else. The drive to satisfy this obsession is so strong that it causes considerable anxiety – even panic – until the obsession is satisfied. This drive to do what it takes to satisfy the obsession is called a compulsion. The classic example of OCD is where the obsession is around hand-washing. The obsession that the hands are dirty is so strong that it causes unbearable anxiety, which can only be satisfied with washing the hands, which is the compulsion. The hand-washing relieves the anxiety from the obsession… for now. The problem is that the obsession starts all over again right away after the hand-washing, and there is an uncontrollable compulsion to hand-wash again. The hand-washing becomes more frequent and more vigorous in an effort to satisfy the obsession. The cycle repeats and the victim ends up with raw hands and an inability to live a normal life because the compulsion takes over. So it is with the alcoholic-addict: the mind obsesses with drinking or using, and there is a compulsion to pick up that first drink or drug. After that first drink or drug, the obsession is there again, and with another drink or hit an arm's length away, our compulsion is to reach for it. And so on. Only sleep interrupts this, and it starts all over again upon awakening.

So, alcoholism-addiction is not so different from OCD. Both are conditions of an obsession and compulsion that prevent us from leading a normal life. In both, no amount of logic can talk us out of our illogical obsession. The difference lies in that OCD is (somewhat) treatable with medication, and alcoholism-addiction is not. Also, the obsession-compulsion in our disease causes considerable changes in our overall psychology, as we have discussed in previous chapters, and involves compulsive use of poisonous substances (our drugs and alcohol).

*

Alcoholism-addiction and Depression

Alcoholism-addiction and depression make the perfect marriage. They are so alike we can barely tell them apart. And they love each other. But it is a mercurial marriage, a suffocating one. They are so woven together that one can kindle the fire of the other. In fact, their romantic dexterity is such that it can be very difficult – sometimes impossible – to figure out which came first and brought the other along. Or even to tell them apart. In this context, we are talking about "clinical depression," not merely a feeling of sadness or having the blahs.

The medical term "depression" refers to a condition where a depressed mood on most days is accompanied by *vegetative symptoms*. These are symptoms which make the person "vegetate:" a loss of interest in doing anything - including things that we normally find fun (sometimes referred to as anhedonia), excessive sleep (although the sleep may be poor in quality or involve simply laying awake), poor or overactive appetite, feelings of guilt (usually excessive and unwarranted), low energy, poor concentration, inability to feel joy in anything. As well, there may be suicidal behavior (fantasizing about, planning, or committing suicide), and psychomotor agitation, which is physical jitteriness, fidgeting. As well, psychosomatic symptoms, also known as *functional symptoms* can appear. These are physical symptoms without a pathological cause. Commonly, these involve pain (particularly in the joints and muscles), headaches, stomach upset, diarrhea, dizziness, fatigue. As well, depression can worsen the symptoms of just about any pre-existing physical symptoms. So, people with low back pain may notice an increase in their pain, people with abdominal disorders may notice their symptoms flare up, and so on.

The statistics for depression and substance use comorbidity are staggering.[2] The lifetime risk of having a mental disorder – of any kind, excluding alcoholism-addiction – is 22.5%. The lifetime risk of alcoholism is 13.5% and 6.1% for other drug addiction. The lifetime rate for any mood disorder (depression or anxiety disorder) is 19.3%. Compared with people with no mood disorder, those with depression were approximately twice as likely, and those with bipolar disorder approximately seven times as likely, to have a substance use disorder. Substance use disorders were shockingly common among people with bipolar disorder: 56%!

[191]

In medical jargon depression is known as a *mood disorder*, which also includes anxiety disorders. Of course – as my fellow medical peacocks like to do – mood disorders have been further complicated by dividing them into many sub-categories with complicated names, such as Generalized Anxiety Disorder with Agoraphobia, Dysthymia, Seasonal Affective Disorder, Schizoaffective disorder, bipolar mood disorder (types I and II, of course), and a number of others. Suffice it to say for our purposes that the mood disorders include depression and anxiety disorders. I would encourage anyone who is interested to research for themselves the variety of depressive and anxiety disorders, as they are all very interesting. The more we know about these things the more we can protect ourselves and those we care about. As always, I strongly advise against trusting a website that has something to sell. A good starting point is the website of the American Psychiatric Association (https://www.psychiatry.org/).

An association between substance use disorders, mood disorders, and suicide is well-established. Intoxication causes us to lose our inhibitions, as well as our judgement and ability to reason. It may magnify our depression and the feelings of despair and hopelessness that go with it. This creates the perfect storm for impulsive, poorly thought-out, and self-destructive acts – including suicide. Many of us find ourselves so desperate to escape our alcoholism-addiction that we see death as our only way out. In studies listed by the National Institute on Drug Abuse (NIDA), two-thirds of people who successfully committed suicide had a substance use disorder. When comparing a number of psychiatric diagnoses, individuals with depression with substance use disorder are at the highest risk for suicide.[3]

Mood disorders and substance use disorders mutually worsen the clinical course, treatment outcome, and prognosis for each other, so it follows that successful alleviation of one condition facilitates recovery from the other. Treating patients' mood disorders will almost certainly reduce their substance craving and improve their overall chances at sobriety. Someone in active alcohol or drug use is unlikely to seek or respond to treatment for a mental illness.

As with all mental health disorders depression is very much a physical illness, involving insufficient production and function of certain neurotransmitters that, as we discussed in previous chapters, are the

[192]

chemicals that brain cells use to communicate with each other. Just as Diabetes is a physical illness involving abnormal production and usage of the chemical insulin, so depression is a physical illness caused by abnormal production and usage of neurotransmitters. The symptoms that are produced by depression are mental and behavioral, so we refer to it as a psychiatric disorder, with all the undeserved and unfortunate social stigma that goes with it. However, depression is no more a problem of character weakness or laziness than is a broken leg.

Depression is an excruciating illness, truly a form of suffering. The depressed person is miserable, low-functioning, and feels guilty, hopeless and alone (sound familiar to our disease?) There was recently a TV ad for an anti-depressant medication that showed a woman laying across her unmade bed in her pyjamas: disheveled, doleful, despairing and down. It was full daylight – when she probably should have been at work or otherwise living her life – and she was tossing and turning, unable to sleep. When I saw this commercial I immediately felt that the image they were projecting successfully personified depression.

I get upset when I hear people tell those suffering with depression that they just need to get out of bed and do things and they'll feel better. This is no different than saying to us in our drinking or using days: "why don't you just stop?" Sure, if we are feeling down, – having "the blues" –and we get out and take a walk or go to a movie with friends, this will probably cheer us up. However, only people who have experienced true clinical depression can know the crushing weight of it on our ability to function (sound familiar to our disease?) The lack of motivation, and the desire to just lay there and vegetate is so overwhelming that we will blow off even urgent chores, ignore the phone, and just lay there staring into space all day. Even showering is too much effort. To discourage people like this from seeking medical help is truly a disservice to them. The Big Book urges us to seek outside help when we need it, and this is certainly one such time.

It's easy to see how people feeling this way, suffering night and day, might easily turn to drink or drugs to try to alleviate the depressive symptoms, something we call "self-medicating." Their desperation to have something – anything – make them feel good even if only for a little while is understandable. Naturally, alcohol and drugs provide only a brief and

[193]

artificial escape from the suffering and, being depressants themselves, will actually worsen the symptoms and lower the depressed person's already diminished level of function.

Depression is common in early recovery. As we saw in our discussion of the "pink cloud" effect, addictive substances affect our brain by artificially causing over-production of dopamine, our feel-good neurotransmitter. In order to try to counter these abnormally high levels of dopamine our brain dials down its natural production and increases its destruction of existing dopamine. After we stop using these substances, the dialed-down dopamine production can take a long time to correct itself back to normal functioning, and until it does we go from having abnormally high levels of our feel-good dopamine to having abnormally low levels of it. The result is the opposite of euphoria – depression. Unfortunately, other neurotransmitters relevant to our mood are affected as well. Two in particular – Norepinephrine and Serotonin – are likewise suppressed. Suppression of these and other neurotransmitters happens to be the cause of clinical depression. After we detoxify it may take some time for production of these neurotransmitters to climb back up to normal levels, and we are left depressed. Often this depression is initially masked by the "pink cloud" effect, but when that abates if our neurotransmitter levels haven't returned to normal levels the curtain drops and we are left suddenly depressed.

The good news is that depression is generally very easy to treat. We have treatments that address these neurotransmitter deficiencies effectively. Most cases are easily treated with a low-dose once a day medication that is well tolerated. The effect of having the suffering of depression alleviated is profound. Doctors like anti-depressant medications because these medications make doctors look like heroes when their patients achieve such a huge relief of suffering in a short period of time with an easy medication. Some cases are tougher to treat than others, and medication doses must be titrated, or other medications used. Psychotherapy, particularly Cognitive Behavioral Therapy (CBT), has a role in treating depression, although it is very time-consuming and expensive to properly pursue. For us alcoholic-addicts, it is crucial to recognize and treat depression. We know that treating depression can decrease substance use and craving. It will help us get sober and stay sober. Even in sobriety, untreated depression is a major risk-factor for relapse.

[194]

With so many overlapping symptoms and causes, it can be unclear which came first and caused the other. Does it matter? It sort of does. If a person is clinically depressed, which is very treatable, it will pave the way to addressing the alcoholism-addiction once the depression is treated. If the person is depressed only as a consequence of substance use, then treating the substance use will likely treat the depression. However, treatment of depression may be impeded by the presence of alcohol or drug use. My clinical experience has been that if people with depression are not responding to treatment, then they are probably drinking or using drugs, and not telling me so. Our tortured minds are not willing to give up our feel-good coping mechanism of our alcohol or drugs, so we are secretive about it. It makes sense that if people are taking anti-depressant medications to restore their neurotransmitters to healthy levels and concurrently using addictive substances that lower these levels, the anti-depressant medications will be blocked from doing their life-saving work.

There remains a frustrating lack of recognition of the intertwining of depression and alcoholism-addiction, and it is reasonable to believe that our treatment of both of these painful life-threatening health problems will improve if that shortcoming is addressed. Twelve Step meetings are a good place to start addressing this, because it is not an "outside issue." Don't be afraid to share your knowledge to this end.

\*

Schizophrenia

Schizophrenia can unleash a special kind of hell on its victims. And the flames can be fanned by a familiar devil: half of all people living with schizophrenia will experience a substance use disorder in their lifetime. Many of them will have had their schizophrenia brought on by their substance use – usually permanently.

Schizophrenia is a "psychotic" disease. We discussed psychosis briefly in chapter One, but we have turned many pages since then, so let's quickly recap. Psychosis is defined as the loss of touch with reality, an inability to

[195]

distinguish between real experiences and ones dreamed up by an uncontrollable mind. There are different types of psychotic symptoms: visual and auditory hallucinations, ideas of reference (belief that people on TV or radio or in crowds are talking about us), paranoia, and catatonia (remaining rigidly still for prolonged periods, like a statue). Besides psychosis, schizophrenia also involves "vegetative" symptoms, similar to those seen in depression. There can be flat emotions, inability to feel pleasure, lack of motivation, and slow speech. Weird behavior is common, especially illogical thinking and planning, and bizarre behaviors and body movements. Not a recipe for fulfilling one's dreams in life.

Psychosis is caused by over-production of the neurotransmitter dopamine (hmm, sound familiar?) in a certain part of the brain. Given that many addictive substances (most notably marijuana, "acid," and MDMA – ecstasy) stimulate over-production of dopamine in the same area of the brain, it is not surprising that psychosis can be a prominent feature of the "high" produced by these drugs, and that use of these drugs can cause permanent psychosis in the user. I had a young patient who developed schizophrenia the very morning after he used the drug ecstasy. He claims that it was the one and only time he had used ecstasy. It ruined his life. At the time he was in his third year of a university degree, but because of his symptoms he had to abruptly drop out. He was unable to hold a job and ended up on government disability, almost certainly for life.

In keeping with the recurrent theme of comorbidity, substance use can bring on schizophrenia, and the reverse is also true. Compared to the general population, people with schizophrenia carry about three times the risk of alcoholism and about five times the risk drug addiction. Wow.

Schizophrenia is characterized by an extreme form of the "lack of insight" that we discussed earlier (remember that word that just glides off the tongue: anosognosia?) Because of this, people with schizophrenia often won't take their medications or attend their medical appointments – why would they, if they don't believe they have a problem? As well, many are paranoid and believe they are being poisoned, which makes them even more resistant to taking their meds. There are effective medical treatments for schizophrenia, but they often go untapped because of this. To be fair, the medications used can be heavily sedating and have other bothersome side-effects, so there are other reasons that compliance with treatment tends to be poor.

People with schizophrenia are impelled to difficulty leading a "normal" life. I remember one of my psychiatry instructors in medical school pointing out to me a clue that a patient whom I had just interviewed may suffer from schizophrenia: she was 38 years and had never been in a serious relationship. People with schizophrenia are prone to other life-smothering psychiatric symptoms and disorders, including depression and anxiety, and are usually completely dysfunctional during episodes of psychosis, which can be prolonged. Their "weird" behavior and vegetative symptoms often dominate in between psychotic episodes. They tend to be awkward or untoward in inter-personal interactions. One can see how all this would make it nearly impossible to be in a long-term relationship, to achieve further education, or to get and hold a job. It's not only be difficult for people with schizophrenia to make and keep friends, but they may also frighten or repel people. This is the life of many of these people, and the result can be a lonely, boring, and economically disadvantaged life. Under these circumstances, it is easy to see how someone with schizophrenia could be particularly vulnerable to the deceitful lure of drugs or alcohol.

I have known many people with schizophrenia and other psychotic disorders who work hard on getting better and overcoming great adversity to live normal, healthy, productive – and sober – lives. People like this inspire me with their acceptance of their situation, ability to look past their misfortune and instead focus on their strengths, and be satisfied with what they have. We alcoholic-addicts can learn from them.

*

Post-Traumatic Stress Disorder (PTSD)

We briefly discussed PTSD in the previous chapter, but we'll take a closer look at it now because of its high likelihood of bringing on alcoholism-addiction. We must keep in mind that although PTSD has garnered a lot of attention in recent times, many people who do not develop full-on PTSD are

[197]

also often anguished by past calamity, and now struggle with life and alcoholism-addiction as a result.

People with PTSD have witnessed or been through a traumatic event, but sometimes just hearing about a traumatic event is enough to bring on the symptoms. Until recently PTSD was unrecognized, and its victims were labelled as "cowards" or "whiners." Its first recognition, albeit in an embryonic way, came in the form of extreme examples of it being labelled by the term "Shell-shock" during and after the First World War, and "Combat Fatigue" during the Second World War and Vietnam War. Even these people were frequently branded as cowards. Victims of debilitating mental symptoms following other traumas – such as rape, assault, fire, natural disaster, witnessing an injury or fatality, or other tragedies – were not given the same acknowledgement.

People with PTSD continue to suffer from the psychological impact of the traumatic event long after it happens. They suffer intrusive thoughts, which can include vivid nightmares, persistent memories, and flashbacks where they re-live the experience. These intrusive thoughts renew the terror and pain of the experience over and over again. They avoid situations, objects, or people that remind them of the event. They often have over-the-top reactions to a sudden unexpected stimulus such as a loud noise or a tap on the shoulder. They are frequently irritable and avoid contact with others, especially when memories of the offending ordeal are strong.

People suffering PTSD have a tendency to internalize their feelings. They don't want to talk about the horrible event nor their feelings around it, and can become violently defensive when asked to do so. They live with a great deal of fear and mistrust. They understandably view the world as a scary, dangerous place. They often blame themselves for their feelings, and may become very down on themselves. Symptoms of depression and anxiety assault their already wounded hearts.

Symptoms usually develop within days of the traumatic event but may appear months later. These persist for months and sometimes many years. For some people the symptoms of PTSD improve or disappear over time. For others it is an ongoing plague on their life.

There is treatment available for PTSD, although it is difficult to treat. There is no "magic bullet" for it, so prevention is key. Post-trauma counselling is a key aspect of this. I was exposed to an event that shocked me deeply when I was an intern working in the ER. The hospital funnelled me into post-traumatic counselling, and I am today very thankful for that. Although I still get occasional clusters of flashbacks, they are only when I see something that reminds me of the event and they are very manageable. I have no doubt that the counselling I received after the event prevented much suffering on my part.

Other than a focus on prevention, treatment involves medications together with psychotherapy, especially Cognitive Behavior Therapy (CBT). The goal is to reduce symptoms until the condition burns itself out. The great danger lies in the PTSD victim seeking relief from their symptoms from "self-medication" with alcohol, drugs, or addictive behaviors. Ultimately, suicide risk is worrisome. PTSD is a very serious illness.

If they come to us for help with their substance use, we must give these unfortunates their space as they work through their issues with professional therapists and their doctor. It is my opinion that the Twelve Step process affords an excellent framework for coming to terms with past events, but those with PTSD will require patience when it comes to discussing these, as will many others with a tormented history. In the meantime, finding sobriety through the Twelve Steps will help the rest of the process along immeasurably.

\*

A more complete outline of mental illness is beyond the scope of this book… it's a huge subject. The standard manual of mental illness – the DSM-5 – is 947 pages long! For our purposes, we have demonstrated the interlacing of mental health illness and alcoholism-addiction, which is, strictly speaking, considered a mental health illness itself.

I have to confess an underlying agenda to this chapter: to prepare all of us for being around people who suffer from these mental illnesses. Because the illnesses discussed carry such a high risk of comorbidity, we will almost certainly run into them in others as our recovery brings us in contact with others "like us." My recovery has been in A.A., and I regularly see people with these problems in the program. An awareness of these illnesses helps us to understand them better, recognize the symptoms in others, and be more helpful as we find our way along in recovery together.

We haven't discussed every mental health illness that we may see, as that would take a book of its own. I have, during my recovery, run into fellow alcoholic-addicts with personality disorders, Tourette's syndrome, Attention Deficit Disorder, Conduct Disorder, Autism Spectrum Disorders, Anorexia Nervosa, and others. The common thread here is that we can be open-minded and accepting when people are afflicted with an illness that may involve behaviors that are odd to us.

We can see that mental health symptoms should be watched for in anyone with alcoholism-addiction issues, and vice-versa. Let's not allow social stigma to prevent us from using this information to help ourselves and others.

# Afterword

Allow me to whisper something in your ear, but don't tell anyone I said it: after reading this book you probably know more about alcoholism and addiction than does your doctor. If you are an alcoholic-addict in recovery then this is definitely the case.

So, what do we do with this information? If you have problems with alcohol or drugs or addictive behaviors, I hope you will use it to help you in your recovery, and to help you as you sponsor others in their recovery. If you have alcoholic-addict friends or loved ones, I hope this information will help you understand them. That understanding will surprise them and help them a lot. If you are a healthcare professional, I hope that you have not been offended by anything I've said, but if so I ask that you remember the poor report card that we all got on our effectiveness in alcoholism-addiction by the National Center on Addiction and Substance Use[1] and reflect on incorporating some of this information into your practice. As we must with any disease, we must always strive to improve on how we approach this savage pandemic affliction.

In the end, we alcoholic-addicts in recovery are all in this together and we need each other. I know I need you. If you have any comments or suggestions or pearls of wisdom you would care to pass on, I'd love to hear from you. Please feel free to email me at alcoholism.addiction@gmail.com.

Well-fed dogs always return to their master. Let's feed the dogs within us known as Acceptance, Willingness, and Open-mindedness. These are the very marks of recovery from our disease. And recovery is its own reward.

## About the author:

Andrew practiced as an ER and Family Doctor for 15 years. More recently he has dedicated himself to research and writing on addictions and recovery. He has been a faculty educator at the medical school of two major universities, but he prefers interacting with the general public on matters of addiction. His passion is for making the stranger-than-fiction marvels and elegant beauty of science accessible for everyone.

## Connect with the author:

**Visit author's website at** www.alcoholism-addiction-psychology.com

**Email the author at** alcoholism.addiction@gmail.com

# Epilogue

## My Story

I'm a product of turbulent but fast-moving times, being born in the late sixties. This was a time of war, social strife, emerging race and feminine rights, and the heyday of a free-loving and drug-tripping culture. Perhaps all a harbinger of the future life that awaited me. Little of the fast times of the sixties touched me, as I was born on an air force base in a sleepy corner of the mid-West. The home of my upbringing was not unhappy, but it was a home of little affection, much oppressed by the black shroud of my father's booming drinking career that slowly descended on our home. My father was drawn in by the immodest sensuality of wine and impossible loves, both of which reached addiction proportions. This culminated in the abrupt break-up of my parents at a time and place where divorce was unheard of.

My mother left my father to his bottle and his women, and loaded my sister and me into an old beater she somehow scrounged and moved us half a continent away to live with her family on the East coast. I was 11. I saw my father twice by the time I was a grown man, neither time in any way fulfilling to my wanting soul. My lot was now living in a small remote fishing community – picturesque but seemingly mired in the 18th century – where I was the only boy without a father. This was a community where every adult would ask you: "whose boy are you?" Fathers took their sons hunting and fishing, taught them to shoot, to drive a car, to be a man. I watched all this as an outsider, and my self-confidence fizzled out of me until it was like a

[203]

month-old balloon. My lack of confidence became a millstone around my neck, well into adult-hood.

I noticed in my late teens that I was developing an obsessive personality. The way it came on resonates perfectly – when I look back at it now – with A.A. co-founder Bill W.'s own experience. At about the same age he began to develop what he called "power drives." He described being seized by compulsive pre-occupation when he set his mind to something... he would work like a fiend to get it done and it had to be done to the utmost. He described it as a desire so fierce that it became a neurosis (what we now call an obsession). That describes very well what happened with me. I became interested in martial arts and boxing, probably in an unconscious desire to boost my dragging self-confidence. I became so heavily into it that I went to two or three classes per day every day of the week. Even between classes I practiced every day, usually for hours on end. I changed my furniture to reflect my new interest in things Japanese. I ended up going at it with this intensity for many years. Even after I received my black belt in two different martial arts and some success as a boxer, I continued at it. I opened my own martial arts and boxing school, and even ran it myself during medical school, no small commitment to take on during such an intense program of study.

One week after my 17th birthday, I fulfilled a life-long dream and left home for the army. I worked hard and was admitted to officer training. I chose the Artillery, which appealed to my penchant for math and big explosions. I finished officer training at age 19, and was posted to my first regiment as a Second-Lieutenant. I was leader of a troop of artillery consisting of six huge tracked guns, and thirty-five men (no women at the time). Ironically, I was the man in charge but I was younger than all my soldiers. My Sergeant-major, who was my second in command, was more than twenty years older than me. This situation wasn't helped at all by my baby-face.

I was constantly burdened by the same lack of confidence that had plagued my teenage years, especially now that I was a "leader of men." It made me second-guess my decisions, too shy to be much of a disciplinary force to aberrant soldiers, and affected my ability to carry out plans. When it came to technical stuff, like tactics and lobbing shells on time and on target, I was an ace, but the leadership thing was something I really had to work at.

[204]

Believe it or not, I purposely started smoking, something that made me nauseous, in an attempt to look older so that people would take me more seriously. Same with drinking.

Oddly enough, my obsession with alcohol at the time was limited to having no "off-switch" once I started drinking. I would drink until I passed out. Every time. I was totally incapable of having one or two drinks, I couldn't stop until I was incapacitated. Fortunately for me, I had not yet developed my daily obsession: the next day I was always able to shake off my hangover and soldier on. I would go weeks or months between episodes of drinking without even missing it. But, the seed of that obsession was there, lying in wait for fertile ground to blossom into alcoholism.

The military is a great place for someone with an obsessive personality to thrive. And I did. By 22 years of age I was promoted to the rank of Captain and was congratulated on being the youngest Captain in the army. However, soon after I made up my mind that I needed a new challenge, so I set my sights on getting a university degree. I started taking night classes at the local university while still serving in the military. I would get home from work around suppertime, eat and hustle to class at the university, get home about 10:30 and then study until 12 or 1 a.m. Up every morning at 5 I would study until 7, hit the gym, then be at work for 8:30. I had to work most weekends, so I kept up this pace all week. What little spare time I found was dedicated to my martial arts and boxing training. An obsessive personality in full expression. And I loved the pace!

When I registered for university, I knew nothing about the process. I was asked at the registration office what my major was to be, but I hadn't even thought about it. So – being an obsessive type – I asked what their hardest degree was. Chemistry, was the reply. So, I said I would major in Chemistry, a subject I had flunked in high school. My usual need to prove something to myself and the world a defence mechanism born of my low self-confidence – made that decision for me. Great reason for choosing a focus of study for the next four years!

After two years of part-time study I had completed my first year of university and decided to leave the military to study full-time. Luckily for me I found chemistry to be an awesome subject of study and I quickly came to love it. Like the military, school is a great place for an obsession person. As

[205]

someone who had to have everything done "perfectly" and who would forego sleep to make sure everything was done just right, I was seen as someone who was "dedicated to his studies." Little did other people know that my "dedication" was actually an obsessive personality that would lead to my great downfall. However, I thrived in university, but was faced with figuring out what to do afterwards. I decided I would try to get into medical school. I would like to say that my intentions were honorable – wanting to heal the sick, save the world, discover the cure for itchy bum-bum syndrome – but when I look back now it was my obsession at work. Medical school was notoriously hard to get into, and for me it was a challenge to beat. Once again, my obsession was making life decisions for me.

Approaching my new goal with my usual obsessive fervor, I succeeded in getting into an excellent "ivy-league" university. The odd thing about it is that I am not a very bright guy. I attribute my success in school to my obsessive personality. I had a psychological need to get every assignment done perfectly, and I wouldn't relax until I had it just right. I was equally obsessed with getting prepared for exams. A truly bright person would have an easy go of it, I had to work for it, driven to it by my obsession.

Medical school was tough, but I enjoyed it. Still only an occasional drinker, I would drink in my accustomed obsessive way at parties – not stopping until I was debilitated – but had no cravings or obsession in the weeks and months in between parties. My obsession with doing well in my studies was – at this point in my life – stronger than my obsession with drinking. One mental defect overpowering another. But, that was to change. Internship and residency were very hard, stressful both mentally and physically, as well as spiritually. Spiritually because I became exposed to many tragedies of health and society from which I had previously been shielded as a non-medical person. During medical school I stayed grounded by my daily workouts at the gym, by running my martial arts and boxing school, and by volunteering as a Boy Scout leader. But I let slip my grounding with God, who had previously been an important part of my life. Yet another ingredient for my future downfall clicking into place.

After finishing my residency training, getting through all the exams and courses I needed to be a fully licenced doctor, my obsession turned to getting married and having a family. In hindsight, getting married was for me at that time my obsessive personality compelling me to check another box on the list of accomplishments in life. I married a girl I barely knew under rushed circumstances and quickly had two very beautiful children. Having kids grounded me considerably, and for once my obsession with things of the world settled down and it came to be more about spending time with my children. I wasn't drinking at all at this point.

The expected unexpected happened, and my wife and I arrived at a point where we couldn't be together anymore. There was no infidelity, no violence, no financial trauma. It was just two people who weren't supposed to be together. So, I left the home and family. Although I still had my kids regularly, an incredible guilt came over me about the failure of my marriage. The guilt grew to the point where I fell under a crushing depression that knocked my feet out from under me. Literally. All I could do was lay in bed all day and all night staring at the ceiling. It halted everything in my life. I wouldn't answer my phone, go to work, eat, or shower. "Miserable" barely describes my state of mind. I fully recognized that I was depressed, and I knew that it was easily treated with medications. But, for some reason I couldn't bring myself to go get help. Such is the nature of mental illness.

As miserable as I felt and as over-powering the desire to just lay in bed and stare at the ceiling, I knew I had to power through it and get myself to work. Many people were relying on me, including my office staff. But untreated depression and having your own prescription pad is a baaaaad combination. I ended up using narcotics to get myself going and keep myself going during the day, and sedatives and alcohol to bring myself down at night. I went downhill fast. Within a few months I was such a wreck that I came to the attention of the medical authorities who told me to get help or else. At that point I wanted help badly. Not only from the drugs and booze but also from the depression. My depression responded quickly to treatment, and the drug and alcohol use fell away. I signed up for a five year recovery program for doctors, a non-Twelve Step-based system.

I managed to stay sober during the time of the program, which came out to just over five years. It consisted of weekly support-group meetings and monitoring in the form of random forensic drug testing. Twelve Step meetings were encouraged, but I managed to get out of going to them. In hindsight, that was a mistake. I see now that it was the drug testing that kept me sober, because after the program – and the drug testing – ended I immediately relapsed. Slowly at first. I never accepted that I could never use substances again. I had no program to keep me learning and focussing – no recovery support system, no book to read, no meetings to attend, no sponsor. Crucially, I had not in any way dealt with what made me drink and use: all the mental debris and carnage that we target when we "clean house" working the Twelve Steps. I still had all the abnormal alcoholic-addict psychology – which we have talked about in this book – partying in my head. We need to "clean house" and we need a program to follow for as long as we wish to remain sober. I had neither. I was defenseless as soon as the drug testing ended.

So began my downward spiral. This time alcohol held a much more commanding place in my affections. As I labored more and more under the lash of my alcoholism-addiction I had less and less left in me for dealing with life. Neglected responsibilities accumulated and multiplied. Small problems, untended, became big. Things piled up and I couldn't handle the stress. I escaped from it all by drinking and using and isolating myself from people and life. Before long I was drinking from morning till night. Life was unmanageable for me, even if I cared enough to try.

I arrived at the point where I pined for a way out of the drinking and using. Each new disaster from my intoxication brought a new sincere vow to stop. I succeeded here and there for a little while, but as soon as I began feeling a little better physically I was back at it. By now my family was involved and deeply concerned. They were pushing me to go to A.A. but I pushed back and never went. I believed I could do it myself, with a little help, but I wanted to pick and choose the help. I attended counselling. Despite the skill of my counselor I continued drinking and using and my life continued to hit bottom after bottom.

By now my physical, mental, and spiritual sickness was profound. Physically, I was spontaneously vomiting all the time. No proper nutrition, no exercise, no break from the constant onslaught of poison drink and drug. Day after day I was so sick I could barely walk, but I kept on. When I drank or took pills, it took great effort to try to keep them down long enough to absorb them into my battered body. Mentally, I had given up on life. I had no relationship to speak of with anyone. I was lonely, broken, ashamed, angry and resentful at the world for what I had become. I was without hope. I had accepted that I could no longer live like this and that the only way out was death. And I was preparing for making that happen. Spiritually, I had abandoned any connection with anything or anyone outside of myself. Meditation, reading, walks lost in thought... all gone. I was resentful of God for allowing my life to end up like this.

One of many days I was unconscious on the floor some true friends (who are in recovery) and my girlfriend (why she was still with me, I don't know) picked me up and deposited me at a detox facility. I went willingly. I was so sick I was promptly transferred me to the hospital where I needed fluid resuscitation – such was my level of dehydration – and then back to detox. There I was introduced to A.A. and N.A. meetings twice daily. I heard talk of the Big Book, which I had never heard of before, and I requested a copy. (Think of how scary that is – a doctor who saw alcoholic and addicted patients on a regular basis and spent 5 years in a recovery program, but had never heard of the Big Book). I dove into it and couldn't put it down. Finally I was seeing an explanation for everything that had been going on inside me. I could finally see that I was not alone, and that there is a way out – even for hopeless souses like me.

I loved what I was getting out of that book and those meetings. By the time I left detox I thought I had it all figured out. I went home and tried living life normally, as if nothing had happened. But my life could never be the same again. I wasn't doing the things that I had learned that were required for me to stay sober. I wasn't going to meetings, I wasn't reading the book, I wasn't contacting other alcoholic-addicts, I wasn't meditating/praying. Within 5 days I was back in detox. I spent one night there sobering up, then, sick and shaking, I signed myself out and went and sat on a park bench. Right then and there I decided that's it! Enough! I'm committing to this program 100%. I'm going to do everything they tell me to do. I surrendered. And I continue giving attention to what I need to do for my recovery every day. Now I have a program of recovery, and I know that as long as I'm following that program I'll be sober and living life. The price of letting go of it is too high. I know too many people who have stopped living in their program and are right back where they were. Not everyone makes it, but many do. Many who don't make it are soon come back the program with some lessons learned and a better go at it. My experience has been that most who don't make it are the ones who didn't get a sponsor and work through the Steps.

Of the Twelve Step programs, A.A. is the one that works best for me. I was surprised to find that many A.A. members – perhaps most – were "cross-addicted" like me. There were many things that had kept me from the Twelve Step program – and thus sobriety – in the past. First and foremost was the insanity of my disease, which kept telling me that I could handle this on my own, or with a little hand-picked help here and there. Second was the impression I had of A.A. as being a group of miserable drunks and addicts sitting in a circle whining to each other; I didn't see how that could get me sober. Nothing could be further from the truth. Also, I feared running into my patients at meetings. Part of surrendering was letting go of that. The fear was unfounded, because when I do run into patients it's always in a setting of brotherhood and it has not caused me any problems. There are other reasons, as we have discussed in this book: alcoholic-addict pride, the desire to keep the door to drink and drugs open a crack, stubbornness.

I have been amazed at what this Twelve Step program has done in my life and in others'. I have seen many walking disasters of humanity turned around, including me. I believe it is the world's best kept secret. I hope to do my part in ending that secrecy.

# Chapter References

## Chapter Two - The Genetics of Alcoholism and Addiction

1 – National Council on Addiction and Drug Dependence. (2015). Family history and genetics. Retrieved from https://www.ncadd.org/about-addiction/family-history-and-genetics

2 – Bevilacqua, L., & Goldman, D. (2009). Genes and Addictions. Clinical Pharmacology and Therapeutics, 85(4), 359–361. http://doi.org/10.1038/clpt.2009.6

## Chapter Four – Our Psychology and Our Disease

1 – Amodeo, John. (2015, Jun 6). Why pride is nothing to be proud of [Web log post]. Retrieved from https://www.psychologytoday.com/blog/intimacy-path-toward-spirituality/201506/why-pride-is-nothing-be-proud

2 – Albrecht, Karl. (2015, Jan 8). The paradoxical power of humility [Web log post]. Retrieved from psychologytoday.com/blog/brainsnacks/201501/the-paradoxical-power-humility

3 - United States National Institute of Health: National Institute on Drug Abuse. (2015). National survey of drug use and health [Data file]. Retrieved from https://www.drugabuse.gov/national-survey-drug-use-health

4 – McGuiness, Kristen. (2011). Drunk dreaming. Retrieved from https://www.thefix.com/content/dream

5 - Dinker, B. (2015) Pink cloud syndrome in recovery, good or bad? Retrieved from http://www.discoveryplace.info/pink-cloud-syndrome-sobriety-good-or-bad

## Chapter Seven – The Twelve Steps as Psychotherapy

1 – Howes, Ryan. (2016, Oct 26). Why people lie to their therapists [Web log post]. Retrieved from psychologytoday.com/blog/in-therapy/201610/why-people-lie-their-therapists

2 - Azar, Beth (2010). A reason to believe. Monitor on Psychology, 41(11), 52.

3 – Maslow, Abraham. (1987). Motivation and personality (3rd ed.). Delhi, India: Pearson India.

4 - Lickerman, Alex. (2011, Dec 4). Why and how to find a mentor [Web log post]. Retrieved from www.psychologytoday.com/blog/happiness-in-world/201112/how-and-why-find-mentor

5 - Levine, Saul. (2016, Feb 1). The importance of friendship [Web log post]. Retrieved from www.psychologytoday.com/blog/our-emotional-footprint/201602/the-importance-friendship

6 - Karbo, Karen. (2006, Nov 1). Friendship: The laws of attraction [Web log post].          Retrieved          from www.psychologytoday.com/articles/200611/friendship-the-laws-attraction

7 - Farsides, Tom. (2007). The psychology of altruism. The psychologist...., 20, 474-477. https://thepsychologist.bps.org.uk/volume-20/edition-8/psychology-altruism

8 - Hofmann, S. G., Asnaani, A., Vonk, I. J. J., Sawyer, A. T., & Fang, A. (2012). The efficacy of cognitive behavioral therapy: A review of meta-analyses. Cognitive Therapy and Research, 36(5), 427–440. http://doi.org/10.1007/s10608-012-9476-1

9 - Columbia University: National Center on Addiction and Substance Use. (2012, June). Addiction medicine: Closing the gap between science and practice. New York, NY: Author.

10 – Harvard Medical School. (2005). National comorbidity survey (NCS). Retrieved from https://www.hcp.med.harvard.edu/ncs/

11 – Staub, Ervin. (2011, Dec 11). Altruism born of suffering: The value of kindness          [Web          log          post].          Retrieved          from https://www.psychologytoday.com/blog/in-the-garden-good-and-evil/201112/altruism-born-suffering

Chapter Eight – Mental Health and Alcoholism / Addiction

1 - United States National Institute of Health: National Institute on Drug Abuse. (2008). Comorbidity: addiction and other mental illnesses [Data file]. Retrieved from https://www.drugabuse.gov/publications/research-reports/comorbidity-addiction-other-mental-illnesses/letter-director

2 - ibid

3 - ibid

Afterword

1 - Columbia University: National Center on Addiction and Substance Use. (2012, June). Addiction medicine: Closing the gap between science and practice. New York, NY: Author.

# Works Cited and Consulted

Alban, D. (n.d.). Fifty amazing human brain facts. Retrieved from https://bebrainfit.com/human-brain-facts/

Albrecht, Karl. (2015, Jan 8). The paradoxical power of humility [Web log post]. Retrieved from psychologytoday.com/blog/brainsnacks/201501/the-paradoxical-power-humility

Alcoholics anonymous (4th ed.). (2001). New York, NY: Alcoholics Anonymous World Services.

American Psychiatric Association. (2013). Diagnostic and statistical manual of mental disorders (5th ed.). Washington, DC: Author.

Amodeo, John. (2015, Jun 6). Why pride is nothing to be proud of [Web log post]. Retrieved from https://www.psychologytoday.com/blog/intimacy-path-toward-spirituality/201506/why-pride-is-nothing-be-proud

Association for Psychological Science. (n.d.). We're only human. Retrieved from http://www.psychologicalscience.org/news/were-only-human

Austin, Michael W. (2012, Jun 27). Humility [Web log post]. Retrieved from www.psychologytoday.com/blog/ethics-everyone/201206/humility

Azar, Beth (2010). A reason to believe. Monitor on Psychology, 41(11), 52.

Azar, Beth (2006). The faces of pride. Monitor on Psychology, 37(3), 24.

Bevilacqua, L., & Goldman, D. (2009). Genes and Addictions. Clinical Pharmacology and Therapeutics, 85(4), 359–361. http://doi.org/10.1038/clpt.2009.6

Boden JM, & Fergusson DM. (2011). Alcohol and depression. Addiction, 106(5), 906-914. http://doi.org: 10.1111/j.1360-0443.2010.03351.x.

Bond J, Kaskutas LA, Weisner C. (2003). The persistent influence of social networks and Alcoholics Anonymous on abstinence. Journal of Studies on

Alcohol, 64(4), 579–588. https://www.ncbi.nlm.nih.gov/pubmed/12921201

Bourg Carter, Sherrie. (2014, Sep 4). Helper's high: The benefits (and risks) of altruism [Web Blog Post]. Retrieved from www.psychologytoday.com/blog/high-octane-women/201409/helpers-high-the-benefits-and-risks-altruism

Brandsma, Jeffery, Maultsby, Maxie, & Welsh, Richard. (1980). Outpatient treatment of alcoholism: A review and comparative study. Baltimore, MD: University Park Press.

Came to believe... (36th ed.). (2012). New York, NY: Alcoholics Anonymous World Services.

Campbell, L. (2010, Aug 15). Relationships in recovery. Retrieved from http://www.hazeldenbettyford.org/articles/campbell/relationships-in-recovery

Carroll, M. (2012). What factors affect memory? Retrieved from http://www.readfast.co.uk/what-factors-affect-memory-recall/

Columbia University: National Center on Addiction and Substance Use. (2012, June). Addiction medicine: Closing the gap between science and practice. New York, NY: Author.

Curd, Martin. (1992). Argument and analysis: An introduction to philosophy. St. Paul, MN: West Publishing.

Dinker, B. (2015) Pink cloud syndrome in recovery, good or bad? Retrieved from http://www.discoveryplace.info/pink-cloud-syndrome-sobriety-good-or-bad

Experience, strength, & hope: stories from the first three editions of Alcoholics Anonymous. (2003). New York, NY: Alcoholics Anonymous World Services.

Farsides, Tom. (2007). The psychology of altruism. The psychologist...., 20, 474-477. https://thepsychologist.bps.org.uk/volume-20/edition-8/psychology-altruism

Gardner, E. L. (2011). Introduction: Addiction and brain reward and anti-reward pathways. Advances in Psychosomatic Medicine, 30, 22–60. http://doi.org/10.1159/000324065

George, Bill. (2015, Sep 28). Know thyself: How to develop self-awareness [Web log post]. Retrieved from http://psychologytoday.com/blog/what-is-your-true-north/201509/know-thyself-how-develop-self-awareness

Groome, D. (2014). *Introduction to cognitive psychology: Processes and disorders* (3rd ed.). New York, NY: Routledge.

H., Fred. (2016). Drop the rock... the ripple effect. Center City, MN: Hazelden.

Harvard Medical School. (2005). National comorbidity survey (NCS). Retrieved from https://www.hcp.med.harvard.edu/ncs/

Harvard Medical School: Harvard Health Publications. (2011). How addiction hijacks the brain. Retrieved from https://www.helpguide.org/harvard/how-addiction-hijacks-the-brain.htm

Herbert, W. (2007, Jun 15). The two faces of pride [Web log post]. Retrieved from http://www.psychologicalscience.org/onlyhuman/2007/06/two-face-of-pride.cfm

Hofmann, S. G., Asnaani, A., Vonk, I. J. J., Sawyer, A. T., & Fang, A. (2012). The efficacy of cognitive behavioral therapy: A review of meta-analyses. Cognitive Therapy and Research, 36(5), 427–440. http://doi.org/10.1007/s10608-012-9476-1

Howes, Ryan. (2009, July 27). The definition of insanity is... perseverance vs. perseveration [Web log post]. Retrieved from http://psychologytoday.com/blog/in-therapy/200907/the-definition-insanity-is

Howes, Ryan. (2016, Oct 26). Why people lie to their therapists [Web log post]. Retrieved from psychologytoday.com/blog/in-therapy/201610/why-people-lie-their-therapists

Humphreys, K., Mankowski, E.S., Moos, & R.H., Finney, J.W. (1999). Do enhanced friendship networks and active coping mediate the effect of self-help groups on substance abuse? Annals of Behavioral Medicine, 21, 54–60. DOI: 10.1007/BF02895034

Jha, A. (2005, Jun 30). Where belief is born. The Guardian. Retrieved from https://www.theguardian.com/science/2005/jun/30/psychology.neuroscience

Karbo, Karen. (2006, Nov 1). Friendship: The laws of attraction [Web log post]. Retrieved from www.psychologytoday.com/articles/200611/friendship-the-laws-attraction

Kaskutas, L.A., Bond, J., & Humphreys, K. (2002). Social networks as mediators of the effect of Alcoholics Anonymous. Addiction, 97(7), 891–900. https://www.ncbi.nlm.nih.gov/pubmed/12133128

Kelly, J.F., Myers, M.G., & Brown, S.A. (2002). Do adolescents affiliate with 12-step groups? A multivariate process model of effects. Journal of Studies on Alcohol, 63(3), 293–304. https://www.ncbi.nlm.nih.gov/pmc/articles/PMC1978185/

Lambert, Brent. (2010, Nov 3). The psychology behind misery and why it loves company [Web log post]. Retrieved from http://www.feelguide.com/2010/11/03/psychology-behind-misery-and-why-it-loves-company/

Levine, Saul. (2016, Feb 1). The importance of friendship [Web log post]. Retrieved from www.psychologytoday.com/blog/our-emotional-footprint/201602/the-importance-friendship

Lickerman, Alex. (2011, Dec 4). Why and how to find a mentor [Web log post]. Retrieved from www.psychologytoday.com/blog/happiness-in-world/201112/how-and-why-find-mentor

Living sober. (2nd ed.). (2012). New York, NY: Alcoholics Anonymous World Services.

Maslow, Abraham. (1987). Motivation and personality (3rd ed.). Delhi, India: Pearson India.

[217]

Mastin, L. (2010). Memory processes. Retrieved from http://www.human-memory.net/processes.html

McGuiness, K. (2011, Apr 22). Drunk dreaming. Retrieved from https://www.thefix.com/content/dream

McPherson, F. (n.d.). The role of emotion in memory. Retrieved from http://memory-key.com/memory/emotion

Moos, R.H., & Moos, B.S. (2006). Participation in treatment and Alcoholics Anonymous: a 16-year follow-up of initially untreated individuals. Journal of Clinical Psychology, 62(6), 735–750. DOI: 10.1002/jclp.20259

Morgenstern, Jon, Labouvie, Eric, McCrady, Barbara S., Kahler, Christopher W., & Frey, Ronni M. (1997). Affiliation with Alcoholics Anonymous following treatment: a study of its therapeutic effects and mechanisms of action. Journal of Consulting and Clinical Psychology, 65(5), 768–777. DOI: 10.1037//0022-006X.65.5.768

Murphy Paul, A. (2016, Jun 9). The nightmare of drug dreams. Psychology Today. https://www.psychologytoday.com/articles/199801/the-nightmare-drug-dreams

National Center on Addiction and Substance Use at Columbia University. (2012). Addiction medicine: Closing the gap between science and practice. Retrieved from https://www.centeronaddiction.org/addiction-research/reports/addiction-medicine-closing-gap-between-science-and-practice

National Council on Addiction and Drug Dependence. (2015). Family history and genetics. Retrieved from https://www.ncadd.org/about-addiction/family-history-and-genetics

Nursing Assistant Central. (2008, Dec 31). 100 fascinating facts you never knew about the human brain [Web log post]. Retrieved from http://www.nursingassistantcentral.com/blog/2008/100-fascinating-facts-you-never-knew-about-the-human-brain/

P., Bill, W., Todd, & S., Sara. (2005). Drop the rock: Removing character defects (2nd ed.). Center City, MN: Hazelden.

Perina, Kaja. (2003, Jan 1). Misery loves company [Web log post]. Retrieved from www.psychologytoday.com/articles/200301/misery-loves-company

Quello, S. B., Brady, K. T., & Sonne, S. C. (2005). Mood disorders and substance use disorder: A complex comorbidity. Science & Practice Perspectives, 3(1), 13–21.

Reddy, M. S. (2016). Lack of insight in psychiatric illness: A critical appraisal. Indian Journal of Psychological Medicine, 38(3), 169–171. http://doi.org/10.4103/0253-7176.183080

Safety Net Recovery. (2016, April 7). Are you suffering from pink cloud syndrome? Retrieved from https://www.safetynetrecovery.com/suffering-pink-cloud-syndrome/

Schizophrenia Society of Canada. (2006). Concurrent disorders and schizophrenia: A national awareness strategy discussion paper. Retrieved from http://www.schizophrenia.ca/docs/CD_Discussion_Paper.pdf

Shatter Proof. (2017). Science of addiction. Retrieved from https://www.shatterproof.org/about-addiction/science-of-addiction

Staub, Ervin. (2011, Dec 11). Altruism born of suffering: The value of kindness [Web log post]. Retrieved from https://www.psychologytoday.com/blog/in-the-garden-good-and-evil/201112/altruism-born-suffering

Tonigan, J.S., Connors, G.J., & Miller, W.R. (2003). Participation and involvement in Alcoholics Anonymous. In: Babor, T.F., & Del Boca, F.K., (Eds). Treatment Matching in Alcoholism (184–204). New York, NY: Cambridge University Press.

Taibbi, Robert. (2011, Nov 8). The art of action [Web log post]. Retrieved from www.psychologytoday.com/blog/fixing-families/201111/the-art-action

Taylor, Jeremy. (2012, Jul 17). Dreams and recovery from addiction [Web log post]. Retrieved from psychologytoday.com/blog/the-wisdom-your-dreams/201207/dreams-and-recovery-addiction

The Little Red Book (Revised ed.). (1986). Center City, MN: Hazelden.

Timko, C., Finney, J.W., & Moos, R.H. (2005). The 8-year course of alcohol abuse: gender differences in social context and coping. Alcoholism: Clinical & Experimental Research, 29(4), 612–621. DOI: 10.1097/01.ALC.0000158832.07705.22

Twelve steps and twelve traditions (18th printing). (2014). New York, NY: Alcoholics Anonymous World Services.

United States National Institute of Health: National Institute on Drug Abuse. (2008). Comorbidity: addiction and other mental illnesses [Data file]. Retrieved from https://www.drugabuse.gov/publications/research-reports/comorbidity-addiction-other-mental-illnesses/letter-director

United States National Institute of Health: National Institute on Drug Abuse. (2014). Drugs, brains, and behavior: The science of addiction [Data file]. Retrieved from https://www.drugabuse.gov/publications/drugs-brains-behavior-science-addiction/drugs-brain

United States National Institute of Health: National Institute on Drug Abuse. (2015). National survey of drug use and health [Data file]. Retrieved from https://www.drugabuse.gov/national-survey-drug-use-health

United States National Institute of Health: US National Library of Medicine. (2017). Genetics home reference [Data file]. Retrieved from https://ghr.nlm.nih.gov/primer/basics/gene

Winklbaur, B., Ebner, N., Sachs, G., Thau, K., & Fischer, G. (2006). Substance abuse in patients with schizophrenia. Dialogues in Clinical Neuroscience, 8(1), 37–43.

Xiong, G.L. (2016, April 18). Wernicke-Korsakoff syndrome. Retrieved from http://emedicine.medscape.com/article/288379-overview

Zemore, S.E. (2007). A role for spiritual change in the benefits of 12-step involvement. Alcoholism: Clinical & Experimental Research, 31(S3), 76S–79S. DOI: 10.1111/j.1530-0277.2007.00499.x

Made in the USA
Columbia, SC
30 May 2020